POPE BENEDICT XVI AND THE LITURGY

Understanding recent liturgical developments

Anselm J. Gribbin, O.Praem.

GRACEWING

First published in 2011
by

Gracewing
2, Southern Avenue
Leominster
Herefordshire
HR6 0QF
www.gracewing.co.uk

ISBN 978 085244 755 0

Cum permissu superiorum:
Rt Rev Jeroen De Cuyper, O.Praem.
Abbot of the Abbey of Our Lady of Tongerlo
18 December 2010

Cover photograph courtesy of Stefano Spaziani.

Contents

Introduction

Joseph Ratzinger, now Pope Benedict XVI, has been a well-known figure in Catholic circles for the last forty years. His views have made him a source of controversy to some, while to others, he is seen as a prophetic and fearless voice in an increasingly secularized world, even against what many view as misguided elements in the Church. The life of Joseph Ratzinger is one of many notable achievements. He was born on 16 April 1927 in Marktl am Inn (Bavaria, Germany) and began his studies after the difficult years of the Second World War, in the Higher School of Philosophy and Theology of Freising, and at the University of Munich (1946–1951), before his priestly ordination on 29 June 1951. He obtained his doctorate in 1953 and later qualified to teach at university. Joseph Ratzinger has spent most of his life as a theologian, writing numerous books, papers and articles, and served the Church as a professor of theology at the universities of Freising, Bonn, Münster, Tübingen and Regensburg. He participated as a *peritus* at the Second Vatican Council (1962–65). In 1977 Joseph Ratzinger was appointed archbishop of Munich, and in the same year he was made a cardinal by Pope Paul VI. In 1981 Pope John Paul II appointed him as Prefect of the Congregation for the Doctrine of the Faith, and he held this post until 2005.[1] Now, as Pope Benedict XVI (2005–), he continues his ministry as the successor of St Peter, shepherding the entire Catholic Church.

---

1. For biographical details and his work as a theologian, see Nichols, *The Thought of Pope Benedict XVI;* Ratzinger, *Milestones: Memoirs 1927–1977.*

A prominent and inescapable feature of Pope Benedict's pontificate is the attention which he has given to the sacred liturgy. Not only have we witnessed the reappearance of many elements used in older papal liturgies, such as the extended use of vestments belonging to Pope Benedict's predecessors—most of which were disused following the wide-ranging reforms after the Second Vatican Council—but also what amounts to be the virtual liberation of the 'Old Latin Mass'. This has come as a great surprise to many people in the Church, some of whom almost regard it as a betrayal of the liturgical reforms. On the other hand, others have viewed liturgical changes in Pope Benedict's pontificate as a positive development, leading to a healthy understanding of the last ecumenical council. Indeed those familiar with the earlier writings of Joseph Ratzinger—a truly gifted theologian in his own right—are quite aware that the theology and celebration of the liturgy has been an important theme for him for a very long time, as well as his negative views about much contemporary liturgical practice, and suggestions to remedy this. This is particularly evident in his book *The Spirit of the Liturgy*. There Cardinal Ratzinger focuses mainly, though not exclusively, on the Eucharist, the very heart of the Church's liturgy.[2]

How do Catholics, and other Christians, then, 'make sense' or 'come to terms' with what has happened recently in the Church in the important field of the liturgy, after the postconciliar changes, and how did all this come about? These are important questions to ask, as so much has been written on the liturgy in recent years, that varies in quality. At times there appears to be so many different liturgical viewpoints, which can often lead to confusion. This book is my own modest attempt to find the answer to these, and other questions, by examining Pope Benedict XVI and the liturgy, which also considers some of the recent literature on the liturgy. This entails pinpointing what Pope Benedict's liturgical theology actually is, and what this means for the

---

2.   Ratzinger, *The Spirit of the Liturgy* (hereafter *TSL*).

concept and celebration of the liturgy, from notable books and papers which the pope has written on this subject, as well as the acts of his papal Magisterium. A significant part of this study will therefore focus on the writings of the pope as a theologian, which were mainly written before his papacy. However this, in itself, raises a fundamental question at the very beginning of this book, which, perhaps, has not been sufficiently addressed elsewhere. In what way do the theological writings of Pope Benedict XVI, as a theologian, relate to the acts of his Magisterium as the supreme pontiff of the Catholic Church? One might suggest—and with good reason—that his theological writings be kept strictly separate from his Magisterium. Joseph Ratzinger, as a cardinal, faced considerable criticism for combining his roles as Prefect for the Congregation for the Doctrine of the Faith with that of a theologian.[3]

It must be indicated that the writings of a pope, as a theologian for instance—including earlier 'pre-papal works'—do not formally constitute a part of his Magisterium. However it is clear that we should look upon the theology of Joseph Ratzinger/Pope Benedict XVI from more than one viewpoint, especially in regard to his papacy. Firstly, as we shall clearly see from my examination of *Sacramentum Caritatis* for instance, Joseph Ratzinger's liturgical theology has had a great influence upon his Magisterium as Pope Benedict. The divide between Pope Benedict's theology and his Magisterium is not so absolute: that is, we should recognize that aspects of Pope Benedict's theology—in this case his theology of the liturgy—has influenced his Magisterium *without* confusing the two as magisterial. A similar instance in papal history also occurred with Pope Benedict XVI's namesake, Pope Benedict XIV (1740–1758), who was also interested in liturgical matters in a 'non-magisterial' sphere, and who hoped to reform the liturgy as pope.[4] More recently, Pope John Paul II's own 'private' thoughts

---

3.   For a discussion of this, see Nichols, *The Thought of Pope Benedict XVI*, 171–73.

4.   Hermans, *Benedictus XIV en de Liturgie*.

and writings in the sphere of morality, especially family life, anthropology, ethics and human sexuality, had a great influence in his development of the 'theology of the body' and magisterial writings on moral issues.[5] Aidan Nichols, a well-respected Dominican theologian from England, comments that Pope Benedict's book *Jesus of Nazareth*, 'is, of course, a study by the pope as a private doctor, not an act of the Roman pontiff in his teaching office', which the pope himself made clear.[6] 'At the same time', continues Nichols, 'for a Catholic reader, there must be something affecting about this selection of topic and genre. It is, after all, the successor of Peter seeking to answer the question put by the God-man to the original Peter, "Who do *you* say that I am?"'.[7] Again, while we should make a suitable distinction between the writings of Pope Benedict as a theologian and his Magisterium, the influence of his theological writings in the latter, particularly in relation to the liturgy, is clearly of no small consequence. Thus when contrasting his theological writings with his Magisterium in general, one should not dismiss them out of hand, even if they are not officially magisterial. This is not to say, of course, that Pope Benedict XVI necessarily intends all his theological opinions to influence his Magisterium, or that his theology is endowed with the same special assistance from the Holy Spirit as his Magisterium. Where the two clearly coincide, we can say that he has used his theology in the service of his Magisterium, which, in turn, is at the service of the Church.[8]

---

5. Asci, *The Conjugal Act as Personal Act*, 13, n. 2; 122, n. 60 and *passim*.

6. Nichols, *The Thought of Pope Benedict XVI*, 242; Pope Benedict XVI/ Ratzinger, *Jesus of Nazareth*, xxiii–xxiv.

7. Nichols, *The Thought of Pope Benedict XVI*, 242.

8. One of Pope Benedict XVI's recent books, *Light of the World*, caused much controversy because of a sentence relating to a specific case involving the use of condoms by a male prostitute, and if the Church's teaching had changed. It would be fair to say that the pope's words—in a non-magisterial interview—were misunderstood and taken out of context: see 'Note of the Congregation

Secondly, we should also appreciate his theological work before and after the beginning of his papacy on its own merits as the work of a great theologian. In fact Joseph Ratzinger's theological writings not only, in part at least, 'reflect' the Magisterium of the Church. A good knowledge of them is useful and 'necessary' in order to understand, and to explain, aspects of Pope Benedict XVI's Magisterium, and, indeed, his entire papacy. This is one of the important roles of theology in the Church. Placing this in the context of the liturgy, we can say that a study of Joseph Ratzinger's liturgical theology is an indispensable aid to understanding Pope Benedict's magisterial teaching on the liturgy, and liturgical praxis. My third, and final point here, should not be lost sight of throughout this book. Although I may refer to the Holy Father as 'Joseph Ratzinger' and 'Cardinal Ratzinger', particularly in chapters one and two, and as 'Pope Benedict XVI' elsewhere, indicating—where appropriate—his life before or after the beginning of his papacy, the theology of Joseph Ratzinger is, and remains, the theology of Pope Benedict XVI. One only has to look at the compilation of the pope's *Opera Omnia* for further confirmation of this which, incidentally, begins with the publication of volume eleven: his liturgical writings.[9]

The first chapter of this book, then, focuses on Pope Benedict's liturgical writings as theologian, primarily *The Spirit of the Liturgy*, with reference to other works, including *The Feast of Faith* (1986). I decided to focus in particular on *The Spirit of the Liturgy*, because it can be rightly viewed as a summary and an adequate account of Joseph Ratzinger's liturgical theology, which he himself has written. Therefore I have also tried to let the author 'speak for himself'. Joseph Ratzinger's theology is not only very precise, but it is eloquent, even in translation. Theology should touch the heart as well as the intellect, and in this regard

---

for the Doctrine of the Faith On the Trivilization of Sexuality', 21 December 2010.

9. For the German edition see Ratzinger/Pope Benedict XVI, *Theologie der Liturgie, Gesammelte Schriften*, vol. 11.

one thinks of the influence of St Bonaventure in the pope's formative years.[10] This chapter is crucial to understanding the pope's liturgical thought, and also aims to provide the reader, especially students, with a convenient and detailed overview of *The Spirit of the Liturgy*. Hopefully he or she will be encouraged to delve deeper into the original book itself, and to analyse Joseph Ratzinger's argumentation. By studying Joseph Ratzinger's/Pope Benedict's 'theology of the liturgy', especially *The Spirit of the Liturgy*, we can be led to a deeper appreciation of what the liturgy actually *is* and its 'otherness' or 'transcendence', which is clearly connected to the daily life of the Christian.

The second chapter concerns criticisms which *The Spirit of the Liturgy* has received, and largely consists of an analysis of the now famous critique made of this book by a prominent liturgical scholar, the late Fr Pierre-Marie Gy, O.P., in *La Maison-Dieu*. This gives prominence to the question of whether or not the-then Cardinal Ratzinger was faithful to the reforms of the Second Vatican Council, particularly in the views and criticisms he expressed about aspects of the post-Vatican II liturgy. Gy's critique and Cardinal Ratzinger's response, has particular relevance to understanding a number of current issues, including the interpretation of the Second Vatican Council, and the celebration of the liturgy under the present pontificate—for example *ad orientem* celebrations of the Holy Eucharist and the so-called 'Benedictine arrangement' of the altar with the cross placed in the middle of the altar facing the celebrant—as well as illuminating further aspects of the pope's theology of the liturgy. I shall also make brief reference in this chapter to a recent publication by John F. Baldovin, S.J., professor of historical and liturgical theology at Boston College School of Theology and Ministry, and some of his comments which 'respond' to Joseph Ratzinger and critics of the liturgical reforms after the Second Vatican Council. For me, Baldovin's book also underlines the relevance of

---

10.   See Ratzinger, *The Theology of History in Saint Bonaventure*; Nichols,
       The Thought of Pope Benedict XVI, 34–44.

examining Gy's critique of Cardinal Ratzinger in coming to a fuller appreciation of the liturgical thought of Pope Benedict, which still receives considerable criticism from liturgical quarters: it is important to respond to such criticism.[11] When reading the first two chapters of this present book, I want to emphasize once again, the importance of bearing in mind that the theology of Joseph Ratzinger is the theology of Pope Benedict XVI. Chapters three and four examine the Magisterium of Pope Benedict XVI and the liturgy, in particular, his post-synodal exhortation *Sacramentum Caritatis* and the motu proprio *Summorum Pontificum*. I attempt to show how the pope's writings and actions—indeed the developments—in the area of the liturgy, are faithful to the Second Vatican Council, and the significance of what has happened to the liturgy since the beginning of his pontificate. It shall also demonstrate how influential Pope Benedict's theology has been in his *Magisterium*, and in coming to understand the liturgical developments in his pontificate. I will also offer some brief remarks on some recent authors who have commentated on *Summorum Pontificum*, including Baldovin. In my general conclusion, I will bring together some thoughts, and concluding comments, concerning the liturgical theology and pontificate of Pope Benedict XVI, and its consequences, especially in relation to understanding what is happening to the liturgy in the Church today, and the way forward.

Although this book is primarily a study of Pope Benedict's theology and vision of the Catholic liturgy, it coincides with the personal journey of the author, no doubt shared by many others, in trying to understand what has happened to the liturgy in the Church since Vatican II—the other central aim of this book—and in seeking what the future path of the liturgy might be, without claiming the gift of clairvoyance. Pope Benedict's writings on the liturgy, and Magisterium, have prompted me to think about my own views on the liturgy, and how to understand the Second Vatican Coun-

---

11. Baldovin, *Reforming the Liturgy*.

cil. This book is, then, in many ways, the fruit, if not the culmination, of twenty years research and reflection on the liturgy, which includes my own involvement in the liturgy as a *caeremoniarius*, and of my experience of praying the liturgy. The latter point is particularly important. Liturgy is primarily the Church's official prayer to God and not solely something to be studied academically, important though this is. My own background, as a historian of Church History—including the liturgy—was also an invaluable help. An essay I wrote in the academic year 2008–9, on Pope Benedict and the liturgy, during my present studies for the sacred priesthood, provided me with the truly wonderful opportunity to collate my thoughts on this important subject, with the view to publishing a book. It has led me to conclude that 'the reform of the reform', *with* the reverent celebration of the missal of Pope Paul VI *and* what is now known as the 'extraordinary form of the Roman Rite' (*usus antiquior*), is the way forward for the Church in the field of the liturgy, as envisaged by Pope Benedict. It is a 'many-sided' viewpoint which is gradually gathering momentum in the Church.[12]

I would like to take this opportunity to extend my gratitude to all those who have helped me over the course of my life, to value the sacred liturgy, especially my first teachers, my mother and father, the late Rev Dr Edward Carey, Rev Michael J. Gallagher, O.Praem., the abbot and monks of Pluscarden Abbey, Scotland, the late Rt Rev Alfred Spencer, O.S.B., and my confreres at the abbey of Tongerlo in Belgium. I am particularly grateful to my liturgy professor, the Rev Christophe Monsieur, O.Praem.—a former student of Pierre-Marie Gy—for allowing me to research the important topic of Pope Benedict XVI and the liturgy, and for the kindness and forbearance which he extended to

---

12.   It is encouraging to see, since I wrote my original essay, that studies on aspects of Pope Benedict XVI's liturgical thought are now just beginning to make some headway. See for example Roy and Rutherford, *Benedict XVI and the Sacred Liturgy: Proceedings of the First Fota International Liturgy Conference, 2008*.

me. I also wish to thank Mgr Gordon Read and Rev Gero P. Weishaupt, particularly for their help with the canonical aspects of *Summorum Pontificum*. I am also very grateful to all the staff of Gracewing Publications, particularly Mr Tom Longford and Rev Dr Paul Haffner for their kindness, support and assistance with the publication of this book, and their dedication to publishing Catholic books. I owe a great deal to the liturgical writings of His Holiness, Pope Benedict XVI, and I thank him heartily for the joy that his writings have brought to me personally. I dedicate this book to my abbot, the Rt Rev Jeroen De Cuyper, O.Praem., whose own love of the sacred liturgy continues to be an inspiration to me, and to my beloved parents.

Frater Anselm J. Gribbin, O.Praem.,
The Abbey of Our Lady of Tongerlo,
The Solemnity of the Immaculate Conception
of the Blessed Virgin Mary,
8 December 2010.

Abbreviations

AAS =   *Acta Apostolicae Sedis*

CCC =   *Catechism of the Catholic Church*

CIC =   *Codex Iuris Canonici* 1983

IGMR =   *Institutio Generalis Missalis Romani*

ST =   Aquinas, T., St, *Summa Theologiae* [*Summa Theologica*]

TSL =   Ratzinger, J., *The Spirit of the Liturgy*

Chapter I

The Spirit and Theology of the Liturgy

The purpose of The Spirit of the Liturgy

In explaining why he wrote *The Spirit of the Liturgy*, Cardinal Joseph Ratzinger recalls that one of the first books he read as a theology student was *Vom Geist der Liturgie* by Romano Guardini (d.1968), whose work had an important influence in his theological and liturgical formation.[1] Guardini's book inaugurated the 'Liturgical Movement' in Germany and, as the cardinal explains, 'helped us to rediscover the liturgy in all its beauty, hidden wealth, and time-transcending grandeur, to see it as the animating centre of the Church, the very centre of Christian life'.[2] Joseph Ratzinger views the liturgy in 1918—when Guardini's book was first published—as a 'fresco' that had been preserved, but obscured by whitewash. The fresco had been revealed by the Liturgical Movement and, 'in a definitive way', by the Second Vatican Council.[3]

Yet while the 'fresco' had been uncovered, Cardinal Ratzinger indicates, in the starkest of terms, that all is not well with the liturgy today. After the Second Vatican Council 'the fresco has been endangered by climatic conditions as well as by various restorations and reconstructions ... *it is threatened with destruction*, if the necessary steps

---

1. Guardini, *Vom Geist der Liturgie.*
2. *TSL*, 7. Concerning the Liturgical Movement, see Brinkhoff and Lescrauwert, 'Liturgische Beweging', 1597–1611; Reid, *The Organic Development of the Liturgy*, 63–284.
3. *TSL*, 7–8; The Second Vatican Council, *The Constitution on the Sacred Liturgy Sacrosanctum Concilium*, 4 December 1963, nos 1–46.

are not taken to stop these damaging influences'.[4] The cardinal's dissatisfaction with the liturgy stems from concerns regarding fundamental aspects of its construction, implementation and interpretation after the council, as if it were a significant break from the liturgy of the past, and—worse—from the Church of the past. Central to this is the question of whether the liturgy after the Second Vatican Council was genuinely an 'organic development' of the previous liturgy. This principle, albeit metaphorically expressed, was employed by key persons throughout the Liturgical Movement and in *Sacrosanctum Concilium*—namely the constitution on the sacred liturgy of the Second Vatican Council—when speaking of liturgical reform:

> In order that sound tradition be retained, and yet the way open to legitimate progress, a careful investigation—theological, historical, and pastoral—should always be made into each part of the liturgy which is to be revised. Furthermore the general laws governing the structure and meaning of the liturgy [*mentis liturgiae*] must be studied in conjunction with the experience derived from recent liturgical reforms and from the indults granted to various places. Finally, there must be no innovations unless the good of the Church genuinely and certainly requires them, and care must be taken that any new forms adopted should in some way grow organically from forms already existing [*ex formis iam exstantibus organice quodammodo crescant*].[5]

Though 'organic development' has no single 'definition' as such, the following 'definition' by Alcuin Reid, illustrates this important concept with great clarity:

---

4. *TSL*, 8 (my emphasis); cf. Bouyer, *The Decomposition of Catholicism*, 119; idem, *The Liturgy Revived*.

5. The Second Vatican Council, *The Constitution on the Sacred Liturgy Sacrosanctum Concilium*, 4 December 1963, no. 23: cf. Reid, '*Sacrosanctum Concilium* and the Organic Development of the Liturgy', 198–215, for a thought provoking essay which deserves careful consideration.

Organic development holds openness to growth (prompted by pastoral needs) and continuity with tradition in due proportion. It listens to scholarly *desiderata* and considers anew the value of practices lost in the passage of time, drawing upon them to improve liturgical tradition gradually, only if and when this is truly necessary. Ecclesiastical authority supervises this growth, at times making prudential judgments about what is appropriate in the light of the needs of different ages, but always taking care that liturgical tradition is never impoverished, and that what is handed on is truly that precious heritage received from our fathers, perhaps judiciously pruned and carefully augmented (but not wholly reconstructed), according to the circumstances of the Church in each age, ensuring continuity of belief and of practice.[6]

Joseph Ratzinger, as we shall see, argues for development in continuity with the past, and for 'the reform of the reform' of the modern Roman liturgy, while acknowledging its positive elements. This is, to some extent, parallel with his views on the organic development of tradition with reference to the Church's Magisterium, which is sensitive to considerations of the internal order and coherence of a tradition. An important influence upon Cardinal Ratzinger's thinking on this subject was Blessed John Henry Newman's notion of the development of doctrine and 'the Tübingen interest in the relationship between history, memory, and tradition'.[7] However an example of his con-

---

6. Reid, *The Organic Development of the Liturgy*, 289–93. See also Bouyer, *The Liturgy Revived*, 54–55; Baumstark, *Comparative Liturgy*; Gamber, *The Modern Rite*, 9–14, 69–75, 77–82; Dobszay, *The Restoration and Organic Development of the Roman Rite*, 64–67. These, and other writings, also show that the Liturgical Movement was not entirely flawless.

7. Rowland, *Ratzinger's Faith*, 45–46; Nichols, *The Thought of Pope Benedict XVI*, 163, 174, which cites Joseph Ratzinger: 'There is a real identity with the origin only where there is at the same time that living continuity which develops the origin, and, in so developing it, guards it', *Ibid*. Concerning 'the reform of the reform',

cern about the organic development of the liturgy and the liturgical changes after the Second Vatican Council, may be found in this passage: 'What happened after the council was something else entirely: in the place of liturgy as the fruit of development came fabricated liturgy. We abandoned the organic, living process of growth and development over centuries, and replaced it—as in a manufacturing process—with a fabrication, a banal on-the-spot product'.[8] Cardinal Ratzinger is not content to let matters lie, indicating that 'necessary steps' have to be taken to avoid the liturgy's destruction and a 'new understanding of [the liturgy's] message and its reality'. *The Spirit of Liturgy* was written 'to assist this renewal of understanding', in a way corresponding to Guardini's book, but with the contemporary situation in mind, 'to give the faith its central form of expression in the liturgy', hoping that it would contribute, in a new way, to 'something like a "liturgical movement"', towards the right way of celebrating the liturgy, inwardly and outwardly.[9] Although Joseph Ratzinger supported the older Liturgical Movement, and was imbued with its spirit, he, and a number of scholars, eventually came to see that it also had its flaws, which became more evident in the implementation of the new liturgy after the Second Vatican Council. This, together with the liturgical practices he saw around him, brought about a development, and, in certain aspects, even modifying some of his earlier liturgical views.[10] In his autobiography, Cardinal Ratzinger, recall-

---

which also has shades of differing opinions, see Kocik, *The Reform of the Reform?*; Nichols, *Christendom Awake: On Re-energising the Church in Culture*, 21–39.

8.   From Ratzinger's preface to Gamber, *The Reform of the Roman Liturgy*, end-cover: the influence of Gamber in the words chosen by the cardinal is unmistakable: cf. Gamber, *The Modern Rite*, 9–14, 69–75, 77–82.

9.   *TSL*, 8–9. Cf. Ratzinger, *Milestones: Memoirs 1927–1977*, 149. For the remainder of this chapter, I have grouped citations to *TSL* for convenience.

10.   See pp. 157–160 on the cardinal's views on the 'Tridentine' Mass.

ing his time as an adviser to Cardinal Frings at the council, makes these comments on *Sacrosanctum Concilium*:

> At the beginning of the council, I saw that the draft of the Constitution on the Liturgy, which incorporated all the essential principles of the Liturgical Movement, was a marvellous point of departure for this assembly of the whole Church, and I advised Cardinal Frings in this sense. I was not able to foresee that the negative sides of the Liturgical Movement would afterwards reemerge with redoubled strength, almost to the point of pushing the liturgy toward its own self-destruction.[11]

The essence of the liturgy

What is the liturgy? For Joseph Ratzinger, the answer has many, interwoven components. He suggests that we approach this question by beginning with the Bible, by examining the Book of Exodus in particular. The flight of the people of Israel from Egypt was done with the desire of reaching the Promised Land, but also, more significantly, 'that they may serve me [that is, God] in the wilderness', in order to worship. The biblical texts enable one to define how these two goals were related. During the Exodus, Israel discovers the kind of sacrifice that God wants; God communicates to the people from the mountain, gives the ten commandments and, through Moses, makes a covenant with them, 'concretized in a minutely regulated form of worship'.[12] Cult and liturgy are part of this worship, but so too is life according to the will of God. Life only becomes 'real life' when it receives its form from looking toward God: 'Cult exists in order to communicate this vision'. According to the cardinal, there is an essential connection

---

11. Ratzinger, *Milestones: Memoirs 1927–1977*, 57: such references to the liturgy, from Ratzinger's biography, could easily be multiplied, especially in relation to the notion of 'organic development', and the disillusionment and sadness which he felt after what happened to the liturgy following the Second Vatican Council.

12. Ex 7: 16; 8: 1, 25, 27; 9: 13; 10: 3;19: 16, 20; 20: 1–17; 24; *TSL*, 15–17.

between worship, law and ethics, as with the covenant of Sinai. Worship—the right way to relate to God—is essential to the right kind of existence in this world.[13] Moses said to pharaoh, '[W]e do not know with what we must serve the Lord' (Exod 10: 26). These words display a fundamental law of all liturgy. 'Real liturgy' implies that God 'responds and reveals how we can worship him'. Liturgy is not a matter of doing 'what you please', a 'feast of self-affirmation' and self-seeking worship, which the Israelites did around the golden calf, in the absence of Moses.[14]

The liturgy also has an important 'cosmic' element. While the idea that liturgy is *either* cosmic *or* historical[15] is not entirely unfounded—an opinion widely accepted in modern theology— 'it is false when it leads to an exclusive opposition.' It underestimates the sense of history, even in the nature religions, and narrows the meaning of Christian worship of God, forgetting that faith in redemption cannot be separated from faith in the Creator. The account of the creation in Genesis (1: 1–2:4) ends with the Sabbath, when creation participates in God's rest, free from subordinate roles. Although nothing directly is said about worship, this account of creation comes from the same source as the Sinai regulations about the Sabbath, and is properly understood when one reads the Sabbath ordinances of the Torah. The Sabbath is the sign of the covenant between God and man, and therefore creation exists to be a place for the covenant, which is the goal of creation. The freedom and equality this brings about for man can only be understood '*theo*-logically'. Man also responds to God with love, 'and loving God means worshipping him'. If creation is a space for the covenant, then it is a space for worship.[16]

---

13.   *TSL*, 17–21.

14.   *Ibid.*, 21–3; Ratzinger, *A New Song for the Lord*, 32.

15.   'Cosmos' refers to the universe, particularly as a well-ordered whole, while 'history' is understood in the sense of God revealing himself in the redemption.

16.   *TSL*, 24–6. Concerning the Christian Sunday, see Ratzinger, *A New Song for the Lord*, 59–77. For a recent study on 'the cosmic liturgy'

Here, according to Joseph Ratzinger, we return to the question of 'What is worship?'. 'Sacrifice' is at the heart of worship in all religions. It is commonly thought of as entailing destruction, the handing over to God of something which is precious to man, which can only occur with its definite removal from man's hands. However such a mechanical act cannot really serve God's glory. True surrender 'is the union of man and creation with God', according to the Fathers, in fidelity to biblical thought. The goal of worship and the goal of creation are the same—divinization, a world of freedom and love. This means that the historical makes its appearance in the cosmic. The cosmos is not a 'stationary container' in which history may by chance take place: 'It is itself movement, from its one beginning to its one end. In a sense, creation *is* history.'[17] However the Fall of man leads to the rejection of love, making him a god of one's own making. Sacrifice also acquires here a new aspect of the 'healing of wounded freedom, atonement, purification, deliverance'. Only the Other (God) can extricate us from our bonds: 'Redemption now needs the Redeemer'. God assumes our flesh and as the God-Man (Christ Jesus), 'carries man the creature home to God'. This sacrifice takes the form of a Cross, 'of the love that in dying makes a gift of himself'. This is an act of creation, the restoration of *creation* to its true identity. Christian worship—a participation in the 'Pasch' of Christ from divine to human, from death to life, to the unity of God with man—'is the practical application and fulfilment' of the words of Jesus: 'I, when I am lifted up from the earth, will draw all men to myself' (Jn 12: 32). This is the Christian understanding of the ancient 'paradigm' of *exitus* and *reditus*: *exitus* is the Creator's free act of creation, which is ordered to a *reditus*, a return of creation to God in love, through Christ. The historical liturgy of Christendom 'is and always will be

---

in the context of Joseph Ratzinger/Pope Benedict XVI's 'biblical theology', see Hahn, *Covenant and Communion*, especially 163–85.

17. *TSL*, 24–8.

cosmic, without separation or confusion, and only as such does it stand erect in its full grandeur'.[18]

Continuing on the theme of sacrifice, in seeking the 'fundamental form' of the Christian liturgy, Joseph Ratzinger points out that the sacrificial system of all the world's religions—including Israel's—rests on the idea of 'representation' (*Vertretung*): representing man by animals or fruits. However this turns out to be not actually representation, the 'real gift', but 'replacement' (*Ersatz*), which replaces worship.[19] Concerning the liturgy of Israel, God was worshipped through an extensive sacrificial system, whose regulations were set out in the Torah. Examining this system more closely 'leads, finally, by its inner logic, to Jesus Christ, to the New Testament'. Reading the New Testament in terms of 'cultic theology', indicates how deeply it is bound up with the Old. At the beginning of 'cultic history', for example, Abraham is given a male lamb by God to be an offering, 'And so representative sacrifice is established by divine command … an expectation of the true Lamb … who comes from God and is for that very reason not a replacement but a true representative, in whom we ourselves are taken to God'. The Apocalypse presents this sacrificed, living lamb 'as the centre of the heavenly liturgy, a liturgy that, through Christ's sacrifice, is now present in the midst of the world and makes replacement liturgies superfluous' (Apoc 5). The institution of the Passover in Exodus 12, concerning the sacrifice of the Passover lamb as the centre of the liturgical year, and of Israel's memorial of faith—which clearly appears as the ransom for the death of the firstborn—can be connected to the 'emphatic way' in which St Luke describes Jesus as the 'first-born' (cf. Lk 2: 7), and helps us understand why the Captivity Epistles present him as the 'first-born of creation', in whom takes

---

18.   *TSL*, 28–34, 44–48. For Ratzinger's response to Catholic critics of 'sacrifice', and hermeneutical aspects, see Ratzinger, 'The Theology of the Liturgy', 18–30.

19.   *TSL*, 35–36 and n.1 concerning the translation of *Ersatz* and *Vertretung*.

place a sanctification of the firstborn that embraces all. The end of the temple in Jerusalem and worship there is also related to Christ as the 'New Temple' (see below).[20]

The cardinal then discusses developments in Jewish worship, particularly in Alexandria, where contact was made with the Greek critique of cult, and the importance of the concept of *logikē latreia* (*thusia*)—worship and sacrifice with spirit and mind, encountered in Romans 12, 1: 'I urge you therefore, brothers, by the mercies of God, to offer your bodies as a living sacrifice, holy and pleasing to God, your spiritual worship [λογικὴν λατρείαν].'[21] The sacrifice is 'the word', the word of prayer, which goes up from man to God, embodying the whole of man's existence and enabling him to become 'word' (*logos*) in himself. The Greek mind elevates *logos* to the idea of a mystical union with 'the *Logos*', 'the very meaning of things'. The Fathers of the Church, in taking up this development, call the Eucharist *oratio* (prayer), 'the sacrifice of the Word', going beyond the Greek concept. The idea of the sacrifice of the *Logos* 'becomes a full reality only in the *Logos incarnatus*, Christ Jesus'. Because of his cross and resurrection 'the Eucharist is the meeting point of all the lines that lead from the Old Covenant, indeed from the whole of man's religious history'.[22]

Cardinal Ratzinger ends this section with some conclusions. Christian worship, 'or rather the liturgy of the Christian faith, cannot be viewed simply as a Christianized form of the synagogue service', however much its actual development owes to it.[23] The effects of this theory

---

20. *Ibid.*, 37–48, which includes a discussion on 'prophetic disquiet' concerning the notion of sacrifice.

21. Cf. Ratzinger, *Pilgrim Fellowship of Faith*, 114–20, where reference is given to the work of Odo Casel, a notable figure in the Liturgical Movement, on the Christian interpretation of 'spiritual worship'.

22. *TSL*, 45–47; Ratzinger, *The Feast of Faith*, 11–32, where the theological basis of Christian prayer is examined.

23. *TSL*, 48. See pp. 11, 13–14 on the relationship between temple and synagogue.

'have been disastrous', making the priesthood and sacrifice no longer intelligible. The temple has been replaced by the 'universal temple of the risen Christ', and so does the new, and definitive sacrifice. Jesus' prayer 'is now united with the dialogue of eternal love within the Trinity. Jesus draws men into this prayer through the Eucharist, which is thus the ever-open door of adoration and the true sacrifice, the Sacrifice of the New Covenant, the "reasonable service of God"'. This means that 'universality' is a feature of Christian worship, which is never 'an event in the life of a community that finds itself in a particular place'. Therefore we must regard St Paul's concept of *logikē latreia*, of divine worship in accordance with *logos*, as the most appropriate way of expressing the essential form of Christian liturgy.[24]

The relationship of the liturgy to time and space

As the liturgy is cosmic, embracing heaven and earth, Joseph Ratzinger asks if there can really be special holy places and times in the world of the Christian faith? Here, in this section, is revealed, in a particular way, the 'eschatological' aspect of his liturgical thought. In the city of the New Jerusalem, God and the Lamb are the Temple (cf. Apoc 21: 22ff.). However 'his City is not yet here'. For this reason the Church Fathers describe the various stages of fulfilment, not just the contrast with the Old and New Testaments, but as the three steps of 'shadow', 'image' and 'reality'. In the 'Church of the New Testament' the shadow has been scattered by the image (cf. Rom 13: 12). But, as St Gregory the Great puts it, it is still only the time of dawn, when darkness and light are intermingled. The time of the New Testament is 'in-between', a mixture of 'already' and 'not yet', as image between shadow and reality. The empirical conditions of life in this world are still in force, but they have been 'burst open', and this process must continue 'in

---

24.   *TSL*, 48–50; Ratzinger, *Called to Communion*, 75–94; idem, *On the Way to Jesus Christ*, 107–28.

preparation for the final fulfilment already inaugurated in Christ.'[25]

Joseph Ratzinger believes that the idea of the New Testament as 'image', between shadow and reality, 'gives liturgical theology its specific form'. This becomes clearer when bearing in mind the three levels on which the liturgy operates, namely, 'the strictly liturgical level', 'the liturgical making present' ('the real liturgical level') and 'the future'. The 'strictly liturgical level' is revealed in the words and actions of Jesus in the last supper, the core of Christian liturgical celebration (the eucharistic prayer), constructed from a synthesis of synagogue and temple liturgies, replacing the temple sacrifices. However this only has meaning in relation to something really happening 'to a reality that is substantially present', Jesus' body and blood, sacrifice become gift, given in love. Without cross and resurrection 'Christian worship is null and void'.[26] Christ's exterior act on the cross is accompanied by an interior act of self-giving: the Body 'is given for you' (cf. Jn 10: 18). As St Maximius the Confessor showed, the obedience of Jesus' will is inserted into the eternal 'Yes' of the Son to the Father. 'The real interior act', the cardinal explains, 'though it does not exist without the exterior, transcends time, but since it comes from time, time can again be brought into it. That is how we can become contemporary with the past events of salvation'. The 'once and for all' (*semel/ephapax*) of Christ's sacrifice, in Hebrews, is bound up with *aiōnios*, 'everlasting'.[27] 'Today' embraces the whole time of the Church, making us contemporaries with what lies at the foundation of that Christian liturgy: the Paschal Mystery of Christ. 'Here is the real heart and true grandeur of the celebration of the Eucharist, which is more, much more than a meal'. Now if the past (level one) has far-reaching power in the present (level two), 'then the future [that is, level three],

25.   *TSL*, 53–54.

26.   *Ibid.*, 54–55.

27.   *TSL*, 56, citing St Bernard, *Sermo 5 de diversis* 1.

too, is present in what happens in the liturgy'. This not only recalls the idea of the *eschaton*, the second coming of Christ, but also 'representation', 'vicarious sacrifice' (*Stellvertretung*). This bears within it the future, in that it 'takes up into itself those whom it represents'. The liturgy is not about sacrificing animals, of 'something that is not me', but is something 'founded on the Passion, endured by a man who with his "I" reaches into the mystery of the living God himself, by the man who is the Son'. It can never be a mere *actio liturgica*. The Church's liturgy has an anthropological reality, the 'logicizing' (*logikē latreia*) of my existence with the self-giving of Christ and has a bearing on everyday life (cf. Rom 12: 1). This 'moral dimension' is at the same time the 'eschatological dynamism of the liturgy', for Christ's sacrifice is only complete when the world has become a place of love.[28] Furthermore, the three stages of salvation history—which progress from shadow to image to reality—and the three dimensions of the *liturgy*—past, present and future— indicate that the liturgy gives 'precise expression to this historical situation ... the "between-ness" of the time of images'. The theology of the liturgy is especially a theology of symbols, which connects us to what is present but hidden. We need sacred space, sacred time and mediating symbols, 'precisely so that, through "the image", through the sign, we learn to see the openness of heaven [to obtain] the capacity to know the mystery of God in the pierced heart of the crucified'. The liturgy is the means by which earthly time is inserted into the time of Jesus Christ.[29]

Joseph Ratzinger then turns his attention to sacred spaces and churches, and here he is indebted to Louis Bouyer, whose contribution to liturgical studies is well

---

28.   *TSL*, 54–59; Ratzinger, *Pilgrim Fellowship of Faith*, 114–18. Time is further discussed, in relation to Sundays, feast days, and the liturgical seasons in *TSL*, 92–111. Concerning the life of Jesus and the Jewish festival calendar, see Pope Benedict XVI/Ratzinger, *Jesus of Nazareth*, 306–7.

29.   *TSL*, 58–61. Concerning the side of Christ and the Eucharist, see Ratzinger, *God is Near Us*, 42–55.

known.[30] The Christian church building, was earlier called *domus ecclesiae* (abbreviated to *ecclesia*), the assembly of the people of God for worship, and convocation (*synagogē-ekklēsia*). Bouyer showed that the Christian house of God 'comes into being in complete continuity with the synagogue and thus acquires a specifically Christian newness, without any dramatic break, through communion with Jesus Christ'. However the cardinal points out that this does not contradict what he said previously about synagogue and temple.[31] The synagogue's orientation 'was always towards the presence of God', which, for the Jews was (and is) indissolubly connected with the temple. The two focal points of the synagogue—the seat of Moses and the shrine of the Torah—are of interest. The seat is where the rabbi presents the Word of God and represents Sinai. The shrine of the Torah, represents the 'Ark of the Covenant' which was the only object allowed in the 'Holy of Holies' of the temple, until it was lost, giving this place a special dignity. The shrine, containing the scrolls of the Torah, the living Word of God, is treated with signs of reverence. The presence of this 'Ark of the Covenant' indicates that the local community it not independent and self-sufficient: 'it is the place where the local community reaches out beyond itself to the temple, to the commonality of the one people of God as defined by one God'. The rabbi and the people gaze at the 'Ark' orientating themselves towards Jerusalem and the 'Holy of Holies' in the temple, connecting the synagogue's liturgy of the Word with the sacrificial liturgy of the temple.[32] The prayers said at the unrolling of the scrolls of scripture, for example, developed from the ritual prayers connected with the sacrificial actions of the temple, and are now regarded 'in accord with the tradition of the time without the temple', as an 'equivalent of sacrifice'.[33]

---

30. *TSL*, 62–63. Bouyer, in turn, relied on E. L. Sukenik.

31. See p. 9 above.

32. *TSL*, 61–67.

33. *Ibid.*, 66–67: there was no special architecture for synagogues: the Greek 'basilica' design was used.

While the synagogue 'exhibits already the essential and constant features of Christian places of worship'—again underling unity between the two Testaments—the cardinal points out that there were three innovations: Firstly the worshipper faces East and not the destroyed temple. 'Christ, represented by the sun, is the place of the *Shekinah*, the true throne of the living God'. The early Church regarded prayer toward the east as an apostolic tradition, and is 'an essential characteristic of Christian liturgy (and indeed private prayer)'. 'Orientation' (*oriens*, 'the East') is firstly a simple expression of looking to Christ as the meeting between God and man. The symbol of the rising sun, in which we find Christ, 'is the indication of a Christology defined eschatologically': we pray east to meet the coming Lord. Parts of Christendom from very early on also emphasized the cross, a sign of victory for the Risen One.[34] The second innovation is the altar at the east wall or apse for the celebration of the Eucharistic Sacrifice. The altar looks towards the *oriens* and forms part of it. 'What the temple had in the past foreshadowed is now present in a new way' on the Christian altar. The third innovation is that while the shrine of the Word remains, even in its position in the church building, the Torah is replaced by the Gospel, which does not abolish the scriptures, but interprets them.[35]

Although Joseph Ratzinger has already indicated some thoughts concerning the Christian altar and the direction of prayer, he develops and highlights these in a separate chapter, with reference to church architecture.[36] Church architecture has developed over the centuries; but, with every new development 'What is in harmony with the

---

34.   *TSL*, 67–70. In this section Joseph Ratzinger cites physical evidence from churches in the Near East. Liturgical 'orientation' in prayer—particularly important for the cardinal—is discussed again shortly.

35.   *TSL*, 70–71.

36.   Concerning church buildings, with particular reference to Christians as 'living stones' in Christ, see Ratzinger, *A New Song for the Lord*, 78–93.

essence of the liturgy, and what detracts from it?'.[37] For him, one thing is clear for the whole of Christendom, despite variations in practice. The early tradition of praying towards the east—in the eucharistic liturgy in this context—is a 'fundamental expression of the Christian synthesis of cosmos and history, of being rooted in the once-and-for-all events of salvation history while going out to meet the Lord who is to come again.' While the Byzantine church has by and large kept the traditional structures, a different arrangement in Rome developed. The bishop's chair was moved to the centre of the apse, and the altar to the nave, which appears to be the case in the Lateran Basilica and St Mary Major's, well into the ninth century. In St Peter's Basilica, however, the *altar* was moved near to the bishop's chair, during the pontificate of Pope St Gregory the Great (590–604). This was probably because the pope wanted to stand as near as possible above the tomb of St Peter, and this ordering was copied in many other stational churches in Rome. Altars above the tomb of the martyrs are very ancient, and identify the martyrs with Christ's sacrifice. However, because of topographical reasons, St Peter's faced west, and in order for the celebrating priest to face east, he had to stand *behind* the people and look *toward* the people. Cardinal Ratzinger indicates that 'Professor Cyrille Vogel has recently demonstrated [that] even when the orientation of the church enabled the celebrant to pray turned toward the people, when at the altar, we must not forget that it was not the priest alone who, then, turned East: it was the whole congregation, together with him'.[38]

Joseph Ratzinger believes that in the twentieth century the liturgical renewal took up this 'alleged model', and developed from it a new idea for the form of liturgy, namely celebrating the Eucharist *versus populum*. The priest and people formed a circle, and this alone was regarded as 'compatible with the meaning of the Christian liturgy,

---

37. *TSL*, 70–74.
38. *Ibid.*, 76–79.

with the requirement of active participation', and alone conformed to the 'primordial model of the Last Supper'. These arguments were so persuasive after the Second Vatican Council (which says nothing about 'turning toward the people') that new altars were set up everywhere. Today celebration _versus populum_, 'really does look like the characteristic fruit of Vatican II's liturgical renewal', bringing a new external arrangement and a new idea of the essence of the liturgy as 'a communal meal'. This is a misunderstanding of the significance of the Roman basilica and of the positioning of its altar, and the representation of the Last Supper is 'to say the least, inaccurate'.[39] Cardinal Ratzinger argues that,

> the Eucharist that Christians celebrate really cannot adequately be described by the term 'meal'. True, the Lord established the new reality of Christian worship within the framework of a Jewish (Passover) meal, but it was precisely this new reality, not the meal as such, that he commanded us to repeat ['Do this']. Very soon the reality was separated from its ancient context and found its proper and suitable form, a form already predetermined by the fact that the Eucharist refers back to the cross and thus to the transformation of temple sacrifice into worship of God that is in harmony with _logos_.[40]

The cardinal admits that these things 'were obscured or fell into total oblivion in the church buildings and liturgical practice of the modern age', leading to the common direction of prayer for priest and people as celebrating 'toward the wall' and 'turning your back on the people'. An 'unprecedented clericalization' arose, whose 'creativity' 'sustains the whole thing', entrusting individuals to 'plan' the liturgy. However the notion of the pilgrim People of God, 'set[ting] off for the _Oriens_, for the Christ who

---

39. _Ibid._

40. _TSL_, 76–78 (at 78). Cf. Ratzinger, _The Feast of Faith_, 33–60; idem, _Pilgrim Fellowship of Faith_, 105–8; Ratzinger, _God is Near Us_, 57–65; idem, _On the Way to Jesus Christ_, 109–12.

comes to meet us', and related matters, are not the products of romanticism and nostalgia for the past. While we cannot simply replicate the past, 'Every age must discover and express the essence of the liturgy anew. The point is to discover this essence amid all the changing appearances'.[41] The cardinal indicates that we cannot reject all the reforms of the twentieth century wholesale—for instance distinguishing the place for the Liturgy of the Word from the eucharistic liturgy proper. In answer to several objections to his ideas by Häussling, the cardinal makes a number of important points concerning the study and interpretation of the liturgy. He sees that the problem with a large part of modern liturgiology is that it tends to recognize only antiquity as a source, and therefore normative. Everything that developed later, in the Middle Ages and through the Council of Trent, is viewed as decadent; 'And so one ends up with dubious reconstructions of the most ancient practice, fluctuating criteria, and never-ending suggestions for reform, which lead ultimately to the disintegration of the liturgy that has evolved in a living way'. This is a reference to the organic development of the liturgy. On the other hand, 'it is important and necessary to see that we cannot take as our norm the ancient in itself and as such, nor must we automatically write off later developments as alien to the original form of the liturgy. There can be a thoroughly living kind of development in which a seed at the origin of something ripens and bears fruit.' For these reasons, Joseph Ratzinger wishes the (general) restoration of the tradition *ad orientem*, in the building of churches and in the celebration of the liturgy, and that the question of the correct position of the altar 'is at the centre of the postconciliar debate.'[42] However, on a practical level, this may not be possible, or desirable at the present time, after so many liturgical changes. The cross—which was linked from early on with the east—'should stand in the middle of

---

41. *TSL*, 78–82.
42. *TSL*, 71, 76–82; Ratzinger, *The Feast of Faith*, 66–67, 139–45.

the altar and be the common point of focus for both priest
and praying community'. In this way *conversi ad Dominum*
is fulfilled. The Lord is the point of reference 'the rising
sun of history.' The cross points to Christ's suffering and
triumph, and expresses the idea of his second coming.[43]

The 'decadence theory' concerning the Christian liturgy
appears again in Joseph Ratzinger's discussion of the reservation of the Blessed Sacrament. In the first millennium the
church did not have tabernacles. In the second millennium
the tabernacle for the living presence of the Lord (*Shekinah*)
developed from 'passionate theological struggles and their
resulting clarifications, in which the permanent presence
of Christ in the consecrated Host emerged with greater
clarity'. The 'decadence theory' canonizes 'the early days'
and a romanticism for the first century: 'Transubstantiation ... the adoration of the Lord in the Blessed Sacrament,
eucharistic devotions with monstrance and processions—
all these things, it is alleged, are medieval errors'. The
Eucharistic gifts 'are for eating, not for looking at'. Joseph
Ratzinger disagrees with this and defends these developments against attacks on the Real Presence of Christ in the
Eucharist. He turns to an important finding of Henri de
Lubac, which has often been misunderstood. 'It has always
been clear that the goal of the Eucharist is our own transformation, so that we become "one body and spirit" with
Christ (cf. 1 Cor 6:17). This ... was expressed up to the early
Middle Ages by the twin concepts of *corpus mysticum* and
corpus verum.' *Mysticum* does not mean 'mystical' in the
modern sense, but, in the vocabulary of the Fathers, 'per-
taining to the mystery, the sphere of the sacrament'. *Corpus
mysticum* was used to express the sacramental Body, the
corporeal presence of Christ in the sacrament, which—
according to the Fathers—'is given to us, so that we may
become the *corpus verum*.' However changes in the use of
language led to the Blessed Sacrament being referred to as

---

43.   *TSL*, 82–84; Ratzinger, *The Feast of Faith*, 141–45.

corpus verum, the 'true body', while *corpus mysticum* related to the 'Mystical ('mysterious') Body'.[44]

It should be acknowledged that a 'spiritual development' occurred with the change in meanings for *corpus mysticum* and *corpus verum*, though 'something of the eschatological dynamism and corporate character (the sense of "we") of eucharistic faith was lost or at least diminished.' However one should not accept the conclusion that many people drew from de Lubac's careful description of the linguistic change, that 'a hitherto unknown realism, indeed naturalism, was now forcing its way into eucharistic doctrine, and the large views of the Fathers were giving way to a static and one-sided idea of the Real Presence'. Despite losses, which we should recover in our own time, there were still gains made overall. The Eucharist can only 'bring us together' and make us his 'true body', because in it the Lord gives us his true body. The early church was aware that the bread once changed remains changed. However in the Middle Ages, 'this awareness is deepened', with a wholly new intensity. Hence the desire grew for a proper place for the Eucharistic Presence of Christ; 'little by little the tabernacle takes shape [taking] the place previously occupied by the now disappeared "Ark of the Covenant", and completely fulfilling what the Ark of the Covenant represented as the "Holy of Holies". Eating this (Eucharistic) Bread—not ordinary bread, as the most ancient traditions constantly emphasize—means worshipping it.' Thus, 'adoration is not opposed to Communion [which] only reaches its true depths when it is supported and surrounded by adoration'. A church where a lamp burns constantly before the tabernacle 'is always alive', and the Lord is always waiting for me, '[...] calling me, wanting to make me "eucharistic"'.[45]

---

44. *TSL*, 85–87.

45. *TSL*, 85–91; Ratzinger, *God is Near Us*, 74–113; idem, *The Feast of Faith*, 127–37.

Art and liturgy

Joseph Ratzinger's discussion on art and liturgy—essentially a theological and historical summary of Christian art—begins by considering 'the question of images' and their use, which indicates continuity between art in the ancient synagogue—particularly from the time of Jesus—and the Christian Church.[46] The first commandment underlines the uniqueness of God and that adoration is due to him alone: 'You shall not make for yourself a graven image, or any likeness of anything that is in heaven above, or that is in the earth beneath, or that is in the water under the earth' (Exod 20: 4; cf. Deut 5: 8). The notable exception to this was something 'at the very centre of the Old Testament', namely the Ark of the Covenant, with its gold covering and two cherubim of gold on either end of the mercy seat (*kapporeth*). Their wings face inwards, protecting the place of divine revelation, 'precisely to conceal the mystery of the presence of God himself' (Exod 25: 18–20). The cardinal links this with the New Testament and St Paul, who saw that the mercy seat foreshadowed the crucified Christ as *the* 'mercy seat', but that God 'lifted the veil from his face' in Christ. The Eastern Church's icon of the resurrection portrays Christ standing on two slabs, which suggest not only the grave, but also the *kapporeth* of the Old Covenant. Christ is also flanked by a cherubim. This transformation of the Ark of the Covenant into the resurrection 'reveals the very heart of the development from Old Testament to New'.[47] The cardinal explores this development in some detail, indicating that, from the time of Jesus, Judaism had a more generous interpretation of the 'image question'. Ancient synagogues were richly decorated with representations from the Bible, in a 'narrative' form (*haggadah*) and not mere images of past events. We can see

---

46.   *TSL*, 115–23. For an illuminating study of Ratzinger/Pope Benedict XVI's views on sacred art ('holy images'), see Nichols, *Redeeming Beauty*, 89–101.

47.   *TSL*, 115–16.

the same continuity here as was seen between synagogue and Christian church. The Christian images, as in the catacombs, 'simply take up and develop the canon of images already established by the synagogue', but now refer to Christ and the sacraments. 'All sacred images are, without exception, in a certain sense images of the resurrection … giving us the assurance of the world to come, of the final coming of Christ'. The portrayal of Christ as the 'good shepherd', was very important in early Christianity 'as an allegory of the *Logos*', through whom all things were made, and who became man to save the lost sheep of humanity.'[48]

Joseph Ratzinger then underlines the importance of the development of iconography in the East, particularly after 'iconoclasm'. In the icon 'it is not the facial features that count'. What matters is 'a new way of seeing … an opening up of the inner senses, from a facilitation of sight that gets beyond the surface of the empirical and perceives Christ, as the later theology of icons puts it, in the light of Tabor.' Cardinal Ratzinger cites Evdokimov: the icon requires—perhaps ironically—a 'fast from the eyes', as the icon painters prepare themselves for the long path of prayerful asceticism. 'This is what marks the transition from art to sacred art'.[49] The icon has become a prayer and leads to prayer. When this interior orientation is understood, only then can the Second Council of Nicaea, and the following councils concerned with icons, be understood, which regarded them as a confession of faith in the incarnation and iconoclasm as a denial of this.[50] We should ask if the theology of the icon from the East is valid for us in the West. From early Christian art until the end of the Romanesque period (thirteenth century), 'there is no essential difference between East and West with regard to the question of images.' Although western synods insisted on the 'purely educative role of the images', in Romanesque art—even with the

---

48. *Ibid.*, 116–19.

49. See Evdokimov, *The Art of the Icon*, 188.

50. *TSL*, 120–3.

development of 'plastic art' — 'it is always the risen Christ, even on the Cross, to whom the community looks as the true *Oriens*. And art is always characterized by the unity of creation, Christology, and eschatology'. Western art is still orientated towards the heavenly liturgy. With Gothic art, a change slowly takes place, though 'much remains the same'. However the central image is the crucified, suffering Christ and not the *Pantocrator*, the Lord of all. 'The separation in iconography between East and West … doubtless goes very deep: very different themes, different spiritual paths, open up. A devotion to the cross of a more historicizing kind replaces orientation to the *Oriens*, to the risen Lord who has gone ahead of us.' However we should not exaggerate the difference. The depiction of Christ dying in pain on the cross is something new, 'but it still depicts him who bore our pains [and] represents the redemptive love of God.' Such images 'belong to the mystery', come from prayer and meditation on the way of Christ, 'and popular piety is enabled to reach the heart of the liturgy, the Mass, in a new way […] to the heart of God.'[51]

On a more controversial note, perhaps, Cardinal Ratzinger says that the Renaissance, while still depicting Christian images, was not 'sacred art' in the proper sense, by focusing on the 'autonomy' of man and 'does not enter into the humility of the sacraments and their time-transcending dynamism', by wanting to enjoy 'today' and to bring redemption through beauty itself.[52] Baroque art 'in its better form', derives from the Counter Reformation and the Council of Trent. It is aligned with the tradition of the West, as Trent emphasized the didactic and pedagogical

---

51.   *Ibid.*, 123–9.

52.   Cf. Nichols, *Redeeming Beauty*, 99, where Renaissance art, in one instance at least — Raphael's *Disputation on the Sacrament* — is shown to 'embody, rather than traduce, the prescriptions for sacred art which Ratzinger offers'; 'the principal message of *Disputation on the Sacrament* concerns eschatology anticipated by the liturgy — absolutely in line, then, with Ratzinger's own theology of the image': *Ibid.*

character of art, but with a fresh start to interior renewal. This art is intended to insert us into the heavenly liturgy. The Enlightenment 'pushed faith into a kind of intellectual and even social ghetto' and contemporary culture 'turned away from the faith and trod another path, so that faith took flight in historicism, the copying of the past, or else attempted compromise or lost itself in resignation and cultural abstinence'. This led to a new iconography, 'which has frequently been regarded as virtually mandated by the Second Vatican Council.' Though the destruction of images—already seen in the 1920s—eliminated a lot of kitsch and unworthy art, it 'ultimately… left behind a void, the wretchedness of which we are now experiencing in a truly acute way'. This 'crisis of art' as a symptom of the crisis of man's very existence, and, coupled with the growth of materialism, man is blinded to the questions of life's meaning 'that transcend[s] the material world.'[53]

From his theological and historical examination of art, Joseph Ratzinger proposes to identify 'the fundamental principles of an art ordered to divine worship'. The complete absence of images 'is incompatible with faith in the incarnation of God', and images of beauty, 'in which the mystery of the invisible God becomes visible', are essential to Christian worship. Sacred art finds its subjects in the images of salvation history which display 'the inner unity of God's action' and have reference to the sacraments, above all to Baptism and the Eucharist, which are essentially connected with what happens in the liturgy. 'Now history becomes sacrament in Christ, who is the source of the sacraments. Therefore, the icon of Christ is the centre of sacred iconography'. The Church in the West does not need to abandon the path it followed from the thirteenth century, but it must achieve 'a real reception of the Seventh Ecumenical Council, Nicaea II, which affirmed the fundamental importance and theological status of the image in

---

53. *TSL*, 129–30.

the Church', while new intuitions and the 'ever-new experiences of piety' should also find a place in the Church.[54]

Joseph Ratzinger, whose fondness for music is well known, then turns to music and the liturgy. Music is very important in biblical religion, and is first mentioned when the Israelites, crossing the Red Sea, had been definitively delivered from slavery (Exod 15). In the Apocalypse, the song of Moses becomes 'the song of the Lamb' (Apoc 15: 3), who conquers the final enemies of the People of God, 'the beast, its image, and the number of its name'. Liturgical singing 'is established in the midst of this great historical tension'. For Israel the event of salvation in the Red Sea 'will always be one of the main reasons for praising God' while for Christians, Christ's resurrection is the true Exodus. However the sufferings of history have still to be endured, and 'all the pain gathered in and brought into the sacrifice of praise, in order to be transformed there into a song of praise'. This is the theological basis for liturgical singing.[55]

The cardinal then examines the 'practical application' of this theological basis for singing, and, once more, in the light of historical developments. As far as scripture is concerned, one of the witnesses to biblical singing is the Book of Psalms. The psalms display the whole range of human experiences, which become prayer and song in the presence of God, for example, lamentation, fear, hope, gratitude and joy. The psalter became the 'prayer book of the infant Church, which, with equal spontaneity, has become a Church that sings her prayers'. The psalms, which also have christological and pneumatological aspects, 'not only concern the text but also include the element of music.' This is due to the Holy Spirit who inspired David to sing and to pray, and to speak of Christ. The Holy Spirit also 'teaches us to sing' for singing surpasses ordinary speech, and is a 'pneumatic' event. Church music comes into being as a

54. *Ibid.*, 131–35.
55. *TSL*, 137–38.

charism of the Spirit. Through the Song of Songs, which were interpreted at a deeper level than human love songs, 'the mystery of the love of God and Israel shines through' in the analogy of marriage. Jesus took this theme up in the parable of the Bridegroom –whom he identifies as himself–and the wedding feast (Mk 2: 19ff.). Christians came to see the Eucharist 'as the presence of the Bridegroom and thus a foretaste of the wedding feast of love'. The spousal mystery, announced in the Old Testament, of the intimate union between God and man 'takes place in the Sacrament of the Body and Blood of Christ'. The singing of the Church comes ultimately out of love. *Cantare amantis est* ('singing is a lover's thing'), says St Augustine.[56]

In time hymns and canticles came into being in the Church, for example, the hymn of Christ in the letter to the Philippians.[57] However restrictions were placed on the composition of these by the Council of Laodicea (360?), due to the dangers of Gnosticism, and post-biblical hymns were almost entirely lost. While we may regret the cultural impoverishment this entailed, 'it was necessary for the sake of a greater good ... the identity of biblical faith, and the very rejection of false inculturation'. In the history of liturgical music one can see 'extensive parallels with the evolution of the image question' (though there are also differences). Eventually, in the West, Gregorian chant developed, and polyphony came in the Later Middle Ages, with the return of musical instruments in the church. However, with artistic licence, secular music influenced Church music, which brought its own dangers, in that music 'was no longer developing out of prayer [and] alienating the liturgy from its true nature.' Reform came with the Council of Trent, subjugating music to the service of the Word and emphasising the clear distinction between secular and sacred music. The age of the Baroque 'achieved an astounding unity of secular music-making with the

---

56.   *TSL*, 139–42.

57.   Phil 2: 6–11: 'though he was in the form of God ...'.

music of the liturgy'. In Bach or Mozart, for example, 'we have a sense ... of what the *gloria Dei*, the glory of God means.' But other dangers appeared, and in the nineteenth century in many places the sacred was obscured by the operatic. More reforms appeared under Pope St Pius X, who declared Gregorian chant, and the great polyphony of the age of the Catholic Reformation, to be the standard for liturgical music.[58]

In response to challenges which Joseph Ratzinger believes that Church music faces today—for example 'pop music'—he gives some principles based on the inner foundations of Christian sacred music, and in relation to *logos*. In liturgical music, built on biblical faith, there is a clear 'dominance of the Word'. This music 'is a higher form of proclamation', rising out of love, and responding to God's love made flesh in Christ. The relation between liturgical music and *logos* is firstly, and simply, 'its relation to the words', which is why singing has priority over musical instruments, though does not exclude them. Biblical and liturgical texts 'are the normative words', but this does not rule out that they can act as inspiration for 'new songs'. Secondly, prayer is a gift of the Holy Spirit, who intercedes for us when we do not know how to pray (Rom 8: 26). He enkindles love in us and thus moves us to sing. This gift 'that surpasses all words', is always related to Christ, *the* Word. The Church's tradition 'has this in mind when it talks about the sober inebriation caused in us by the Holy Spirit. There is always an ultimate sobriety, a deeper rationality, resisting any decline into irrationality and immoderation.' It is a form of *logikē latreia* (reason-able, *logos*-worthy worship). Thirdly the Word incarnate in Christ, the *Logos*, is not just the power that gives meaning to the individual and to history, but is 'the creative Meaning from which the universe comes and which the universe, the cosmos, reflects'. In the Mass we insert ourselves into this cosmic liturgy, 'and all our singing is a singing and praying with

---

58.   *TSL*, 142–47.

the great liturgy that spans the whole of creation'.[59] The cosmic character of liturgical music—grounded ultimately in the ordering of all Christian worship to *logos*—stands in opposition to modern tendencies of seeing music as pure subjectivity, and as an expression of mere will. Cardinal Ratzinger ends his discussion on art and music on a very positive note, while acknowledging that the problems of the present day pose 'without doubt a grave challenge to the Church and the culture of the liturgy'. What in museums is only a monument of the past 'is constantly made present in the liturgy in all its freshness' and in our time important works of art, inspired by faith, are being produced. Such artists need not regard themselves as the 'rearguard of culture'. 'Humble submission to what goes before us releases authentic freedom and leads to the true summit of our vocation as human beings'.[60]

Liturgical form

In considering what 'liturgical form' is, Joseph Ratzinger makes the observation that for many people today, the word 'rite' has many negative connotations, and is viewed as restrictive. But what actually is 'rite'? Although he was not a Christian, the Roman jurist Pomponius Festus defined *ritus* as 'an approved practice in the administration of sacrifice'. Man is always looking for the 'right way' of honouring God, for a form of common prayer and worship. Originally the word 'orthodoxy' (*doxa* means 'opinion' or 'splendour') meant the right way to glorify God, the right form of adoration. We know how we should truly glorify God 'by praying and living in communion with the Paschal journey of Jesus Christ, by accomplishing with him his *Eucharistia*, in which the incarnation leads to the resurrection—along the way of the cross'. Initially 'rite' is defined

---

59. Ratzinger draws upon St Augustine's *On Music: TSL*, 152–53.

60. *TSL*, 148–56; Ratzinger, *The Feast of Faith*, 97–126; idem, *A New Song for the Lord*, 94–110: further important insights into Joseph Ratzinger's 'theology of music' may be gained from these books.

for Christians as 'the practical arrangements made by the
community, in time and space, for the basic type of worship received from God in faith'. While rite has a primary
place in liturgy, it, too, has ethical dimensions, by including the whole conduct of one's life.[61]

Joseph Ratzinger then provides an overview of the
major rites that have left their mark upon the Church. The
existence of the primatial sees of Rome, Alexandria, Antioch and Byzantine, indicates a point of 'crystallization' in
the liturgical tradition. Antioch was the capital of Syria,
and here we also find the West Syrian rites, including the
Syro-Malankar Rite, traced back to the apostle James, and
still in use in India. These rites were characterized by 'an
extraordinary missionary zeal' and spread as far as China.
There is also the Chaldean liturgical family, which has preserved very ancient traditions, originating from the apostle
Thomas and two disciples: that Thomas was a missionary
in India 'definitely has to be taken seriously at the historical level'. Alexandria includes all the Coptic and Ethiopian
rites. The Liturgy of St Mark, developed in Alexandria,
and bears strong Byzantine influence. The Armenian Rite,
is traced back to the apostles Bartholomew and Thaddeus.
Byzantium took up the tradition of Antioch (the Liturgy
of St John Chrysostom), and influences from Asia Minor
and Jerusalem. This liturgy was adopted by a large part
of the Slavic world. With the Roman liturgy—which was
very similar to the Latin liturgy of Africa—stood the Old
Gaulish or 'Gallican' liturgy, to which the Celtic and the
old Spanish or 'Mozarabic' liturgies were closely related.
These rites were very similar, but Rome was more sober
and conservative. It began to adopt the Gallican heritage,
which, after the liturgical reform following the Second Vatican Council, more or less completely disappeared. Joseph
Ratzinger is critical of this, indicating that (in general) for
the first time a radical standardisation of liturgy was car-

---

61.   *TSL*, 159–60.

ried out. What began as a process of making everything uniform 'has swung to the opposite extreme'.[62]

From this brief sketch, some important conclusions about liturgical form can be drawn. Individual rites are related 'to the places where Christianity originated and the apostles preached: they are anchored in the time and place of the event of divine revelation'. 'Always' (*semper*) can only come from 'once for all' (*semel*). 'The Church does not pray in some kind of mythical omnitemporality', and nor can she cannot forsake her roots. Rites are not, therefore just the products of inculturation, even if they have incorporated elements from different cultures. 'They are forms of the apostolic tradition'.[63] This is essential to what defines them, and it follows on from that 'that there can be no question of creating totally new rites'. However rites are not rigidly fenced off from each other, and there is exchange and cross-fertilization between them. They not only incorporate the diachronic aspect, 'but also create communion among different cultures and languages... Unspontaneity is of their essence'.[64] Here again the notion of organic development appears. The cardinal cites J. A. Jungmann, who tried to sum up the Western view in the phrase 'the liturgy that has come to be', wanting to show that this 'coming-to-be' still goes on, 'as an organic growth, not as a specially contrived production.' It grows as a plant, 'whose laws of growth determine the possibilities of future development.' Joseph Ratzinger then makes, what some may view as blunt comments on perceptions concerning the authority of the pope in liturgical matters, which, while providing 'a juridical element' in the liturgy, has its limits:

---

62. *TSL*, 160–63; Ratzinger, *The Feast of Faith*, 61–68.

63. On tradition and the importance of the liturgical inheritance of the patristic age, see Ratzinger, *Principles of Catholic Theology*, 85–152, especially 150–51.

64. For further comments on the theme of 'liturgy and inculturation' —which is not unconnected—see *TSL*, 200–3; Ratzinger, *The Feast of Faith*, 80–82.

> After the Second Vatican Council, the impression
> arose that the pope really could do anything in
> liturgical matters, especially if he were acting on
> the mandate of an ecumenical council. Eventually,
> the idea of the givenness of the liturgy, the fact that
> one cannot do with it what one will, faded from the
> public consciousness of the West. In fact, the First
> Vatican Council had in no way defined the pope as
> an absolute monarch. On the contrary, it presented
> him as the guarantor of obedience to the revealed
> Word. The pope's authority is bound to the tradi-
> tion of faith, *and that also applies to the liturgy.* It is not
> 'manufactured' by the authorities. Even the pope
> can only be a humble servant of its *lawful develop-
> ment* and abiding integrity and identity.[65]

Concerning divergences in the East, the cardinal comments
that while there is—as with icons (and sacred music)—
freedom and historical development, 'it would lead to the
breaking up of the foundations of Christian identity if the
fundamental intuitions of the East, which are the fundamental intuitions of the early church, were abandoned',
repeating that 'The authority of the pope is not unlimited;
it is at the service of sacred tradition'.[66] In the context of the
Christian liturgy, rite is, 'the expression, that has become
form, of ecclesiality and of the Church's identity as a historically transcendent communion of liturgical prayer
and action', where 'creativity' cannot be considered as an
authentic category. The life of the liturgy 'does not come
from what dawns upon the minds of individuals and planning groups', but is 'God's descent upon our world, the
source of real liberation'. The more we humbly surrender
ourselves to this 'the more "new" the liturgy will constantly be, and the more true and personal it becomes.' In
conclusion, Joseph Ratzinger asks if it must still be explicitly stated that 'all this has nothing to do with rigidity?'.

---

65. *TSL*, 165–66 (my emphasis). Papal/conciliar authority is discussed
     again in chapter two.

66. *Ibid.*

Christians know that God has spoken through man and that the human and historical factor, is part of the way God acts. That is the reason why there can be development, 'a development, though, that takes place without haste or aggressive intervention.' The connection to apostolic origins is essential to what defines them. Thus, Ratzinger repeats again, that from this there can be 'no question of creating totally new rites', while not discounting variations within liturgical families.[67]

The body and the liturgy

Joseph Ratzinger begins his consideration of the body and the liturgy by examining the phrase *participatio actuosa*, the 'active participation' of everyone in the liturgy, used by the Second Vatican Council to express one of its main ideas for the shaping of the liturgy.[68] The council was 'quite right to do so', but what does it mean? Unfortunately the phrase was 'very quickly misunderstood to mean something external, entailing a need for general activity, as if as many people as possible, as often as possible, should be visibly engaged in action.' Yet 'part-icipation' refers to a principal action in which everyone has a part. To understand *participatio actuosa* we need to determine what this central *actio* is. By the *actio* of the liturgy 'the sources mean the eucharistic prayer', called the *oratio* by the Fathers. This is the essence,

---

67. *TSL*, 163–69.

68. 'Mother Church earnestly desires that all the faithful should be led to that full, conscious, and active participation [*ad plenam illam, consciam atque actuosam liturgicarum celebrationem participationem ducantur*] in liturgical celebrations which is demanded by the very nature of the liturgy, and to which the Christian people … have a right and obligation by reason of their baptism. In the restoration and promotion [*instauranda et fovenda*] of the sacred liturgy the full and active participation [*plena et actuosa participatio*] by all the people is the aim to be considered before all else, for it is the primary and indispensable source from which the faithful are to derive the true Christian spirit': The Second Vatican Council, *The Constitution on the Sacred Liturgy Sacrosanctum Concilium*, 4 December 1963, no. 14.

fundamental form and centre of the liturgy. This *oratio*,
the 'Canon', 'is *actio* in the highest sense of the word'. The
human *actio* 'steps back' and makes way for the *actio divina*.
The priest says the 'I' of the Lord, 'This is my Body', 'This
is my Blood'. Man can 'part-icipate' in this because of the
incarnation. Although the Sacrifice of the *Logos* is accepted
already and forever, 'we must still pray for it to become *our*
sacrifice that we ourselves ... may be transformed into the
Logos (*logisiert*), conformed to the *Logos*, and so be made
the true Body of Christ'. In this real 'action' there is no difference between priests and laity, though the 'I' of Jesus
Christ has to done by the priest. Participation in that which
no human being does, is a question of being united to the
Lord, and thus becoming 'one spirit with him' (1 Cor 6:
17). External action—for example reading and singing—
can be distributed in a reasonable way, but participation
in the Liturgy of the Word is to be distinguished from
the sacramental celebration proper. 'External actions are
quite secondary here'. It is not now a matter of looking at
or toward the priest, 'but of looking together toward the
Lord'.

But what about the body? In the liturgy, Christ offers
himself to us in his Body and Blood 'and thus in a corporeal way', the new corporality of the risen Lord. 'The
true liturgical action is the deed of God and for that very
reason the liturgy of faith [once again] always reaches
beyond the cultic act into everyday life'. It is more than
'carrying objects' and other such activities. Surrendering
ourselves to God's action, in order to cooperate with him
'begins in the liturgy', in the liturgy's orientation towards
the risen Christ. The body has a place within divine worship, expressed liturgically 'in a certain discipline of the
body ... in gestures that have developed out of the liturgy's
inner demands and that make the essence of the liturgy, as
it were, bodily visible.'[69]

---

69.   *TSL*, 171–75; Ratzinger, *The Feast of Faith*, 68–72, 88–90.

Having discussed liturgical gestures generally, Joseph Ratzinger then examines a series of specific gestures, namely, the sign of the cross—'the most basic Christian gesture in prayer'—kneeling; standing and sitting; the *orans* (praying with arms extended); joining one's hands; bowing; and striking one's breast. To seal oneself with the sign of the cross 'is a visible and public Yes to him who suffered for us', a confession of faith in Christ's death and resurrection, and of hope in salvation. We place ourselves under the protection of the cross, which shows us the road to life, the 'imitation of Christ'. It also confesses the triune God, Father, Son and Holy Spirit, and in it we accept our Baptism anew. It sums up 'the whole essence of Christianity', and it displays 'what is distinctively Christian'. It is interesting to note that Jewish graves from the time of Jesus have been discovered with the sign of the cross, the *Tav*—the last letter of the Jewish alphabet—which, among certain Jewish circles, was used as a widespread sacred sign 'of confession of faith in the God of Israel and at the same time a sign of hope in his protection', which derived from Ezekiel's vision of the salvific *Tav*.[70] Christians—as far as we know—did not at first adopt this Jewish symbol of the cross, 'but they found the sign of the cross from within their faith and were able to see in it the summing up of their whole faith'. But was Ezekiel's vision 'not bound to appear to Christians later as a glimpse of the One who was to come?', who has transformed the *Tav* 'into the power of salvation?'. The cardinal indicates that the cross as 'the key to all reality', is one of the fundamental ideas in patristic theology. In fact the Fathers connected the sign of Christ's cross with Plato's *Timaeus* (34ab and 36bc), where the Greek letter *Chi* (X) is 'inscribed upon the cosmos'. The sign of the cross also became the characteristic gesture of blessing for Christians, and the cardinal advocates its return 'in a much

---

70.   Ez 9: 4ff.

stronger way into our daily life and permeate it with the
power of the love that comes from the Lord'.[71]

In regards to kneeling (*prostratio*), there are groups 'of
no small influence' who try to discourage it and consider
it inappropriate for redeemed man. However kneeling is
biblical, and its central importance can be found in a very
concrete way. In the New Testament, for example, the word
proskynein occurs fifty-nine times, twenty-four of which
are in the Apocalypse 'the book of the heavenly liturgy',
which is the standard for the Church's liturgy.[72] There are
three forms of this posture in the Bible, though they can be
merged with each other. Firstly there is 'prostration' — lying
with one's face to the ground before the overwhelming
power of God. In Joshua (5:15) God appears to Joshua, who,
'seeing the commander of the army of the Lord' and, having recognized who he is, throws himself to the ground.
Origen, commenting on this passage, says that 'Is there
any other commander of the powers of the Lord than our
Lord Jesus Christ?'. In the New Testament, there is Jesus'
prayer on the Mount of Olives (Mt 22: 39; Mk 14: 35; Lk 22:
40–46). Luke, whom Joseph Ratzinger terms as 'the theologian of kneeling prayer', indicates that Jesus prayed on his
knees: his use of the expression *theis ta gonata*, to describe
the kneeling of Christians, 'is unknown in classical Greek'.
Our Lord, before entering his Passion, gives us an example
of the 'fall of man' in anguish, and the union of the human
will with the divine. The liturgy today has the prostration
on Good Friday and at ordinations.[73] The prostration on
Good Friday, expresses fittingly 'our sense of shock at the
fact that we by our sins share in the responsibility for the

---

71.   *TSL*, 177–84; Ratzinger, *Pilgrim Fellowship of Faith*, 110–11.

72.   *TSL*, 184–85.

73.   One could also mention, for instance, religious professions, in
      a liturgical context, and the beautiful ceremony of prostration
      after the reading of the martyrology on Christmas Eve in the Pre-
      monstratensian Rite ('use' is more accurate): *Ordinarius seu Liber
      Caeremoniarium ad usum Sacri et Canonici Ordinis Praemonstratensis*,
      no. 792.

death of Christ ... We throw ourselves down, as Jesus did, before the mystery of God's power present to us'. During ordinations the prostration 'comes from the awareness of our absolute incapacity, by our own powers, to take on the priestly mission of Jesus Christ'.[74]

Secondly—especially in the New Testament—there is falling to one's knees before another, described four times in the Gospels (Mk 1: 40; 10: 17; Mt 17: 14; 27: 29) by the word *gonypetein*. For example, in Mark 1: 40, a leper comes to Jesus and begs for help. He falls to his knees before him and says 'If you will, you can make me clean'. This is not a proper act of adoration, 'but rather a supplication expressed fervently in bodily form'. The classical word for adoration, *proskynein*, is used elsewhere in the Gospels, especially in St John's Gospel.[75] It is clear from these passages, from the structure of the narrative, that this gesture, 'acknowledging Jesus as the Son of God is an act of worship'. The spiritual and bodily meaning of *proskynein* 'are really inseparable'. 'Worship is one of those fundamental acts that affect the whole man', which is why kneeling before God 'is something we cannot abandon'.[76] Thirdly, there is kneeling, on one or both knees. Kneeling is a Christological as well as a Christian gesture, and for Joseph Ratzinger the most important passage for the theology of kneeling is the great hymn of Christ in Philippians 2: 6–11: 'at the name of Jesus every knee should bow, in heaven and on earth and under the earth'.[77] Here the cardinal issues a stark 'wake-up' call. The man who learns to believe learns also to kneel, 'and a faith or a liturgy no longer familiar

---

74. *TSL*, 185–94.

75. For example. Jn 9: 35–38; 4: 19–24: the story of the blind man and the Samaritan woman.

76. *TSL*, 188–91.

77. Cf. Is 45: 23: 'To me every knee shall bow, every tongue shall swear'.

with kneeling would be sick at the core. Where it has been lost, kneeling must be rediscovered'.[78]

Standing and sitting 'are not very controversial these days, and the importance that each has is not hard to see'. In the Old Testament standing is a classic posture for prayer, and various New Testament texts show that in Jesus' time standing was the ordinary posture of prayer among the Jews.[79] Among Christians, standing was the customary form of prayer at Easter, which was decreed in the twentieth canon of Nicaea: 'It is the time of the victory of Jesus Christ, the time of joy … even in the posture of our prayer'. Standing is also an expression of readiness. 'Christ is standing up at the right hand of God, in order to meet us'. We unite ourselves to the victory of Christ, and show reverence when standing to listen to the Gospel. When hearing the Word 'we cannot remain sitting; it pulls us up'. Concerning the familiar image of the catacombs, the *orans* female figure standing and praying with out-stretched hands, recent research indicates that the *orans* normally represents, not the praying Church, but the soul that stands before God in Heaven. The prayer represented here 'is not the earthly liturgy, the liturgy of pilgrimage … but prayer in the state of glory'. To the extent that liturgical prayer anticipates what has been promised, standing is its proper posture. However, 'insofar as liturgical prayer belongs to that "between" time in which we live, then kneeling remains indispensable to it as an expression of the "now" of our life'.[80]

Sitting is permitted during the readings, the homily and the 'meditative assimilation of the Word'. Some deny its sacred character and view it as purely practical. Here Joseph Ratzinger believes that further research is necessary; though he discounts the possibility that the 'lotus position' of oriental meditation has a place in the liturgy,

---

78.   *TSL*, 191–94. Unfortunately this is certainly the case in a number of European countries.

79.   Cf. 1 Sam 1:26; Mt 6:5; Mk 11:25 and Lk 18:11ff.

80.   *TSL*, 194–96.

as man does not look to himself, but to God. He also discounts dancing as a form of expression for the Christian liturgy. In about the third century certain Gnostic-Docetic circles tried to introduce it into the liturgy. For them the crucifixion was only an appearance and before that Christ abandoned the body that he had not really assumed. Different religions had different purposes for dance, including incantation, imitative magic and mystical ecstasy, 'none of which is compatible with the essential purpose of the liturgy of the "reasonable sacrifice"'. None of the Christian rites includes dancing: 'what people call dancing in the Ethiopian Rite or the Zairean form of the Roman liturgy', for example, 'is in fact a rhythmically ordered procession, very much in keeping with the dignity of the occasion'.[81]

The cardinal comments further on the *orans*, the oldest gesture of prayer, with arms extended. It is one of the primal gestures of man in invoking God, and is found in many world religions. It is a gesture of non-violence, of openness to another person, of seeking and hoping: 'Man reaches out to the hidden God.' It is also Christological, as one thinks, too, of Christ extending his arms on the cross. By extending our arms, we resolve to pray with the Crucified, to unite ourselves to his 'mind' (Phil 2: 5); as an act of worship which unites the human will with the will of the Father, and of love of neighbour (Jn 12: 32). Praying with hands joined was a later development, from the world of feudalism. While feudalism is questionable, the act of joining one's hands is 'a wonderful symbolic act': 'I lay my hands in yours, allow yours to enclose mine', an expression of trust as well as of fidelity. This gesture has been retained in priestly ordination, and, we might also add, during religious professions. Its true meaning is found in the relationship between the believer and Christ the Lord.[82] Bowing is, again, where 'the bodily gesture and the spirit-

---

81. *TSL*, 196–99. Concerning dance as 'popular piety' and the 'Dancing Procession' in Echternach in the Grand Duchy of Luxembourg, see *ibid.*, 199–200, esp. n.1.

82. *TSL*, 203–5.

ual process are inseparable and flow into each other'. One of the petitions of acceptance in the Roman Canon begins with the word *supplices*, 'Bowing low, we implore thee'. It expresses humility, which is the 'ontologically appropriate attitude, the state that corresponds to the truth about man': in fact St Augustine constructed his whole Christology on the concept of *humilitas*. The man who wishes to become close to God must learn to bend, as God has bent himself down.[83] 'Striking the breast' (for example, Lk 18: 9–14) 'remains a meaningful gesture of prayer', when we point not at someone else but at ourselves as the guilty party. We need to do this time and time again, and to beg for forgiveness. When saying *mea culpa* (through my fault)—in the *Confiteor*—we turn to ourselves, asking God for forgiveness, the saints and the people around us, whom we have wronged. Although it is not explicitly required in the rubrics of the revised liturgy of the Mass, Joseph Ratzinger indicates that, as previously, at the *Agnus Dei*, we look upon the Shepherd who became the Lamb, and that 'it is only right and proper that we should strike our breasts and remind ourselves, even physically, that our iniquities lay on his shoulders, that 'with his stripes we are healed'' (Is 53: 5).[84]

Although Cardinal Ratzinger spoke earlier on singing, he comments further on the human voice, and also on silence in the liturgy. Certain things said in the liturgy are reserved to the bishops, priests and deacons. There is also 'the response to the Word [*Ant-Wort*]'. The structure of Word and response, which is essential to the liturgy, is modelled on the basic structure of the process of divine revelation, in which the Word and response, the speech of God and the receptive hearing of the bride, the Church, go together. One of the most important results of the liturgical renewal is that the people 'really do again respond in the acclamation and do not have to leave it to a representative,

---

83.   *Ibid.*, 205–6.
84.   *TSL*, 206–7.

the altar server'. God, the Revealer, 'did not want to stay as *solus Deus, solus Christus* … No, he wanted to create a Body for himself, to find a Bride—he sought a response'. Then there is the 'new song', the great song which 'the Church sings as she goes off toward the music of the New Heaven and New Earth.' This explains why—in addition to congregational singing—'Christian liturgy of its very nature finds a suitable place for the choir, and for musical instruments, too, which no purism about collective singing should be allowed to contest'.[85] Joseph Ratzinger does not comment on the use of Latin and the vernacular in the Roman liturgy in *The Spirit of the Liturgy*, but he did so in his book *God is Near Us*.[86] The change from Greek to Latin came about because, in the words of the Roman Canon, the action of the Mass is *rationabile obsequium*. However later on the Church was cautious in changing the liturgy into the vernacular languages of Europe, because 'for a long time they had not attained the literary level or the unity of usage that would have permitted a common celebration of the Eucharist over a wide area'. There was also a question of avoiding the possibility of giving the Eucharist 'a national identity', and thus Latin was retained. Although comprehension in the Eucharist is important, the Eucharist is also 'more than comprehension'. The Church knew that 'the heart must also understand'. However the use of the vernacular is also justified, so long as the Eucharist is not dragged into the realm of national culture. We should not, however, forget to pray, and love, 'the common language of the Church over the centuries', so that we can worship God together in this unsettled world, where nations interact.[87]

We respond by singing and praying to God who addresses us. However 'the greater mystery, surpassing all words, summons us to silence … a silence with content and

---

85. *Ibid.*, 207–9.

86. Ratzinger, *God is Near us*, 71–73.

87. *Ibid.*

not just the absence of speech and action.' It should not just be a pause, but a time of recollection, 'giving us an inward peace, allowing us to draw breath and rediscover the one thing necessary'. Silence is one of man's deepest needs and the cardinal says, quite explicitly, that it is a need 'not being met in our present form of liturgy'. For example, the silence after the homily has not proved very satisfactory, and is a bit artificial, 'with the congregation just waiting for as long as the celebrant feels inclined to let it go on', and the homily often leaves questions and contradictions in people's minds 'rather than an invitation to meet the Lord.' Silence after communion, has been 'more helpful and spiritually appropriate', which is, in truth, 'the moment for an interior conversation with the Lord', although it is sometimes curtailed if the distribution of Holy Communion is lengthy. However this silence should be used, and the faithful should be given some guidance on interior prayer. In some places the 'preparation of the gifts' is intended as a time for silence, which 'makes good sense and is fruitful, if we see the preparation, not just a pragmatic external action, but as an essentially interior process', asking the Lord, 'to make us ready for transformation', to share in Jesus Christ's act of self-offering to the Father. The silence of the consecration and elevation of the consecrated species, is an invitation 'to direct our eyes toward Christ … in a gaze that is at once gratitude, adoration, and petition for our own transformation'. The reformed missal of 1970 places on our lips a greeting directed to the Lord: 'We proclaim your death, O Lord, and we confess your resurrection, until you come [in glory]!'. The moment when the Lord comes down and transforms bread and wine to become his Body and Blood cannot fail to stun … we cannot do other than fall on our knees and greet him.' The consecration is 'the moment of God's great *actio* in the world for us … For a moment the world is silent, everything is silent, and in that silence we touch the eternal'.[88]

---

88.   *TSL*, 209–14: I discuss the priest's 'private/silent prayers' in the next chapter; Ratzinger, *The Feast of Faith*, 72–73.

Joseph Ratzinger also reiterates a point he made in 1978, that 'in no sense does the whole canon always *have* to be said out loud'. Liturgists in Germany, he explains, have said that the eucharistic prayer is in crisis, and attempts to combat this led to the creation of new eucharistic prayers after the reform of the liturgy. In the process, 'we have sunk farther and farther into banality' and the possibility of silence is excluded. 'It is no accident that in Jerusalem, from a very early time, parts of the canon were prayed in silence and that in the West the silent canon—overlaid in part with meditative singing—became the norm'. Dismissing these as the result of misunderstandings is all too easy. 'It really is not true that reciting the whole eucharistic prayer out loud and without interruptions is a prerequisite for the participation of everyone in this central act of the Mass'. The faithful, the cardinal suggests, ought to be made familiar with the essential meaning and fundamental orientation of the canon. The first words of the prayers could be said aloud 'as a sort of cue for the congregation, so that each individual in his silent prayer can take up the intonation and bring the personal into the communal and the communal into the personal.' Anyone who has experienced a church united in the silent praying of the canon, 'will know what a really *filled* silence is. It is at once a loud and penetrating cry to God and a Spirit-filled act of prayer.'[89]

The cardinal then moves onto the liturgical attire worn during the Mass. This, he explains, should first and foremost indicate, that the priest is not a private person during the liturgy, 'but stands in place of Another—Christ,' acting *in persona Christi*. In reference to 'putting on the Lord Jesus' in St Paul's Letter to the Romans,[90] Joseph Ratzinger indicates that 'The image of putting on Christ is [...] a dynamic image, bearing on the transformation of man and the world, the new humanity. Vestments are a reminder

---

89.   *TSL*, 214–16.
90.   Rom 13: 14; cf. Eph 4: 24, Col 3: 10ff.; Gal 3: 27.

of all this, of this transformation in Christ, and of the new community that is supposed to arise from it'. They also remind those participating in the Mass 'of the new way that began with Baptism and continues with the Eucharist, the way that leads to the future world already delineated in our daily lives by the sacraments.' Here he further elaborates on the 'eschatological orientation of clothing', drawing from St Paul's letters to the Corinthians and the traditional formula for the distribution of Holy Communion: 'The Body of Our Lord Jesus Christ preserve thy soul unto everlasting life'. Cardinal Ratzinger then comments on the parable of the Prodigal Son, where the father instructs his servants to 'Bring quickly the best robe [...]' for his returning son (Lk 15:22). The Greek text actually says the *first* robe, and, indeed this is how the Fathers of the Church read and understood this text. For them 'the first robe is the robe in which Adam was created and which he lost after he had grasped at likeness to God.' They also referred this text to the Fall of man and his reconciliation with God. The white robe given in Baptism—which points to salvation history and the white garments of eternity (cf. Apocalypse 19:8)—and liturgical vestments, link with the 'great arch' connecting Adam's creation and fall: the cornerstone supporting the whole arch is Christ.[91]

Although Joseph Ratzinger does not intend to present a complete theology of the sacraments in *The Spirit of the Liturgy*, he briefly discusses the use of 'matter' in the liturgy at the very end of this book.[92] Catholic liturgy is the liturgy of the Word made Flesh, and is a cosmic liturgy. 'Thus it is clear that not only do the human body and signs from the cosmos play an essential role in the liturgy but that the matter of this world is part of the liturgy'. Matter is used in the liturgy in the form of symbols—for example the holy fire of Easter night and liturgical objects such as bells and the altar cloth: and, even more importantly, the way in which matter

---

91. *TSL*, 216–20.

92. For this subject, in relation to the Eucharist, see, in particular, Ratzinger, *God is Near Us* and idem, *Pilgrim Fellowship of Faith*, 108–10.

comes into the liturgy in the sacraments, whose substance
was given by the Lord himself. Here the cardinal refers to
Baptism, Confirmation, the Eucharist and the Anointing of
the Sick, which use water, (olive) oil, (wheaten) bread and
wine. The Church's tradition discerns a twofold symbolism
in water. Water flowing from a spring 'is a symbol of the
source of all life, *the* symbol of life', which is why the early
Church insisted on Baptism being administered by means
of living water, spring water. The Fathers always had at
the back of their minds the blood and water flowing from
the opened side of Christ on the cross.[93] Baptism and the
Eucharist spring from the pierced side of Christ. Jesus said
that streams of living water would flow from the man who
came to him and drank: 'Now this he said about the Spirit,
which those who believed in him were to receive' (Jn 7: 39).
The baptized man 'himself becomes a spring'. When thinking about the great saints of history, 'from whom streams of
faith, hope, and love really came forth, we can understand
these words and thus understand something of the dynamism of Baptism, of the promise and vocation it contains.'
When considering olive oil, wheaten bread and wine, we
are dealing with the typical gifts of Mediterranean culture.
They are mentioned in Psalm 104:15: 'wine to gladden
the heart of man, oil to make his face shine, and bread to
strengthen man's heart'. These elements 'express the goodness of creation, in which we receive the goodness of the
Creator himself. And now they become the gift of an even
higher goodness, a goodness that makes our face shine
anew in likeness to the 'Anointed' God, to his beloved Son,
Jesus Christ, a goodness that changes the bread and wine
of the earth into the Body and Blood of the Redeemer, so
that, through the Son made man, we may have communion
with the triune God himself'. To the objection that these
gifts—typical of the Mediterranean—should be replaced
by elements more appropriate in other growing regions,
Joseph Ratzinger reiterates that God has 'acted in history

---

93.   Cf. Jn 19: 34ff.; 1 Jn 5: 6.

and, through history'. He has given the gifts of the earth their significance. The incarnation 'does not mean doing what we please [and] binds us to the history of a particular time', the form of history willed by God. 'It is with [a] particular face, [a] particular human form, that Christ comes to us, and precisely thus does he make us brethren beyond all boundaries. Precisely thus do we recognise him: "It is the Lord" (Jn 21: 7)'.

Conclusion

We have now examined what we may call, the 'core' and summary of Joseph Ratzinger's/Pope Benedict XVI's theological account of the spirit of the liturgy. It is a well-constructed, rich synthesis, a veritable 'cosmos', composed mainly from a blend of elements in scripture and the Church Fathers—two essential components of Catholic theology—with a particular sensitivity for what we might call the Church's journey through historical and theological development. It is also very christological, eschatological and cosmological, going beyond much of the subjectivism and individualism of the modern world. The idea of history as an *egressus* (*exitus*) from God—and cosmologically 'of' God—and the *regressus* (*reditus*) to him of everything through our Lord Jesus Christ, is fairly central in Joseph Ratzinger's theological vision. How, then, can we summarize his account of the liturgy? Liturgy/worship is something that God reveals to us. It is cosmic, embracing heaven and earth, time and space, past, present and future (an eschatological element), in which mankind participates in the Paschal mystery of Jesus Christ, the God-man, the *Logos incarnatus*, and redeemer, who offers His life on the cross to the Father. The shadows of worship in the Old Testament are realized in the New Testament. In this Christ restores creation and calls us to participate (*participatio actuosa*) in this sacrifice of love and in the Eucharist (*oratio*), in order to be sanctified and united with the Holy Trinity. St Paul's concept of *logikē latreia*, of divine worship in accordance with *logos*, with its implications for morality and daily life, is 'right worship', and is 'orientated' towards the *Logos*, uniting the human race, with its myriad of cultures, in the adoration of God. Liturgy is not based on the 'cult of man', but directed towards God. Liturgy grows and develops organically through the ages, with room for legitimate diversity of rites, built upon apostolic tradition, and it is served by the Church in fidelity to tradition. These elements permeate, and have a practical application, in the design of Church buildings, the position of the Christian altar, the direction of liturgical prayer, liturgical art and music, gesture and silence.

However, and more controversially, the cardinal questioned a number of aspects of the liturgical reforms after the Second Vatican Council, including elements of its implementation and composition, calling for 'a new liturgical movement' and a general rediscovery of liturgy. It would be clearly wrong to view these aspects as drawing a 'negative cloud' over the solid, and very positive vision of the liturgy which is presented in *The Spirit of the Liturgy*. It is a vision that one must respond to: it is the foundation and essence of the liturgical theology of Pope Benedict XVI. However Joseph Ratzinger's liturgical theology and the criticisms he made of current liturgical practices, have caused a degree of disagreement, particularly among liturgists. This important matter, and criticism of *The Spirit of the Liturgy*, shall be the focus of our second chapter.

Chapter II

Sed Contra: Pierre-Marie Gy's Critique of Cardinal Ratzinger's *The Spirit of the Liturgy*

Background to Pierre-Marie Gy's critique and Cardinal Ratzinger's response

Cardinal Ratzinger intended that *The Spirit of the Liturgy* would simply be an 'aid to the understanding of the faith and to the right way to give the faith its central form of expression in the liturgy', rather than involve himself with 'scholarly discussion and research'. Nevertheless we have seen that this book is a profoundly theological work, a summary of his liturgical theology and, indeed, one should not forget his other liturgical writings, which are no less scholarly. Joseph Ratzinger is clearly no newcomer to the field of liturgy.[1] It is therefore not surprising that some liturgists, and other scholars, have, indeed, engaged in a 'scholarly discussion' in their response to *The Spirit of the Liturgy*. One of them was Fr. Pierre-Marie Gy, O.P. (1922–2004), a widely known, and respected, liturgical scholar, historian and theologian, particularly in sacramentology. He knew, and was influenced by, some of the great names of the Liturgical Movement, including Dom Bernard Botte, O.S.B., of Louvain, and J. A. Jungmann, S.J.. Gy played a not insignificant role in the construction of the new liturgical books, and was one of the principal authors of *Sacrosanctum Concilium*, the constitution on the liturgy from the Second Vatican

---

1. *TSL*, 8.

Council.[2] Given Gy's prominence and background, he is representative of the viewpoint of many liturgists after the council.

In 2002 Gy wrote a largely critical review of *The Spirit of the Liturgy* in *La Maison-Dieu*, and, in the same year, the same periodical graciously published Cardinal Ratzinger's personal response.[3] Though this dialogue may be said to possess a certain 'historical' value, in light of Joseph Ratzinger's papacy, Gy raised a number of important issues, as well as criticisms of the former's theory of liturgy, which have bearing on the celebration of the liturgy under the present pontificate, the 'question of the liturgy' in the contemporary Church, prevailing trends in liturgiology, and the authority and interpretation of the Second Vatican Council. It is also very important to address criticisms of Joseph Ratzinger's liturgical writings, because I believe that, by doing so, we shall be bringing more light to bear on the theology of the liturgy of Pope Benedict XVI, and that the enduring value of his work will shine through. The truth, which all scholars seek, can be brought one step closer. This chapter, then, evaluates Gy's main criticisms, beginning with the notion of *participatio actuosa* and orientation, and the cardinal's response. However we must also examine Gy's most important, and indeed, fundamental question: is *The Spirit of the Liturgy* faithful to the Second

---

2.   For an overview of his life and thought see Gy, *The Reception of Vatican II, passim*.

3.   Gy, 'L'Esprit de la Liturgie du Cardinal Ratzinger est-il Fidèle au Concile ou en Réaction Contre?', 171–78; Ratzinger, 'Réponse du Cardinal Ratzinger au Père Gy', 113–20: I have used the following English translations by S. Maddux—Gy, 'Cardinal Ratzinger's *The Spirit of the Liturgy*: Is it Faithful to the Council or in Reaction to It?', 90–96; Ratzinger, '*The Spirit of the Liturgy* or Fidelity to the Council: Response to Father Gy', 98–102. It is should be noted that Gy responds to Ratzinger as an academic and not as a (cardinal) member of the Roman Curia.

Vatican Council, or is it a reaction against it and the authority of the pope in liturgical matters?[4]

As I have said above, Gy is representative of the viewpoint of many liturgists after the council. It is also useful here to take the opportunity—where appropriate—to reply to certain comments made in a recent book by one of those liturgists, John F. Baldovin, S.J., which also attempted to 'respond' to Joseph Ratzinger and critics of the recent liturgical reforms.[5] This is all the more interesting, as he is well aware that Joseph Ratzinger is now Pope Benedict XVI. In fairness to Baldovin, he does see much that is positive in the writings of Ratzinger and the critics of the recent liturgical reforms, more so than Gy,[6] and he generally presents his criticisms in a respectable and non-polemical manner. However Baldovin, as we shall see, still reflects the position of many liturgists today, in their views concerning the reformed liturgy and those who wish to see 'the reform of the reform', despite having an excellent grasp of the issues at stake. Many, but certainly not all of his criticisms against 'the reformers' *et alia*, and recent changes under Pope Benedict, still show the prevalent tendency of many liturgists of not responding in a sufficient manner to 'substantial issues', and their counter positions remain unconvincing, to me at least. Nevertheless this contribution to the current liturgical debate in the Church, by Baldovin—a charitably open-minded, though critical liturgist—ought to be read, not only in order to consider a suitable response to his viewpoint, but also to fine-tune one's own outlook on the Roman liturgy, if need be.

---

4.   I have decided to avoid addressing elements which may be perceived as purely polemical, and which blur the most important issues; for example, Gy's reference to Ratzinger's attendance at the 'traditionalist' conference at Fontgombault in 2001.

5.   Baldovin, *Reforming the Liturgy,* esp. 65–89: he also labels the liturgical legislation under the pontificate of Pope John Paul II as 'conservative': *Ibid.,* 99.

6.   See p. 61 below for his comments on *versum populum* celebrations of the Holy Mass.

Participatio Actuosa

Pierre-Marie Gy begins his critique by suggesting that Ratzinger's references to the Second Vatican Council—he counts about ten—do not mention 'important aspects of the Constitution on the Liturgy *Sacrosanctum Concilium* with the single exception of 'active participation' [*participatio actuosa*]', which Ratzinger views as a 'dangerous' concept, because it seems to involve 'a risk that the Church may celebrate itself''. The cardinal shows in his book, according to Gy, 'no concern for how active participation deepens the piety of the faithful, nor for spiritual values, such as that of the role (expressly mentioned in the council documents) of the faithful in the Eucharistic Sacrifice, or of communion under both species'. Ratzinger does not refer—for example—to article 48 of *Sacrosanctum Concilium*:

> The Church, therefore, earnestly desires that Christ's faithful, when present at this mystery of faith [the Mass], should not be there as strangers or silent spectators; on the contrary, through a good understanding of the rites and prayers, they should take part in the sacred action conscious of what they are doing, with devotion and full collaboration. They should be instructed by God's Word and be nourished at the table of the Lord's Body; they should give thanks to God; by the offering the Immaculate Victim, not only through the hands of the priest, but also with him ... they should learn also to offer themselves.[7]

Gy comments that 'To see in this article ... a risk of "self-celebration" would assuredly be an error in need of reform!'.[8]

In his response, Joseph Ratzinger rejects as 'simply false' Gy's suggestion that he views *participatio actuosa* as 'a risk that the Church may celebrate itself', indicating that

---

7. Gy, 'Cardinal Ratzinger's *The Spirit of the Liturgy*', 90–91; The Second Vatican Council, *The Constitution on the Sacred Liturgy Sacrosanctum Concilium*, 4 December 1963, no. 48.

8. Gy, 'Cardinal Ratzinger's *The Spirit of the Liturgy*', 91.

the entire second chapter of the fourth part of his book, was dedicated to this topic 'as an essential component of a proper celebration of the liturgy'. However he does reject a 'false and superficial interpretation of this fundamental notion: active participation cannot consist in assigning exterior activities in the liturgy to all the faithful gathered for the eucharistic celebration'. Active participation 'means something greater' requiring a proper liturgical formation and knowledge of the liturgical texts, 'without which the purely exterior activities remain empty and meaningless'.[9] Ratzinger says that participation, which makes possible a close union of the whole being, of thought and action, must also be expressed corporally, and that 'succeeding paragraphs of the chapter [cited above] give a whole series of indications along these lines that are developed on the basis of the great liturgical traditions of the East and the West and are carried on up to the present.'[10]

While all this indicates that Gy's general criticism was misplaced, did the cardinal ignore other important aspects of *Sacrosanctum Concilium*? It is apparent that his concept of liturgy ties in very favourably, and actually reflects, Vatican II's teaching on what the liturgy *is*. The teaching of Vatican II 'flavours' and is clearly evident in Joseph Ratzinger's liturgical theology. One can favourably compare, for instance, the following excerpts from *Sacrosanctum Concilium* and the cardinal's emphasis on the heavenly/earthly/cosmic liturgy and the *Logos incarnatus* (Jesus Christ), and the connections which he makes to liturgy and ethics—that is, the liturgy lived out in the ordinary circumstances of life—and between 'right worship' and 'right living', and the fidelity to and the adaptation of liturgical rites:

> In the earthly liturgy we take part in a foretaste of
> that heavenly liturgy which is celebrated in the holy
> city of Jerusalem toward which we journey as pil-
> grims, where Christ is sitting at the right hand of

---

9. Ratzinger, *'The Spirit of the Liturgy* or Fidelity to the Council', 98; *TSL*, 175.

10. Ratzinger, *'The Spirit of the Liturgy* or Fidelity to the Council', 98.

God, a minister of the holies and of the true tabernacle. With all the warriors of the heavenly army
we sing a hymn of glory to the Lord; venerating the
memory of the saints, we hope for some part and
fellowship with them; we eagerly await the Saviour,
Our Lord Jesus Christ, until he our life shall appear
and we too will appear with Him in glory... For it is
the liturgy through which, especially in the divine
sacrifice of the Eucharist 'the work of our redemption is accomplished', and it is through the liturgy,
especially, that the faithful are enabled to express
in their lives and manifest to others the mystery of
Christ and the real nature of the true Church. The
Church is essentially both human and divine, visible but endowed with invisible realities, zealous
in action and dedicated to contemplation, present
in the world, but as a pilgrim, so constituted that
in her the human is directed toward and subor-
dinated to the divine... and this present world to
that city yet to come, the object of our quest. The
liturgy daily builds up those who are in the Church,
making them a holy temple of the Lord, a dwelling-
place for God in the Spirit, to the mature measure
of the fullness of Christ. At the same time it marvel-
lously increases their power to preach Christ, and
thus shows forth the Church, a sign lifted up among
the nations... a sign under which the scattered children of God may be gathered together, until there
is one fold and one shepherd... Finally, in faithful
obedience to tradition, the sacred Council declares
that Holy Mother Church holds all lawfully recognized rites to be of equal right and dignity; that she
wishes to preserve them in the future and to foster
them in every way. The Council also desires that,
where necessary, the rites be revised carefully in
the light of sound tradition, and that they be given
new vigour to meet present-day circumstances and
needs.[11]

---

11.   The Second Vatican Council, *The Constitution on the Sacred Liturgy
      Sacrosanctum Concilium*, 4 December 1963, nos 2, 4, 8: I have not

Gy is correct in saying that Joseph Ratzinger does not directly mention communion under both species: though the latter says the following in relation to the 'spousal mystery', announced in the Old Testament and the central theme in the Apocalypse ('the wedding feast of the Lamb'):

> Since, in the visions of the heavenly liturgy, that wedding seems always to be already anticipated, Christians came to see the Eucharist as the presence of the Bridegroom and thus as a foretaste of the wedding feast of God. In the Eucharist a communion takes place that corresponds to the union of man and woman in marriage... [this] spousal mystery, announced in the Old Testament, of the intimate union of God and man takes place *in the Sacrament of the Body and Blood of Christ*.[12]

Gy is also correct in saying that Joseph Ratzinger says 'nothing regarding the importance that the Constitution on the Church *Lumen Gentium* attaches to the Eucharist', but only explicitly.[13] However *The Spirit of the Liturgy* clearly correlates with *Lumen Gentium*, for instance, in relation to 'the People of God':

> Though they differ essentially and not only in degree, the common priesthood of the faithful and the ministerial or hierarchical priesthood are none the less ordered one to another; each in its own proper way shares in the one priesthood of Christ. The ministerial priest, by the sacred power that he has, forms and rules the priestly people; in the person of Christ he effects the Eucharistic Sacrifice and offers it to God in the name of all the people. The faithful, indeed, by virtue of their royal priesthood, participate in the offering of the Eucharist... Taking part in the Eucharistic Sacrifice, the source and summit of the Christian life, they [the faithful] offer

---

quoted these consecutively; and cf. *TSL* and Ratzinger, *The Feast of Faith, passim*, and the references indicated on p. 64, n. 51 below.

12.   *TSL*, 142.

13.   Gy, 'Cardinal Ratzinger's *The Spirit of the Liturgy*', 90.

the Divine Victim to God, and themselves along
with It. And so it is that, both in the offering and in
Holy Communion, each in his own way, though not
of course indiscriminately, has his own part to play
in the liturgical action. Then, strengthened by the
Body of Christ in the Eucharistic Communion, they
manifest in a concrete way that unity of the People
of God which this holy sacrament aptly signifies
and admirably realizes.

To those whom he [Jesus Christ] intimately joins
to his life and mission he also gives a share in his
priestly office, to offer spiritual worship for the
glory of the Father and the salvation of man ... In
the celebration of the Eucharist these [that is, spiritual sacrifices] may most fittingly be offered to the
Father along with the body of the Lord. And so,
worshipping everywhere by their holy actions, the
laity consecrate the world itself to God.[14]

In Joseph Ratzinger's bibliography—which readers should
pay close attention to when seeking his sources—mention
is made to 'the theology of the liturgy in the *Catechism of
the Catholic Church*', based on the Second Vatican Council,
which the cardinal describes as 'fundamental'.[15]

Celebrating Mass ad orientem

The issue of celebrating Mass *ad orientem* or *ad apsidem*—in
which the matter of Christian prayer *ad orientem* is central—has been much discussed in recent years. Joseph
Ratzinger believes that the correct position of the altar is at
the heart of the postconciliar debate.[16] However Gy judges
Ratzinger's discussion of this 'unsatisfactory both historically and with regard to the issue of active participation
[examined above]'. According to Gy,

---

14.   The Second Vatican Council, *Dogmatic Constitution on the Church
       Lumen Gentium*, 21 November 1964, nos 10, 11, 34; cf. *TSL*, 45–47,
       171–75; Ratzinger, *Called to Communion*, 125–28.

15.   *TSL*, 225.

16.   See p. 17, n. 42 above.

On the historical side, it relies explicitly on Louis Bouyer's *Liturgy and Architecture* (1991), in which this great voice of the Liturgical Movement ... not necessarily a great historian, thought he could apply to the entire West the eucharistic 'orientation' characteristic of the liturgies in the regions east of the Mediterranean [that is, praying East] ... whereas in the churches of the western Mediterranean celebration with the priest facing the people is clearly attested, for example in Rome and Africa.[17]

Gy further believes that Bouyer and Ratzinger have not taken into account 'the fundamental work' of Otto Nussbaum, on the place of the celebrant at the altar, published in 1965, which was refined and completed for North Africa by the French scholars Yvette Duval and Noël Duval. Furthermore, as far as Rome and Italy were concerned, '*versus orientem* was not introduced into the papal liturgy until Avignon, and that St Charles Borromeo, the archbishop of Milan ... was careful to respect the tradition of the Roman basilicas.'[18] The celebration of the Eucharist *versus populum* after the Second Vatican Council, 'was the immediate and spontaneous consequence of the dialogue Mass in the vernacular, recognized and authorized by Roman authority less than a year after the Constitution on the Liturgy and while the council was still going on', citing the instruction *Inter Oecumenici* (1964).[19]

Joseph Ratzinger begins his response by indicating that Nussbaum's work—based on his thesis—was examined in an article by Albert Gerhards, professor of liturgy at Bonn, where Nussbaum was a doctoral student and Joseph

---

17. Gy, 'Cardinal Ratzinger's *The Spirit of the Liturgy*', 92; cf. Baldovin, *Reforming the Liturgy*, 89: 'As Gy points out in his review, Ratzinger's reliance on the tendentious work of Louis Bouyer does not show much historical sophistication'. Note that, in his bibliography, Ratzinger also cites two other works: TSL, 228–29.

18. Gy, 'Cardinal Ratzinger's *The Spirit of the Liturgy*', 92–93, and n. 12, where Gy cites the work of Sible de Blaauw, who is quoted as saying that *versus populum* is 'the classic Roman disposition'.

19. *Ibid.*

Ratzinger was a professor. After examining the question of celebration, Gerhards clearly showed 'the universal value of prayer *versus orientem*', including the corrections which Nussbaum added to his original thesis.[20] Rejecting as 'incomprehensible' Gy's suggestion that the question of 'orientation' was only valid for the eastern half of the Mediterranean, the cardinal suggested that Gy visit the early and medieval Christian churches of the West, 'to see that the principle of orientation was respected practically everywhere that specific local circumstances did not pose an obstacle to it.'[21] Concerning the Roman basilicas, Joseph Ratzinger says that 'there can ... be no doubt that the liturgical call *conversi ad Dominum*, after the sermon, was an invitation to the faithful to turn to the East, in those cases where the disposition of the building as such did not already provide for it'. Furthermore, he indicates three points already discussed in his book, namely, the space proper to the liturgy of the Word (ambo); provision of altars closer to the people where existing altars are too far away (not unknown in the Middle Ages); and the tradition of 'orientation', the act of turning toward the 'Orient' as the image of the return of Christ, which 'no way requires that all altars must once again be reversed and that the priest's place be changed as a consequence', making the cross the focal point in the middle of the altar.[22]

In order to ascertain the validity of Gy's criticisms and Joseph Ratzinger's responses, it is important to look at the conclusions made in the comprehensive study of the question of liturgical orientation by U. M. Lang, which appeared in English in 2004.[23] Lang indicates that the issue here 'is not so much the celebration of Mass 'facing the people'

---

20. Ratzinger, '*The Spirit of the Liturgy* or Fidelity to the Council', 100, n. 2.

21. *Ibid.*, 100.

22. Ratzinger, '*The Spirit of the Liturgy* or Fidelity to the Council', 101.

23. Lang, *Turn towards the Lord*, which should be referred to for more detailed discussion, especially for the theological aspects, which are more important.

as the orientation of liturgical prayer'.[24] He expresses the view that Gy's critique of Ratzinger's view on this subject in *La Maison-Dieu*, 'reflect[s] neither the current state of historical research nor the present theological debate'.[25] That being said, Lang also examines the question of *versus populum* celebration—with reference to Sible de Blaauw—and indicates that its history 'in the proper sense began in the late Middle Ages and the Renaissance, when the Christian principle of praying towards the east was little understood and began to fade away ... Nonetheless, the common direction of liturgical prayer was retained, with very few exceptions'.[26] Lang notes that St Charles Borromeo, in his *Instructiones fabricae et supellectilis ecclesiasticae* of 1577—an important work on church architecture after Trent—indicated that the *capella major* must be oriented, with the main altar, facing east. Westward 'facing the people' was to be the exception rather than the rule, if it was impossible to erect an eastward-facing building: he believes that Gy is 'misleading' on this point.[27] The idea that the priest should face the people during Mass 'only gained currency in the Catholic Enlightenment of the eighteenth century... [when] Christian worship was supposed to be useful for the moral edification of the individual and for the building of society [which] was at the expense of its latreutic and mystical nature'.[28]

Concerning two of the main arguments advanced in favour of facing the people during the Eucharist—that it

---

24. Lang, *Turn towards the Lord*, 15, 32–33, citing Reinhard Messner. Lang holds that 'the intrinsic sense of facing east in the Eucharist is the common direction of priest and people orientated towards the triune God' (*Ibid.*).

25. *Ibid.*, 19, n. 15.

26. Lang, *Turn towards the Lord*, 56, 119. Cf. St. Thomas Aquinas, *ST*, II–II, q. 84, a.3 ad 3 and Berger, *Thomas Aquinas and the Liturgy*.

27. Lang, *Turn towards the Lord*, 96–97 and n. 16–18. Concerning references to *versus [ad] populum* in liturgical sources before the Second Vatican Council—and the context—see *Ibid.*, 30ff.

28. Lang, *Turn towards the Lord*, 119.

was the practice of the early Church and should be the norm for our age, and that 'active participation' demands celebrating towards the people—Lang counters these by indicating that 'an examination of the historical evidence will show that the orientation of priest and people in the liturgy of the Eucharist is well-attested in the early Church and was, in fact, the general custom', and that—significantly—'the common direction of liturgical prayer has been a consistent tradition in both the East and the West'.[29] It is interesting to note—and this has bearing on how we define *participatio actuosa*—that where references to *versus populum* can be found in liturgical sources,

> it is by no means suggested here that nothing should limit, let alone block, the faithful's view of the ritual acts of the celebrant. Such an interpretation would have seemed alien to the understanding of the liturgy that was common from Christian antiquity until well into the Middle Ages and is still found in the Eastern Churches. Thus it is hardly surprising to find that even with altars *versus populum* the sight was significantly restricted, for example, by curtains that were closed during certain parts of the liturgy or already by the architectural layout of the church.[30]

According to Lang, celebration *versus populum* 'in the modern sense was unknown to Christian antiquity, and it would be anachronistic to see the eucharistic liturgy in the early Roman basilicas as its prototype'. There is 'strong evidence' from literary sources, for eastward prayer from most parts of the Christian world from the second century onwards, and he cites, among others, Tertullian, Clement of Alexandria, Origen, and Augustine.[31]

---

29. Lang, *Turn towards the Lord*, 28–9.

30. *Ibid.*, 31, citing Nussbaum and Jungmann, and 63–64 concerning large basilicas.

31. Lang, *Turn towards the Lord*, 42ff., 86, citing Dölger and Vogel. On the interpretation of references in St Augustine's sermons to *conversi ad Dominum* as a liturgical call for the people to face east

Concerning Nussbaum's study of the liturgical sources in the first millennium, and issues such as *versus populum* — which he argues was the more ancient practice in some regions, such as in Egypt and Italy for instance — Lang indicates that scholars have been very critical of Nussbaum's interpretation of the sources, and concluded that facing east in prayer 'became decisive for early Christian liturgy and church architecture. As a rule, the eastward direction determined the position of the celebrant at the altar'.[32] A major weakness in Nussbaum's arguments was that one should automatically take *versus populum* celebration for granted 'unless the plan of a church shows otherwise', basing *versus populum* on a theory concerning the original form of the Eucharist, and that, in c.400, there was a change in emphasis away from the meal aspect of the Eucharist to the sacrifice: thus the celebrant turned away from the people. This theory is undermined by references to sacrifice in early documents, such as the *Didache*. One should also bear in mind the substantial lack of early sources concerning the position of the celebrant in the first two hundred years and that we can only hypothesize.[33] Most ancient churches had an orientated apse, and concerning those *small* number of churches with an eastward-facing entrance — mainly found in Rome and North Africa — circumstances, such as location and geographical problems, burial sites of saints, and the conversion of older buildings to Christian use, meant that

---

as well as its spiritual connotations, see *Ibid.*, 51–53. See also St Augustine, *De Sermone Domini in Monte* II, 5, 17–18: 'When we rise to pray, we turn East, where heaven begins. And we do this not because God is there, as if He had moved away from other directions on earth ... but rather to help us remember to turn our mind towards a higher order, that is, to God' (*cum ad orationem stamus, ad orientem convertimur, unde caelum surgit; non tamquam ibi habitet Deus, quasi ceteras mundi partes deseruerit ... sed ut admoneatur animus ad naturam excellentiorem se convertere, id est ad Deum*) : cited in Gamber, *The Reform of the Roman Liturgy*, 79–80, 153–54.

32. *Ibid.*, 56ff., utilising, in particular, the work of Marcel Metzger.

33. Lang, *Turn towards the Lord*, 58–63.

the apse could not be built facing east.[34] Lang concludes
that it is wrong to ask, 'as Nassbaum does, at what time
in any given region a transition was made from the celebration "facing the people" to the priest's "turning away"
from the congregation'.[35]

We should ask what is to be made of Gy's statement
that *versus populum* celebrations were 'recognized and
authorized by Roman authority less than a year after the
Constitution on the Liturgy and while the council was
still going on', citing *Inter Oecumenici*.[36] Firstly, it must be
stated that, whatever one's position on *versus populum*,
Sacrosanctum Concilium does not mention *versus populum*
nor the erection of new altars in churches. *Inter Oecumenici*
states that 'It is better for the main altar to be constructed
away from the wall so that one can easily walk around the
altar and celebrate [Mass] facing the people'.[37] According
to Jungmann, 'It is only the *possibility* [of *versus populum*]
that is emphasized. And this [separation of the altar from
the wall] *is not even prescribed*, but is only *recommended*, as
one will see if one looks at the Latin text of the directive'.[38]
In a letter to the heads of bishops' conferences from Cardinal Giacomo Lercaro, president of the liturgical consilium
(25 January 1966), it is explained that 'Above all because
for a living and participated liturgy, it is not indispensable
that the altar should be *versus populum*: in the Mass, the
entire liturgy of the word is celebrated at the chair, ambo
or lectern, and therefore facing the assembly; as to the

---

34. Lang, *Turn towards the Lord*, 65–66; see *Ibid.*, 72–88 also for further
     discussion on *conversi ad Dominum* in buildings with an eastward
     entrance, altars positioned in the nave, early Roman and African
     church architecture, and the imitation of Roman basilicas in some
     places.

35. Lang, *Turn towards the Lord*, 66.

36. Gy, 'Cardinal Ratzinger's *The Spirit of the Liturgy*', 93; Sacred Con-
     gregation of Rites, *Instructio ad Exsecutionem Constitutionis de Sacra
     Liturgia Recte Ordinandam (Inter Oecumenici)*, 26 September 1964,
     877–900.

37. Lang, *Turn towards the Lord*, 22 (Lang's translation).

38. Cited in Lang, *Turn towards the Lord*, 22 (my emphasis).

eucharistic liturgy, loudspeaker systems make participation feasible enough'.[39] The *Missale Romanum* of Pope Paul VI 'presuppose[s] *a common direction* of priest and people for the core of the eucharistic liturgy' indicated by instructions for the priest *to turn towards the people* at the *Orate fratres, Pax Domini, Ecce, Agnus Dei* and the *Ritus conclusionis*. The third *editio typica* (published in 2002) 'retains these rubrics'.[40] This interpretation has received official confirmation.[41] Lang also indicates that 'One cannot appeal to the Second Vatican Council for a justification of the radical alterations that historic churches have undergone in recent times. It is entirely consistent with the intention of Vatican II that the Congregation for Divine Worship gives preference to the celebration at an existing [high] altar over the construction of another altar directed towards the people'.[42] John L. Baldovin, while strongly favouring *versus populum*, agrees that, 'historical honesty requires us to admit that the idea that the early liturgy was habitually celebrated *versus populum* was mistaken... it must also be admitted that the priest can "hijack" the liturgy and that the celebration can seem to be purely horizontal [and that] we need to acknowledge that it has never been forbidden to celebrate the liturgy with the priest facing the liturgical east—even in the Missal of Paul VI'.[43] It would appear that

---

39.   *Ibid.*, 22–3.

40.   Lang, *Turn towards the Lord*, 23–4 (my emphasis); *IGMR*, nos 146, 154, 157, 165; cf. *Ibid.*, nos 181, 243 and 244.

41.   Congregation for Divine Worship and the Discipline of the Sacraments, 'Editoriale: Pregare "ad orientem versus"', 247; Lang, *Turn towards the Lord*, 23–5.

42.   Congregation for Divine Worship and the Discipline of the Sacraments, 'Responsa ad quaestiones de nova *Institutione Generalis Missalis Romani*', 171–74, concerning the interpretation of *IGMR*, no. 299—*Altare exstruatur a pariete seiunctum, ut facile circumiri et in eo celebratio versus populum peragi possit, quod expedit ubicumque possibile sit*; Lang, *Turn towards the Lord*, 26–7, 125.

43.   Baldovin, *Reforming the Liturgy*, 112.

we should view Joseph Ratzinger's position on *ad orientem* celebrations favourably.

'Private' prayers, liturgy and spirituality

Gy also questions Joseph Ratzinger's fidelity to *Sacrosanctum Concilium* in the context of piety and spirituality: 'Spiritually, the author [that is, Cardinal Ratzinger] antedates Vatican II. He is faithful to the piety of his Christian childhood and of his priestly ordination, but insufficiently attentive, on the other hand, to the liturgical rules currently in place (should he not, when he writes on this subject, give an example of attentiveness and fidelity?) and, on the other hand, to the liturgical values affirmed by the council.' According to Gy, this piety is marked 'by an attachment to the priestly prayers said in a low voice ... He [Ratzinger] seems unaware of the distinction, which is constant in tradition, between the private prayers of the priest and the prayers said by him as celebrant—and he situates himself *de facto* in the untraditional line, begun at Trent, of the private Mass as the fundamental form of the Mass', when music could cover the silent canon, now contrary to the rubrics, which insist that speaking aloud the presidential prayers is 'something of their very nature'.[44] Baldovin has even made the suggestion that Ratzinger has 'a somewhat romantic view of the liturgical glories of the past'.[45]

The issue of Joseph Ratzinger's attachment to 'private prayers' was not directly addressed when responding to Gy. However we find discussion of these prayers where *The Spirit of the Liturgy* discusses silence, and it is important to see it in its original context. Gy's criticism could be conditioned here by the cardinal's views against the role of the

---

44.   Gy, 'Cardinal Ratzinger's *The Spirit of the Liturgy*', 94–95, citing *IGMR*, nos 32 and 33, promulgated after *TSL* was published. Gy's point concerning Cardinal Ratzinger and Vatican II's liturgical values has already been discussed, and also in the next section ('Questioning Cardinal Ratzinger's fidelity to Vatican II, the papacy and the Church').

45.   Baldovin, *Reforming the Liturgy*, 89.

priest as a mere 'presider' at the liturgy, which some interpret as a sort of 'liturgical animator', to the detriment of the spirituality of the priesthood, as someone who is ordained to offer God sacrifice on behalf of the Church: 'Those who hold a sociological or activistic view of the priest's duties in the Mass frown upon these prayers, and, whenever possible, they leave them out'. The priest is viewed as a 'presider' at the liturgical celebration, 'which is thought of as a kind of meeting.' The priest, however, '*presides over an encounter with the living God* [and] the silent prayers… invite him to make his task truly personal, so that he may give his whole self to the Lord.'[46] These prayers—while reduced— still exist in the new missal, and 'they have to exist, now as before.' Joseph Ratzinger believes that old prayer books contain—'alongside a lot of kitsch'—much that is a valuable resource for prayer. St Paul's comment in his letter to the Romans—that we do not know how to pray as we ought (Rom 8: 26)—applies even more today, and the Holy Spirit, who teaches us how to pray, 'also uses human mediation'. Ratzinger is correct to point out that these prayers have risen up from the hearts of believers.[47] Prayers, such as those recited by the priest after communion—the *apologiae* according to liturgists— and that for offering the host in the extraordinary form of the Roman Rite, *Suscipe, sancte Pater*, were originally recited by lay people, and made their way into the official liturgical prayers: such prayers may still be beneficial to the laity today.[48]

In the *Missale Romanum* (*IGMR* 2002), the 'presidential prayers' of the priest, 'addressed to God in the name of the entire holy people and all present by the priest who presides over the assembly in the person of Christ', are the eucharistic prayer, the collect, prayer over the gifts, and the

---

46. *TSL*, 212–13; cf. *IGMR*, nos 27, 30–33, 37–38.
47. *TSL*, 213–14.
48. Suarez, *The Sacrifice of the Altar*, 106–7; Cabié, *The Eucharist*, 131, 166: *IGMR*, no. 142 on circumstances when the non-presidential prayers beginning *Benedictus es, Domine* can be recited aloud by the priest and responded to by the laity.

prayer after communion.[49] Although the 'private' prayers are said silently by the priest, they are not 'private prayers' in the strictest sense. While they are not 'presidential' prayers, they remain real 'liturgical' prayers stipulated by the Church, which the priest prays, for himself, in the singular tense—though not entirely so (see below)—*as celebrant*, 'asking that he may exercise his ministry with greater attention and devotion', *pace* Gy. Such prayers occur before the proclamation of the Gospel, at the preparation of the gifts, and also before and after the Communion of the priest.[50] Considering the importance which *IGRM* 2002 places upon these prayers, it is hard to see how they are contrary to the Second Vatican Council or that sound spirituality and piety—exhibited in the lives of the saints before the council—are now somehow irrelevant.[51] Indeed, it is also hard to justify Baldovin's claim that the offertory prayers of the extraordinary form, 'communicated a notion of individual priestly offering (prayers said in the first-person singular)', to the detriment of the fact that 'the whole Church [in different ways] offers the Eucharistic Sacrifice', when one considers the prayers themselves: for example, '*Offerimus tibi, Domine, calicem salutaris* ... pro *nostra* et totius mundi salute'; 'In spiritu humilitatis ... et sic fiat sacrificium *nostrum* in conspectu tuo hodie'; 'Suscipe, sancta Trinitas, hanc oblationem, quam tibi *offerimus*'.[52] The new prayers for the preparation of the gifts in the *Missale Romanum* (2002), also use the plural. For example, ... *accepimus panem, quem tibi offerimus* ... *ex quo nobis fiet panis vitae* and *accepimus vinum,*

49.　　*IGMR*, no. 30.

50.　　*IGMR*, no. 33.

51.　　The Second Vatican Council, *The Constitution on the Sacred Liturgy Sacrosanctum Concilium*, 4 December 1963, no. 13; Congregation for the Clergy, *Directory on the Ministry and Life of Priests*, no. 39; Congregation for Divine Worship and the Discipline of the Sacraments, *Directory on Popular Piety and the Liturgy*.

52.　　Baldovin, *Reforming the Liturgy*, 145 (my emphasis).

quod tibi offerimus ... ex quo nobis fiet potus spiritalis.[53] On the subject of popular piety in general, Joseph Ratzinger has also said—in line with *Sacrosanctum Concilium*—that it 'is the soil without which the liturgy cannot thrive. Unfortunately, in parts of the Liturgical Movement and on the occasion of the postconciliar reform, it has frequently been held in contempt or even abused. Instead, one must love it, purifying and guiding it where necessary, but always accepting it with great reverence.'[54]

Though the form of the 'private Mass' before the council—that is, the Mass said by a single priest—certainly had an influence upon the performance of the more 'solemn' form, it is hard to see where Joseph Ratzinger situates himself in an absolute *'de facto'* manner 'in the untraditional line, begun at Trent, of the private Mass as the fundamental form of the Mass' because of his comments on reciting the canon quietly, which was done for centuries in the Latin Church before Trent. It is true that the *IGMR* 2002 indicates that the nature of the 'presidential' texts 'demands' 'that they be spoken in a loud and clear voice'.[55] The cardinal is not advocating direct disobedience of the rubrics, but is

---

53.   Ratzinger, *God is Near Us*, 65–69: I would politely disagree with the-then Cardinal Ratzinger, in respect of his reason for supporting the change or removal of the old offertory prayers (as expressed in 1978), as sufficient justification for the change: i.e. that the old prayers led to misunderstanding(s) with those outside 'the world of faith', because they combined elements of preparation with Christ's actual sacrifice. For a detailed study of the old offertory prayers, see Quoëx, 'Historical and Doctrinal Notes on the Offertory of the Roman Rite', 53–75. However in *TSL*, 210–11, 213 (in 2000) Cardinal Ratzinger questioned the preparation of the gifts, 'the significance of which in the new rite is not entirely clear', in respect of the *rite* itself, while approving of the period of silence which can accompany this, relating it to preparation towards sharing in Christ's sacrificial offering to the Father: see p. 40 above. For Pope Benedict XVI's Magisterium on this section of the liturgy, see pp. 107–8 and p. 108, note 56.

54.   *TSL*, 202, and see n. 51 above.

55.   *IGMR*, no. 32; Gy, 'Cardinal Ratzinger's *The Spirit of the Liturgy*', 94–95.

merely suggesting a change in practice, in that the canon need not 'always' be said aloud, in the context that the laity have received appropriate catechesis on the canon.[56] However it has to be admitted that the current practice was not mandated by the Second Vatican Council.

Concerning Joseph Ratzinger's 'somewhat romantic view of the liturgical glories of the past', according to Baldovin—a similar description of the cardinal was also made by Häussling—[57] we do well to recall what the cardinal said in *The Spirit of the Liturgy* concerning the 'decadence theory' held by many modern liturgists[58] in the context of the cardinal's views on *ad orientem* prayer and liturgical celebrations. We can see how balanced the cardinal's argumentation is in his understanding of 'the liturgical glories of the past':

> … is this not all romanticism and nostalgia for the past [that is, *ad orientem*]? Can the original form of Christian prayer still say something to us today, or should we try to find our own form, a form for our own times? Of course, we cannot simply replicate the past. Every age must discover and express the essence of the liturgy anew … It would surely be a mistake to reject all the reforms of our century wholesale … On the other hand, a common turning to the east during the eucharistic prayer remains essential… As I see it, the problem with a large part of modern liturgiology is that it tends to recognize only antiquity as a source, and therefore normative, and to regard everything developed later, in the Middle Ages and through the Council of Trent, as decadent.[59]

The last sentence of this quotation really goes to the root of the charge of 'romanticism' and 'nostalgia' which is frequently made against those who have a deep appreciation

---

56.   *TSL*, 214–16.
57.   *Ibid.*, 80–84.
58.   See pp. 17–19 above.
59.   *TSL*, 80–82.

for the Church's liturgical past, and of its enduring value in the future.

Questioning Cardinal Ratzinger's fidelity to Vatican II, the papacy and the Church

We have thus far seen in our discussion of Gy's critique that Joseph Ratzinger's loyalty and adherence to the Second Vatican Council is continually queried. Gy, in effect, has personally answered the question he posed in the title of his article: that Ratzinger is not wholeheartedly faithful to the council, and is reacting against it. Indeed further criticism of the cardinal by Gy concerns the area of papal authority in the liturgy. Gy accuses him of appearing 'egocentric' 'with regard to the rules of the Church' in that it would be appropriate for him to have mentioned 'the reservation of liturgical law (*droit*) to the pope by the Council of Trent, and the reaffirmation of this role both by the Constitution on the Liturgy of Vatican II and by current canon law'. Gy asks why 'not a whisper is breathed about the way Paul VI constantly followed the work of the consilium' for the implementation of the constitution on the liturgy, as witnessed, not only by Annibale Bugnini—who oversaw the liturgical reforms—but also by its principal architects.[60] The attention of Pope Paul to this work is so detailed 'that it does seem to merit the qualification—well known to Cardinal Ratzinger, as well as to Roman canonists past and present—of papal approval *in forma specifica*,[61] that is, applying even to the details'. Gy also wonders if Ratzinger is afraid of 'paying the closest possible attention to both the *lex orandi* and the tradition'.[62]

---

60. In fact Bugnini is regarded as 'the major architect of the liturgical reform'; Baldovin, *Reforming the Liturgy*, 53.

61. I discuss this canonical term shortly.

62. Gy, 'Cardinal Ratzinger's *The Spirit of the Liturgy*', 92, 95; *CIC*, c. 838, §1 and 2; Bugnini, *The Reform of the Liturgy (1948–1975)*; and now also see Marini, *A Challenging Reform*. Unfortunately this important book has been criticized: for example, for not indicating all its sources and for less information on the period after 1965.

In responding to this, Joseph Ratzinger indicates agreement with Gy in being 'altogether on his side in his effort to be faithful to the liturgical forms transmitted to us in the [current] liturgical books', and that the right to change the liturgy is 'at least in the Latin Church, reserved to the pope'. However Ratzinger points out that 'such is not the attitude of a considerable portion of the liturgists who continually bombard us, on the contrary, with newly proposed texts and forms and who have thereby contributed not a little, in divers places, to a certain anarchy in the liturgical domain ... [which] *constitutes the principal obstacle to a general and positive reception of the missal of Paul VI*. The liturgy is often so different from one parish to another, that the common missal is scarcely visible anymore. It would be easy to provide a good number of examples in this regard'. This is very evident indeed.[63] Despite his criticisms, one should also note that Pierre-Marie Gy also indicates agreement between himself and the cardinal on 'emphasizing the absolute necessity of faithfulness to the rules and doctrines concerning the liturgy and the sacraments (in particular the Real Presence and the Eucharistic Sacrifice)'. This is also agreement on 'the place given in the liturgy in our day to the vernacular language; conjointly, if I may say so, the renewal of biblical readings in the Mass; and lastly the importance of the Fathers of the Church, whose renewed place in the Liturgy of the Hours I imagine he appreciates'.[64]

Joseph Ratzinger's response to Gy's specific points concerning the pope and liturgical law, indicates, once more, his adherence to the new missal, though with reservations,

---

63. Ratzinger, '*The Spirit of the Liturgy* or Fidelity to the Council', 98–99; Pope John Paul II, *Apostolic Letter Vicesimus quintus annus*, 4 December 1988, no. 13; *idem, Encyclical Letter Ecclesia de Eucharistia*, 17 April 2003, no. 52. For a balanced discussion of what Ratzinger terms the 'crisis in the Church' and the liturgy, see Robinson, *The Mass and Modernity*, 31–54: cf. Crouan, *The History and the Future of the Roman Liturgy*, 194–217, 239–46.

64. Gy, 'Cardinal Ratzinger's *The Spirit of the Liturgy*', 91, 93–94.

and his commentary here is noteworthy: 'It is true that Paul VI approved the missal published in 1970 *in forma specifica* [now in its third edition], and that I hold to it with an inner conviction, even if I regret certain deficiencies and do not consider each of the decisions made the best possible'. He then briefly refers—significantly—to the historical circumstances concerning the preparation of the Pauline missal and if 'the wishes of the pope were truly sought out and maintained in detail'. However while questions, such as Bugnini's dismissal by Pope Paul VI in 1975, then secretary of the Congregation for Divine Worship 'naturally change nothing in the obligatory character of the missal', that the impression should arise 'that nothing in this missal must ever be changed, as if any reflection on possible later reforms were necessarily an attack on the council—such an idea I can only call absurd'. While stability needs to be regained in the liturgy, says the cardinal, 'we also need to reflect on the means for correcting the deficiencies of the reform, deficiencies that are more obvious today. Why we should not call such a possible future investigation and development a "reform of the reform" is something I have still not figured out'.[65] He also expressed his belief that the missal should last longer than the twenty or thirty years which Bugnini estimated for its lifespan, arguing that it is situated 'in the great continuity of the history of the liturgy, in which there is always growth and purification, but not ruptures'. One again we detect here the idea of the organic development of the liturgy.[66]

Although we have seen the publication of books such as Bugnini's memoirs, the recent book of Piero Marini, former papal master of ceremonies, Nicola Giampietro's book on Cardinal Ferdinando Antonelli and the liturgical

---

65. Ratzinger, '*The Spirit of the Liturgy* or Fidelity to the Council', 99; cf. Ratzinger, *God is Near Us*, 66–73; idem, *The Feast of Faith*, 79–95, which indicates the development of his thought on the post-Vatican II *Missale Romanum*. Concerning Bugnini's dismissal, see Marini, *A Challenging Reform*, 148–50.

66. Ratzinger, '*The Spirit of the Liturgy* or Fidelity to the Council', 99.

reform, the precise circumstances surrounding the composition of the new Pauline missal, and the necessity to study more documentation, still needs to be fully explored to give more comprehensive and critical answers to the historical questions. Yet it is evident that serious mistakes and errors of judgement were made.[67] However what is to be made of Joseph Ratzinger's views on the regulation of the liturgy by the papacy, 'deficiencies' in the missal, the possibility of future change, and a 'reform of the reform' without slighting the Second Vatican Council? The pope, indeed, regulates the liturgy for the whole Church, and has done so since Trent: though earlier examples of papal intervention in the liturgy can be found.[68] Theologically speaking, the 'ordinary Magisterium' is the basis of the liturgy, and 'magisterial decisions in matters of discipline [and liturgy], even if they are not guaranteed by the charism of infallibility, are not without divine assistance and call for the adherence of the faithful'. Again, according to theological opinion, 'it is to be held [generally that] from the time of their express approval by the Holy See one can, and must, regard liturgies as used in the Catholic Church today *as free of errors regarding the Faith and God-given moral norms'*.[69] The law of prayer is the law of faith: the Church believes as she prays. Liturgy is a constitutive element of the holy and living tradition. For this reason, says the *Catechism of the Catholic Church*, 'no sacramental rite may be

---

67. Giampietro, *The Development of the Liturgical Reform: As seen by Cardinal Ferdinando Antonelli from 1948 to 1970*; Rowland, *Ratzinger's Faith*, 127–28; Gy, *The Reception of Vatican II*, 1–19.

68. The Second Vatican Council, *The Constitution on the Sacred Liturgy Sacrosanctum Concilium*, 4 December 1963, no. 22 (1); Pope John Paul II, *Apostolic Letter Vicesimus quintus annus*, 4 December 1988, no. 19; Rubin, *Corpus Christi*, 176.

69. Schumacher, 'The Liturgy as *Locus Theologicus*', 87, 89–90 (my emphasis); Congregation for the Doctrine of the Faith, *Instruction on the Ecclesial Vocation of the Theologian Donum veritatis*, 24 May 1990, no. 17; Gamber, *The Reform of the Roman Liturgy*, 34–35: and see the comments at the end of this section concerning 'prudential judgement'.

modified or manipulated at the will of the minister or of
the community. Even the supreme authority in the Church
may not change the liturgy arbitrarily, but only in the obedience of faith and with religious respect for the mystery
of liturgy'.[70] A comparison with Joseph Ratzinger's views
on these elements demonstrates that he has not expressed
anything contrary to the Church's teaching—let alone
denied any article of faith and morals—while stating his
opinion concerning papal authority and liturgy after the
council.[71] In his book *On the Way to Jesus Christ*, when
examining the *Catechism* and the liturgy, the cardinal actually cites the above quotation from the *Catechism*.[72] It is
also clear—and this, indeed, is frequently forgotten—that
a pope, and other clergy, *can* (in)frequently err in liturgical
and disciplinary matters, the most famous example being
the introduction of the breviary of Cardinal Quignonez in
the sixteenth century—abolished, and eventually replaced
by the *Breviarium Romanum* after Trent. One could also
mention the alteration —or perhaps 'mutilation'—of
the hymns of the breviary in the seventeenth century.[73]
Though Joseph Ratzinger does not question or challenge
papal authority or its prerogatives over the liturgy *per se*, or
counsel disobedience of current rubrics, even when speaking about 'deficiencies' in the missal and its formulation,
we must admit—at the very least—that it is theoretically
possible that papal approval was given to certain 'deficiencies', where these exist, with the best intentions. Such
deficiencies are the result of human scholarship, which

---

70. *CCC*, nos 1124–25.

71. See above pp. 29–30 for excerpts from *TSL*, 165–66. For more
     discussion of papal authority and liturgical change, see Gamber,
     The Reform of the Roman liturgy, 27–39. However Ratzinger would
     certainly not agree entirely with the latter's views on the Pauline
     missal.

72. Ratzinger, *On the Way to Jesus Christ*, 153–58, at 154–55; *CCC*, no.
     1125.

73. Reid, *The Organic Development of the Liturgy*, 25–30, 37–38; Her-
     mans, *Het Getijdengebed*, 45.

does not have a guarantee of absolute infallibility.[74] Some
might, for example, legitimately ask if the new prayers for
'the preparation of the gifts', really grew 'organically' from
the previous liturgy, or even if such a radical re-casting of,
or removal of many beautiful prayers from, the Catholic,
Latin liturgy, and certain newer elements, was really for
'the good of the Church'.[75] Wide scale changes made to the
ceremonies and prayers of the Mass—despite their objective theological correctness—or their removal, might also
weaken the presentation and reception of the faith, albeit
unintentionally. Joseph Ratzinger has, himself, said the
following, on the 'watering down' of the use of the word
'soul' (*anima*) in the revised missal: 'Indeed, the Missal of
Paul VI dared to speak of the soul only here and there,
and that in timorous fashion, otherwise avoiding all mention of it where possible. As for the German rite of burial,
it has, so far as I can see, obliterated it altogether'.[76] The
notion of the organic development of the liturgy, and
that liturgy is not a fabricated product, is one of the main
points of proponents for 'the reform of the reform', such
as Ratzinger, who (before and after becoming pope), in
any case, substantially accepts, and daily uses, the new
Roman Missal.[77] Despite somewhat ambiguous doubts
over Alcuin Reid's understanding of the organic develop-

---

74. For an interesting discussion on the use of liturgical history, see
     Baldovin, 'The Uses of Liturgical History', reproduced in Bald-
     ovin, *Reforming the Liturgy*, 158–73.

75. The Second Vatican Council, *The Constitution on the Sacred Liturgy
     Sacrosanctum Concilium*, 4 December 1963, nos 4, 23; The Second
     Vatican Council, *Decree on the Catholic Eastern Churches Orientalium
     Ecclesiarum*, 21 November 1964, no. 2; Pope John Paul II, *Apostolic
     Letter Vicesimus quintus annus*, 4 December 1988, no. 4 (a 'pruden-
     tial judgement'); and see n. 53 above.

76. Ratzinger, *Eschatology: Death and Eternal Life*, 248; Schumacher,
     'The Liturgy as *Locus Theologicus*', 90; Hitchcock, *The Recovery of
     the Sacred*, 141–45.

77. See the interesting discussion of 'the reform of the reform' in the
     light of *Sacrosanctum Concilium* in Harrison, 'The Postconciliar
     Eucharistic Liturgy: Planning a "Reform of the Reform"', 151–93.

ment of the liturgy, discussed by Reid in his well-known book, Baldovin admits that, '… if one were to understand the council's language [that is, the organic growth of newer forms from existing forms] to refer to the pace and extent of the reforms, one could certainly take issue with the finished product … [Alcuin Reid's] assessment of the need for reform is balanced'.[78] That the current missal is subject to reform and change is evident, for instance, by its third edition (2002), mainly in the general instruction. Further 'reform' should not be definitively precluded.

We should also add here that Joseph Ratzinger has a point when he briefly refers to the question of whether 'the wishes of the pope [Paul VI] were truly sought out and maintained in detail' concerning the preparation of the Pauline missal, while agreeing that 'It is true that Paul VI approved the missal published in 1970 *in forma specifica*', despite deficiencies.[79] An ecclesial document, act, or law—for example, that which comes from some Vatican dicastery—which is given *in forma specifica*, means that the pope has approved this document, act, or law in a special way such that no further appeal to the pope directly is possible, unless he should specifically mandate such an appeal. The expression *in forma specifica* indicates that the pope has reviewed the document and makes it his own by express approbation. The document then acquires the canonical force of a formal papal act.[80] To carry the added weight of *in forma specifica* the document must have the precise formula *in forma specifica approbavit;* otherwise the document would be understood to be approved *in forma communi* ('in common/usual form'). *In forma communi* means that the pope has reviewed a Vatican curial document and orders it to be published. However this document retains the juridical weight of the particular curial

---

78. Baldovin, *Reforming the Liturgy*, 57. Cardinal Ratzinger wrote a favourable preface to the Ignatius Press' edition of Reid's book, *The Organic Development of the Liturgy*, 2nd ed.

79. Ratzinger, '*The Spirit of the Liturgy* or Fidelity to the Council', 99.

80. Cf. *CIC*, cc. 1404 and 1405, §2.

dicastery which has formulated it, and does not carry the added weight of a papal document or papal act.[81] However distinguishing these forms of confirmation is not entirely straightforward in every instance, and various formulas could be used, especially under the old *Codex Iuris Canonici*, which was replaced in 1983.[82] Pierre-Marie Gy—who was closely involved with the formulation of the new missal— has, in another publication, commented on the canonical nature of the approval which Pope Paul gave to various elements of the new missal, during this process. However, from our examination of *in forma specifica*, it is clear that his suggestion that 'There are so many ... examples of the Pope's [that is, Paul VI] involvement [in the reform of the liturgy] that we can say that most of the documents of the liturgical reform during his papacy have been approved *in forma specifica*, that is, directly by the Pope, *without a specific expression of such an approval* ...', is extremely doubtful, from a canonical perspective.[83]

   We can see from all this that, for those who propagate 'the reform of the reform', it is also a question of the hermeneutics used to interpret the Second Vatican Council: and Gy's comments on Ratzinger's spirituality as 'antedating' Vatican II are revealing. Since the council there is a common misperception in the Church, even though it may be innocent and unconscious, that since Vatican II there has been a break—to some a decisive break—with the 'Church of pre-Vatican II', and with a generally corrupted, liturgical past.[84] With this mindset, official texts, such as conciliar

---

81.   Bretzke, '*In forma specifica*'; Huels, 'Interpreting an Instruction Approved *in forma specifica*', 5–46.

82.   For a discussion of this in the context of the liturgy, with fuller canonical references, Capponi, 'Alcune considerazioni giuridiche in materia di riforma liturgica': English translation, *Some Juridical Considerations on the Reform of the Liturgy*, especially 16–18.

83.   Gy, *The Reception of Vatican II*, 18 (my emphasis).

84.   For instance, concerning faulty interpretations concerning lay liturgical participation in the Middle Ages—while acknowledging 'unsatisfactory elements'—see Gribbin, 'Lay Participation in the Eucharistic Liturgy of the Later Middle Ages', 51–69.

documents, liturgical texts (whether or not they contain deficiencies), and also catechetical teaching and theology, are expounded in a vacuum from the council and the Magisterium. A brief look at the footnotes of the council documents, demonstrates how much the Second Vatican Council *is* in line with previous Church teaching, and it is partly the role of theologians, working under the Magisterium, to harmonize, and present, this council with previous church teachings.[85] This has consequences for the liturgy and *vice versa*. On the subject of liturgical reform, Cardinal Francis George has said that 'My own belief is that liturgical renewal after the council was treated as a programme or movement for change, without enough thought being given to what happens in any community when its symbol system is disrupted'. Liturgical theology, understood correctly, is important for liturgical praxis.[86] While Cardinal Ratzinger has not suggested abandoning certain 'disciplinary' elements which appeared in *Sacrosanctum Concilium*, Aidan Nichol's comments on distinguishing the doctrinal aspects of *Sacrosanctum Concilium* from other elements, have particular relevance to interpreting the council, and

---

85.   Congregation for the Doctrine of the Faith, *Instruction on the Ecclesial Vocation of the Theologian, Donum veritatis*, 1990. For models of this in respect of *Sacrosanctum Concilium*, see Jackson, 'Theology of the Liturgy', 101–28; Folsom, 'The Hermeneutics of *Sacrosanctum concilium*: Development of a Method and its Application', 2–9; and see Cardinal Ratzinger's discussion of *Sacrosanctum Concilium* — especially his comments on 'comprehension', *participatio actuosa* and 'simplicity' ('Simplicité ... ne signifie pas fonctionnalisme') in Heinz, 'Rencontre avec le cardinal Joseph Ratzinger', 45–49; Ratzinger, '40 Jahre Konstitution über die heilige Liturgie. Rückblick und Vorblick', 209–21. More controversial—but nonetheless noteworthy—is Mgr Brunero Gherardini's discussion of Vatican II in *The Ecumenical Vatican Council II: A Much Needed Discussion*.

86.   George, '*Sacrosanctum Concilium* Anniversary Address: The Foundations of Liturgical Reform', 46. Denis Crouan—a strong advocate of the recent edition of the *Missale Romanum* (2002)—also admits that mistakes were made: see Crouan, *The History and the Future of the Roman Liturgy*, 137–38.

the possibility of further development, which has consequences for liturgical expression:

> The habit of obedience makes good Catholics slow
> to criticize. But absence of critical comment cannot
> be taken without further ado to imply approval of
> the manners of celebrants at the altar, the quality of
> church music, or the casual atmosphere that too fre-
> quently reigns in our churches ... one must frankly
> say that, while the doctrinal sections of *Sacrosanc-
> tum Concilium* ought to be regarded, along with all
> teaching on faith and morals by general councils, as
> sacrosanct (no pun intended!), the bishops [at the
> council] enjoyed no assistance of the Holy Spirit—
> even negatively—in matters of the aesthetics of rit-
> ual. In that realm they had only human prudence to
> guide them, a prudence that, sadly, lacked access to
> resources of anthropological understanding more
> fully available to us now.[87]

Similar points, from an historical perspective, could also
be made. In the spirited words—but nonetheless accurate
observations—of J. P. Parsons,

> Are we really *obliged* to believe that the Holy Spirit
> demanded the launching of a crusade at the Fourth
> Lateran Council in 1215? And *must* we hold that in
> 1311 the Holy Spirit dictated the Council of Vienne's

---

87. Nichols, 'Salutary Dissatisfaction: An English View of "Reform-
     ing the Reform"', 198–99, 206. See also *Ibid.*, *Looking at the Liturgy:
     A Critical View of its Contemporary Form*, especially chapter two;
     Flanagan, *Sociology and Liturgy*; Pickstock, *After Writing: On the
     Liturgical Consummation of Philosophy*. Although John F. Baldovin
     may label Pickstock's view of the medieval liturgy as 'romanti-
     cism'—a charge he also makes about Klaus Gamber, Alcuin Reid
     and, indeed, Joseph Ratzinger, concerning their views of the litur-
     gical past—and even that her work 'is of little use to those who
     want to know how to reform the liturgy', he admits that Pickstock's
     analysis of medieval liturgy 'does raise some very important and
     fundamental philosophical questions about the nature of the post-
     Vatican II reform as well as its charter in *Sacrosanctum Concilium*':
     Baldovin, *Reforming the Liturgy*, 25–6, 31, 55, 89. Concerning his
     views about the critique of sociology and anthropology—which
     are somewhat contradictory—see *Ibid.*, 90–104, 161.

rules regulating the use of torture by the Inquisition? ... As to the liturgy, is it mandatory to believe that in 1963 the Holy Spirit wanted the abandonment of the principle of the weekly recitation of all 150 psalms [or] *de fide* that God wanted the Hour of Prime suppressed from January 1964? ... It is not Catholic teaching that the Church is infallible in pastoral or prudential judgements. We are therefore logically free to hold that any council can be ill-advised when making these kinds of decision.[88]

However one must certainly not counsel disobedience. In his discussion on recognising possible errors on an official level, Brian W. Harrison (2003) indicates that he is 'not saying we should be *disobedient* to the Holy See. My point is not that obedience in liturgical matters is unnecessary; but rather, it is insufficient'.[89]

Conclusion

Pierre-Marie Gy's review of *The Spirit of the Liturgy*, and Joseph Ratzinger's response, brings into a sharper focus, not only a clarification of certain, central opinions of Ratzinger, but liturgical issues of great importance today, as the liturgy is at the summit of the Church's activity. These issues also have a bearing on the interpretation of the Second Vatican Council.[90] Though not without polemics, this frank dialogue was more peaceable than the sad 'liturgical wars' which have been raging in the Church since the last council, with individuals going to extremes, in either

---

88. Parsons, 'A Reform of the Reform?', 248–49; cf. Rowland, *Ratzinger's Faith*, 127–28. On prudential judgement—though here in the context of doctrine—see Congregation for the Doctrine of the Faith, *Instruction on the Ecclesial Vocation of the Theologian Donum veritatis*, no. 24. The Magisterium's prudential judgement, in doctrinal matters, cannot 'habitually' be mistaken, though progress can be made.

89. Harrison, 'The Postconciliar Eucharistic Liturgy', 166 (the author's emphasis).

90. The Second Vatican Council, *The Constitution on the Sacred Liturgy Sacrosanctum Concilium*, 4 December 1963, no. 10.

a very liberal or conservative way. How do *we* answer, here, Gy's 'title question' concerning Cardinal Ratzinger? It is clear from our examination of Gy's criticisms, that Joseph Ratzinger is faithful to the council and is not reacting against it, while critical of the implementation of the liturgical reform, the manner of its production, and individual elements. There is a major drawback, in that Gy did not sufficiently examine in depth the predominantly theological, and hence other fundamental aspects of *The Spirit of the Liturgy*, which aids one's understanding of 'liturgy' and liturgical practice.[91] Nevertheless Gy's and Ratzinger's dialogue is clearly valuable, especially in relation to what Pope Benedict XVI has said and done in regards to the liturgy, as we shall see.

It was unfortunate that Gy, who should still be esteemed for his scholarly achievements, took issue with the cardinal's loyalty to the Second Vatican Council, especially as the latter's writings are permeated with the council's documents to a significant degree. However it is a valid point—despite being disputed by many liturgists—that the actual implementation and interpretation of the council should not be viewed entirely *a priori* as fulfilling what the council actually desired, in its doctrine, general principles, and practical decrees: even at an official level. Legitimate, respectful, and 'obedient' criticism, from individuals such as Joseph Ratzinger, can help one rediscover the council. One would certainly not be violating the Magisterium in pointing 'liturgical deficiencies' out. In this connection, one should be very careful not to elevate those recent liturgical innovations—even if they are ancient—which, while important, are *not* of divine origin, to a higher doctrinal level than they possess, saving liturgical 'Tradition'. The notion of a fundamental break between the Church before and after Vatican II remains, sadly, a serious problem in many sections of theological, historical and liturgical

---

91.   Ratzinger, '*The Spirit of the Liturgy* or Fidelity to the Council', 101–
      2. Baldovin, at least, in *Reforming the Liturgy*, made an attempt to
      do this: see *Ibid.*, 65–89.

studies, and also at the pastoral level, which, in my own experience and that of many others, not infrequently shows signs of a certain liturgical and spiritual mediocrity. A change in mindset is required, which reads and interprets the decrees of the council in terms of continuity with the past.[92] We should also add, concerning problems in theology, that the way we regard and 'define' the person of Christ can also produce a negative effect upon liturgical theory and practice, if we depart from the Magisterium. Indeed Ratzinger believes that the criteria for liturgical renewal cannot be separated from the question which Jesus asked his disciples at Caesarea Philippi, 'Who do you say that the Son of Man is?'.[93]

At the same time, the positive liturgical fruits after the council, also acknowledged by Joseph Ratzinger, should be recognized, and the work of many theologians and liturgists. The prescriptions of the Holy See should be obediently followed, something which Ratzinger has also underlined, according to recognized forms of rubrical interpretation, and, above all, in a proper liturgical spirit. The Holy See has attempted to rectify the widespread liturgical abuses in the Church, and to cultivate veneration and love for the Holy Eucharist, for example, in *Redemptionis Sacramentum*: Cardinal Ratzinger is recognized as 'one of the driving forces' behind this instruction.[94] The recent edition of the *Missale Romanum* can be beautifully celebrated, and though little may appear to have practically changed, it is a step in the right direction, with more emphasis on liturgical tradition in the *Institutio Generalis* and features, such as the restored—though optional—form of the vigil of Pentecost. However, it has to be said, that any mistakes, made at an official level in the formulation of the new lit-

---

92. In the next chapter we shall see that Pope Benedict XVI appreciates this point.

93. Mt 16: 13; See Ratzinger, *A New Song for the Lord*, esp. 29–36.

94. Congregation for Divine Worship and the Discipline of the Sacraments, *Instruction Redemptionis Sacramentum*, 25 March 2004; Reid, 'Looking Again at the Liturgical Reform', 4.

urgy, and anything which gives the impression of breaking
with the liturgical tradition of the Church, should be humbly recognized. Along with this, the possibilities offered
by a 'reform of the reform' should also be considered, in
order to produce a liturgy *more* in continuity with the heritage of the Church's living liturgical past, and with the
Second Vatican Council. It is not only a question of *solely*
correcting liturgical abuses. There needs to be a more open
and courageous dialogue between those great number of
liturgists who oppose 'the reform of the reform' and any
trace of 'preconciliar liturgy'—which is frequently carica-
tured[95]—and may have a less 'transcendental' approach to
the sacred liturgy,[96] with those who also accept Vatican II,
but have reservations about its implementation in liturgical matters, and wish to reform the current liturgical rite.

Characterisations and generalisations of previous liturgical practices—for example, priests whose voices could
barely be heard in the Church during Mass, or who advised
people to receive communion before Mass—clearly indicate less than perfect models of liturgical celebration of
the pre-Vatican II liturgy in particular instances. However
by almost presenting them as the 'state of affairs' before
the reforms which followed the Second Vatican Council,
actually ignores the valuable achievements of the Liturgical Movement—endorsed by the Magisterium—which
were *also* apparent before Vatican II, and the experience,
and sound liturgical piety, of many ordinary people, and
the liturgy in the lives of the saints, which puts matters in
a broader, theological and historical perspective.[97] While
one should be conscious of a constant need for 'liturgical
education' of clergy and laity in the Church, the necessity
'for a *radical* reform' of the liturgy as a response to possible

95.   For example, see Baldovin, *Reforming the Liturgy*, 55.

96.   For example, de Jong, 'Enkele overpeinzingen naar aanleiding van
      de buitengewone misorde', 250–67.

97.   Again, we shall see that these points have not escaped the atten-
      tion of Pope Benedict XVI in the chapters which follow, especially
      chapter four.

'liturgical deficiences' of the past, has surely proved to be a significant problem and not the answer.[98] It would also be wrong to view entirely those individuals who attend 'old rite' masses as 'regressionists' desiring a wholesale return to the 1950s, or the Middle Ages. Yet, generally speaking, both periods in history, made a very positive contribution to the development of the liturgy,[99] as with other periods, a fact which is too frequently dismissed by liturgists today, many of whom still believe in making liturgy 'relevant' to modern man, with a constant creation and re-working of texts, to the spiritual detriment and instability of modern man.[100] To my mind Baldovin has not dealt sufficiently with Jonathan Robinson's book *The Mass and Modernity*, nor the work of Aidan Nichols *et al.*, in order to offer a convincing alternative 'scenario' to the problems they indicate concerning modernity, philosophy, anthropology, and the liturgy. Saying that Joseph Ratzinger 'seems haunted by the Enlightenment and its privileging of historical-critical analysis', does not seem to be enough.[101] However, what can be done about those many individuals who desire access to the 'Pre-Vatican II' Roman Rite? The cardinal clearly favoured the harmonization, or rather the continuity of the Second Vatican Council and the modern liturgy with the previous, centuries-old liturgy. Attempts at progress in these, and other issues concerning the liturgy, in the current pontificate of Pope Benedict XVI, will be the focus of the chapters which follow.

---

98. Baldovin, *Reforming the Liturgy*, 55.

99. Here one might cite the institution of the feast of Corpus Christi in the thirteenth century and the papal encyclical *Mediator Dei* of Pope Pius XII in 1947, for example.

100. Baldovin, *Reforming the Liturgy*, 157.

101. *Ibid.*, 89.

Chapter III

Pope Benedict XVI and the Liturgy —
Towards a *Pax Liturgica*[1]
Part One

Introduction

On 19 April 2005, Cardinal Joseph Ratzinger became Pope Benedict XVI. His election brought to the throne of St Peter a man who is undoubtedly one the greatest theological minds of the present day. The pope continues to write as a theologian, as we have recently seen with *Jesus of Nazareth* and other publications. It was also mentioned in the introduction that he had previously combined the role of theologian with his task as Prefect for the Congregation for the Doctrine of the Faith.[2] The pope's active concern for the liturgy, which was evident throughout his life as a priest and cardinal, is a notable hallmark of his pontificate. What, then, has Pope Benedict, after six years since the beginning of his pontificate, said about the liturgy, and how has his theological thought flowed into his Magisterium and in his celebration of the liturgy? In what way does all this relate to the liturgy of the Church as a whole? In answering these questions, we shall indicate, in the following chapters, what he has taught in his papal Magisterium concerning the liturgy, and what he has thus far done to harmonize the new liturgy with the old — the 'hermeneutic of continuity' — and 'the reform of the reform'. We shall examine in particular, Pope Benedict's post-synodal exhortation on the

---

1.   I borrowed the phrase *Pax Liturgica* from Geffroy, *Benoît XVI et la Paix liturgique.*

2.   Pope Benedict XVI/Ratzinger, *Jesus of Nazareth*; Pope Benedict XVI/ Ratzinger, *Waarden in tijden van ommekeer*; see p. vii.

Eucharist *Sacramentum Caritatis* together with a number of other sources of his magisterial teaching, particularly his motu proprio, *Summorum Pontificum*. It is not easy—nor wholly desirable—to separate the pope's eucharistic theology from his liturgical theology, as both are interlinked and must remain so when considering what the liturgy is. An evident fault of recent years is that some experts of the liturgy do not pay sufficient attention to sound eucharistic or liturgical theology. However in line with Joseph Ratzinger's *The Spirit of the Liturgy*, I have sought to lay emphasis on the liturgical aspects rather than present a complete eucharistic or sacramental theology of Pope Benedict XVI, while not ignoring the importance of the latter.[3]

Liturgy and related issues in Pope Benedict XVI's Magisterium

In the first year of his papacy, Pope Benedict made some very important, pivotal statements, which were to set the background for his words and actions concerning the liturgy, and wider theological and pastoral issues in the Church. It is significant that in his first address to the cardinals at the end of a concelebrated Mass in the Sistine Chapel, the day after his election, he drew attention to the correct interpretation of the Second Vatican Council—an important theme of 'the reform of the reform'—and 'The Year of the Eucharist', inaugurated by Pope John Paul II. Pope Benedict wished 'to affirm with force my decided will to pursue the commitment to enact Vatican Council II, in the wake of my predecessors and in faithful continuity with the millennia-old tradition of the Church.' The significance of that special Year of the Eucharist to Pope Benedict, who is particularly attentive to the importance of the liturgy, is noteworthy: 'my pontificate starts as the Church is living the special Year dedicated to the Eucharist. How

---

3.   For a recent collection of texts of Pope Benedict XVI concerning the Holy Eucharist, see Pope Benedict XVI, *Heart of the Christian Life*.

can I not see in this providential coincidence an element that must mark the ministry to which I have been called? The Eucharist, the heart of Christian life and the source of the evangelizing mission of the Church, cannot but be the permanent centre and the source of the petrine service entrusted to me'.[4] The pope's reference here to pursuing the enactment of the Second Vatican Council 'in faithful continuity with the millennia-old tradition of the Church', was further underlined in his address to the Roman Curia in December 2005, which touched upon, at greater length, the correct hermeneutics to be used in interpreting the Second Vatican Council and the Holy Eucharist. For example, he says the following concerning 'worship/adoration', where there are clear parallels with his liturgical theology:

> Before any activity, before the world can change there must be worship. Worship alone sets us truly free; worship alone gives us the criteria for our action. Precisely in a world in which guiding criteria are absent and the threat exists that each person will be a law unto himself, it is fundamentally necessary to stress worship. ... It is moving for me to see how everywhere in the Church the joy of eucharistic adoration is reawakening and being fruitful. In the period of liturgical reform, Mass and adoration outside it were often seen as in opposition to one another: it was thought that the Eucharistic Bread had not been given to us to be contemplated, but to be eaten, as a widespread objection claimed at that time. The experience of the prayer of the Church has already shown how nonsensical this antithesis was ... Indeed, we do not merely receive something in the Eucharist. It is the encounter and unification of persons; the person, however, who comes to meet us and desires to unite himself to us is the Son of God. Such unification can only be brought about by means of adoration. Receiv-

---

4.   Pope Benedict XVI, 'First Message of His Holiness Benedict XVI at the End of the Eucharistic Concelebration with the Members of the College of Cardinals in the Sistine Chapel', 20 April 2005, 29.

ing the Eucharist means adoring the One whom we receive. Precisely in this way and only in this way do we become one with him. Therefore, the development of eucharistic adoration, as it took shape during the Middle Ages, was the most consistent consequence of the Eucharistic Mystery itself: only in adoration can profound and true acceptance develop.[5]

Concerning the implementation and interpretation of the Second Vatican Council, Pope Benedict asks, quite openly,

What has been the result of the council? Was it well received? What, in the acceptance of the council, was good and what was inadequate or mistaken? What still remains to be done? … Why has the implementation of the council, in large parts of the Church, thus far been so difficult? Well, it all depends on the correct interpretation of the council or—as we would say today—on its proper hermeneutics … On the one hand, there is an interpretation that I would call 'a hermeneutic of discontinuity and rupture'; it has frequently availed itself of the sympathies of the mass media, and also one trend of modern theology. On the other, there is the 'hermeneutic of reform', of renewal in the continuity of the one subject-Church which the Lord has given to us … The hermeneutic of discontinuity risks ending in a split between the preconciliar Church and the postconciliar Church. It asserts that the texts of the council as such do not yet express the true spirit of the council. It claims that they are the result of compromises in which, to reach unanimity, it was found necessary to keep and reconfirm many old things

5.   Pope Benedict XVI, 'Address of His Holiness Benedict XVI to the Roman Curia Offering them His Christmas Greetings', 22 December 2005: cf. *TSL*, 85; Ratzinger, *God is Near Us*, 89; Pope Benedict XVI, *Post-synodal Exhortation Sacramentum Caritatis*, 22 February 2007, no. 66 (hereafter, Pope Benedict XVI, *Sacramentum Caritatis*): and see chapter one, where Joseph Ratzinger is seen to discuss 'worship' very frequently (e.g. *TSL*, 22–50). I have had recourse to the official Latin text of *Sacramentum Caritatis* in *AAS* 99 (2007), 105–80, where it was judged appropriate.

that are now pointless. However, the true spirit of the council is not to be found in these compromises but instead in the impulses toward the new that are contained in the texts ... In a word: it would be necessary not to follow the texts of the council but its spirit. ... The nature of a council as such is therefore basically misunderstood ... The hermeneutic of discontinuity is countered by the hermeneutic of reform, as it was presented first by Pope John XXIII in his Speech inaugurating the council on 11 October 1962 and later by Pope Paul VI in his Discourse for the council's conclusion on 7 December 1965 ... The Church, both before and after the council, was and is the same church, one, holy, catholic and apostolic journeying on through time.[6]

The 'hermeneutic of reform' or 'the hermeneutic of continuity' in interpreting the council and the liturgy, will be seen time and time again in Pope Benedict's Magisterium and is a key concept in understanding his pontificate and Magisterium.

Pope Benedict XVI's Post-synodal Apostolic Exhortation Sacramentum Caritatis

Sacramentum Caritatis (2007) is particularly noteworthy among Pope Benedict's magisterial statements on the eucharistic liturgy, because the Eucharist is explored more broadly and in greater depth. Although an exhaustive commentary of every aspect of this document is beyond the scope of this present work, we will indicate a number of its important, noteworthy elements, mainly from parts two and three of the document.[7] It will be seen that this document reflects the pope's own theology of the liturgy, as the attentive reader of the first chapter of this book will surely

---

6. Pope Benedict XVI, 'Address of His Holiness Benedict XVI to the Roman Curia Offering them His Christmas Greetings', 22 December 2005.

7. Note that I shall not necessarily follow the subject matter in sequence, as presented in *Sacramentum Caritatis* itself.

note. Among the themes from *Sacramentum Caritatis* which
will be highlighted here, are the hermeneutic of continuity (reform) in action—in a liturgical context—the theology
of beauty, art, mystagogy, *participatio actuosa*, the *ars celebrandi*, 'spiritual worship'—*logiké latreía*—and eschatology.

In *Sacramentum Caritatis*, Pope Benedict 'takes up' the
reflections and proposals from the synod on the Holy
Eucharist (no. 5) 'to offer some basic directions aimed at
a renewed commitment to eucharistic enthusiasm and
fervour in the Church'. The pope emphasizes the 'hermeneutic of continuity', which attempts to connect the liturgy
of today with the Church's liturgical heritage, and highlights—significantly—that the Church's liturgy was very
much alive in the past too. He does so in a brief commentary on the development of the liturgical rites:

> If we consider the bimillenary history of God's
> Church, guided by the wisdom of the Holy Spirit,
> we can gratefully admire the orderly development
> of the ritual forms in which we commemorate the
> event of our salvation. From the varied forms of the
> early centuries, still resplendent in the rites of the
> Ancient Churches of the East, up to the spread of
> the Roman Rite; from the clear indications of the
> Council of Trent and the Missal of Saint Pius V to
> the liturgical renewal called for by the Second Vati-
> can Council: in every age of the Church's history the
> eucharistic celebration, as the source and summit of
> her life and mission, shines forth in the liturgical
> rite in all its richness and variety.[8]

However he also indicates that there were difficulties with
the liturgy after the Second Vatican Council, as well as
acknowledging the recent fruits of liturgical reform and the
validity of the liturgical renewal, whose riches remain to be
appreciated.[9] It is necessary, therefore, that, 'the [liturgical]
changes which the council called for need to be understood

---

8.   Pope Benedict XVI, *Sacramentum Caritatis*, no. 3.

9.   Pope Benedict XVI, *Sacramentum Caritatis*, no. 3: *Multum sane aes-
      timavit. Difficultates nonnullique cogniti etiam abusus — dictum est*

within the overall unity of the historical development of the rite itself (*quae historicum ipsius ritus progressum*), without the introduction of artificial discontinuities (*absque inductis facticiis fractionibus, designat*).' Here the pope explicity refers to 'the need for a hermeneutic of continuity (*explicationis continuationis*) also with regard to the correct interpretation of the liturgical development which followed the Second Vatican Council.'[10] This is something which we will also see when examining the pope's 'reconciliation' of the liturgy of the Mass, as promulgated after Vatican II with the 'Missal of Pope St Pius V'. Again, Pope Benedict is also conscious that 'This great mystery [that is, the Holy Eucharist] is celebrated in the liturgical forms which the Church, guided by the Holy Spirit, develops in time and space. We need a renewed awareness of the decisive role played by the Holy Spirit in the evolution (*efficiendis*) of the liturgical form and deepening understanding of the sacred mysteries'.[11] Here the pope is emphasising the reverence and appreciation that we should have for the liturgical texts of the Church, where the Holy Spirit plays a decisive role in their 'formulation'. However the pope is not saying that everything that came about with the liturgical reforms after the Second Vatican Council was necessarily well implemented, or even free from human error. Here we should also bear in mind what was said earlier about the

---

    — *bonitatem et renovatae liturgiae validitatem opacare non possunt, quae adhuc haud plane perspectas continet divitias.*

10.   Pope Benedict XVI, *Sacramentum Caritatis*, no. 3, n. 6 (Pope Benedict XVI, 'Address of His Holiness Benedict XVI to the Roman Curia Offering them His Christmas Greetings', 22 December 2005: *AAS* 98 (2006), 44–45).

11.   *'Magnum mysterium' hoc in liturgicis formis celebratur, quas Ecclesia, a Spiritu Sancto ducta, per tempora locaque fingit. Quocirca oportet in nobis conscientiam iterum excitemus officii decretorii, quod in liturgicis formis efficiendis itemque in divinis mysteriis intellegendis Spiritus Sanctus detinet*: Pope Benedict XVI, *Sacramentum Caritatis*, no. 12. 'Evolution' is a bad translation for *efficiendis*, which is better translated as 'to make', 'to accomplish', in a productive manner (*efficientia*).

'prudential judgment' of the Church, and that the liturgical tradition of the Church is a 'constitutive element' of the
holy and living tradition. This entails, in the words of the
Catechism of the Catholic Church, that, 'no sacramental rite
may be modified or manipulated at the will of the minister or the community. Even the supreme authority in the
Church may not change the liturgy arbitrarily, but only in
the obedience of faith and with religious respect for the
mystery of the liturgy'.[12] It is not without significance that
the pope, when talking of the 'hermeneutic of continuity',
as he did when he was a cardinal, that 'artificial discontinuities' have been introduced into the liturgical life of
the Church—such as the liturgical abuses of recent years
and ruptures with liturgical tradition—which require cor-
rection. In talking about the 'hermeneutic of continuity',
we also see here something which, quite clearly, acknowledges the organic development of the liturgy. It should be
recalled that Cardinal Ratzinger said that 'What happened
after the council was something else entirely: in the place of
liturgy as the fruit of development came fabricated liturgy.
We abandoned the organic, living process of growth and
development over centuries, and replaced it—as in a manufacturing process—with a fabrication, a banal on-the-spot
product'; he later commented on 'the great continuity of the
history of the liturgy, in which there is always growth and
purification, but not ruptures'. This is surely akin to proper
'organic development'.[13] One can also bring to mind here,
the pope's address to the Roman Curia in 2005 ('What,
in the acceptance of the council, was good and what was
inadequate or mistaken?'). The celebration of the liturgy
has a connection with what we believe, and Pope Benedict
begins the second part of *Sacramentum Caritatis* by recalling that the Synod of Bishops spent much time reflecting

---

12.   *CCC*, nos 1124–25.

13.   Gamber, *The Reform of the Roman Liturgy*, end-cover; Ratzinger,
      'The Spirit of the Liturgy or Fidelity to the Council', 99; Pope Ben-
      edict XVI, *Letter to the Bishops on the Occasion of the Publication of the
      Apostolic Letter "Motu Proprio Data"*, 7 July 2007.

upon the 'intrinsic relationship between eucharistic faith and eucharistic celebration, pointing out the connection between the *lex orandi* and the *lex credendi*, and stressing the primacy of the liturgical action.' Both our faith and the eucharistic liturgy have their source in Christ's gift of himself in the Paschal Mystery.[14]

Following on from 'faith and the eucharistic liturgy', and in relation to them, the pope gives, what we may call, a 'theology of beauty' and the 'splendour of the liturgy', which have a central place in his theology of the liturgy:

> This relationship between creed and worship is evidenced in a particular way by the rich theological and liturgical category of beauty. Like the rest of Christian Revelation, the liturgy is inherently linked to beauty: it is *veritatis splendor* ... This is no mere aestheticism, but the concrete way in which the truth of God's love in Christ encounters us, attracts us and delights us, enabling us to emerge from ourselves and drawing us towards our true vocation, which is love. ...[15]

It is worth 'mulling over' this excerpt, from one of the many 'beautiful' theological passages of *Sacramentum Caritatis* (it is surely a theological masterpiece): liturgy is, like the rest of Christian Revelation, 'inherently' linked to beauty, a *veritatis splendor*, a 'concrete' way of encountering Christ drawing us to our true vocation of love, in communion with him. Christ demonstrated how the truth of love transformed 'the dark mystery of death into the radiant light of the resurrection'. Here is revealed 'the splendour of God's glory', which surpasses all worldly beauty. The pope connects the beauty of the liturgy with God and Revelation, with Our Lord Jesus Christ, and his transformation of death into life and resurrection through the cross—the paschal mystery—in which the beauty of the liturgy is a part, a 'sublime expression of God's glory and, in a certain

---

14.   Pope Benedict XVI, *Sacramentum Caritatis*, no. 34.

15.   *Ibid.*, no. 35.

sense, glimpse of heaven upon earth': here the eschatological aspect of the liturgy is present. Pope Benedict ends his 'meditation' on beauty on a practical note: 'These considerations should make us realize the care which is needed, if the liturgical action is to reflect its innate splendour'.[16] It is noteworthy how time and again here, Pope Benedict underlines that beauty 'is an essential element of the liturgical action': it is not purely a question of taste. His insistence on the connection between liturgy and beauty is, in fact, very poignant, particularly if one considers that the 'noble simplicity' called for, in sacred furnishings for example,[17] has frequently been misinterpreted in a very sterile way, often with the destruction of beautiful vestments, liturgical fittings and altars, to the clear detriment of the liturgy. The pope gives here a very important, and a much needed theological 'concept' that can truly help individuals to rediscover the 'essence' of the liturgy and that it is not a 'simple meal', but something much greater, going to the heart of Christ's redemption, to God and Heaven.[18] We also find the pope's 'theology of beauty', and its connection with liturgy, in the sections of *Sacramentum Caritatis* which concern art (including vestments and other liturgical artefacts), architecture and music—particularly Gregorian chant—which are integral features to the liturgy:

> The profound connection between beauty and the liturgy should make us attentive to every work of art placed at the service of the celebration … Here it is important to remember that the purpose of sacred architecture is to offer the Church a fitting space for the celebration of the mysteries of faith, especially the Eucharist … This same principle holds true for sacred art in general, especially painting and sculpture, where religious iconography should be directed to sacramental mystagogy … Every-

---

16. *Ibid.*
17. *IGMR*, no. 325: this does not rule out the use of more older, traditional forms of liturgical items: see below pp. 133–34.
18. Cf. *TSL*, 58–61, 76–79.

thing related to the Eucharist should be marked by beauty. Special respect and care must also be given to the vestments, to the furnishings and the sacred vessels, so that by their harmonious and orderly arrangement they will foster awe for the mystery of God, manifest the unity of the faith and strengthen devotion ... In the *ars celebrandi*, liturgical song has a pre-eminent place ... In the course of her two-thousand-year history, the Church has created, and still creates, music and songs which represent a rich patrimony of faith and love. This heritage must not be lost ... Gregorian chant [is to] be suitably esteemed and employed as the chant proper to the Roman liturgy'.[19]

Here we see exactly where those 'considerations' concerning beauty are related to the care needed 'if the liturgical action is to reflect its innate splendour'.[20] We shall discuss later how these 'considerations' are being carried out in the papal liturgy of Pope Benedict. It is worth noting here that, in addition to encouraging Gregorian chant, Pope Benedict XVI also referred elsewhere in *Sacramentum Caritatis* to the use of the Latin language in the liturgy, particularly in relation to international gatherings. In general, however, he asked that future priests 'from their time in seminary, receive the preparation needed to understand and to celebrate Mass in Latin, and also to use Latin texts and execute Gregorian chant': one hopes that this advice is heeded in seminaries.[21]

We should remind ourselves that the pope has already written on art and music in *The Spirit of the Liturgy* and in other publications, which we can connect here to this section of *Sacramentum Caritatis*, and which helps to shed more light on these aspects of the liturgy.[22] We have seen

---

19.   Pope Benedict XVI, *Sacramentum Caritatis*, nos 41–42; *TSL, passim.*

20.   *Ibid.,* no. 35.

21.   Pope Benedict XVI, *Sacramentum Caritatis*, no. 62.

22.   *TSL,* 115–56: this constitutes part three of Cardinal Ratzinger's book.

that, after his theological and historical examination of art in *The Spirit of the Liturgy*, for example, Joseph Ratzinger proposed to identify the fundamental principles of an art ordered to divine worship (that is, the liturgy). From these principles we should draw attention to the following points: the encounter that the pope speaks of in *Sacramentum Caritatis*, between Christ and ourselves, through beauty, is paralleled—and explained—in the central place of Christ in art. Again, art and beauty in liturgy, with God, the redemption, the paschal mystery, eschatology and 'going beyond' this world, go hand-in-hand:

> The complete absence of images [in the liturgy] is incompatible with faith in the Incarnation of God. God has acted in history and entered into our sensible world, so that it may become transparent to him. Images of beauty, in which the mystery of the invisible God becomes visible, are an essential part of Christian worship ... Images thus point to a presence; they are essentially connected with what happens in the liturgy. Now history becomes sacrament in Christ, who is the source of the sacraments. Therefore the icon of Christ is the centre of sacred iconography. The centre of the icon of Christ is the Paschal Mystery: Christ is presented as the crucified, the risen Lord, the One who will come again and who here and now hiddenly reigns over all ... The image of Christ and the images of the saints are not photographs. Their whole point is to lead us beyond what can be apprehended at the merely material level ... The sacredness of the image consists precisely in the fact that it comes from an interior vision and thus leads us to such an interior vision ... The image is at the service of the liturgy.[23]

Concerning art and beauty, in the context of *Sacramentum Caritatis* and the pope's theology, Aidan Nichols comments that 'Pope Benedict is to be lauded for the rapid way in which, on assuming the office of the bishop of Rome, he

23.   *TSL*, 131–33.

sought to put into effect his high view of the place of holy images in Christian catechesis and mystagogy.'[24] Pope Benedict not only referred to the relationship between art and 'mystagogy' in *Sacramentum Caritatis* (no. 41) but also discussed 'mystagogical catechesis' in relation to *participatio actuosa* (no. 64). 'Mystagogy' is 'the interpretation of mystery', and 'mystagogical catechesis', and is apparent in the writings of some of the most important Church Fathers, in relation to the sacraments of initiation. It may be defined — in the present context—as the explanation of the spiritual and theological significance of the various signs, symbols and gestures of the rites, and liturgical texts.[25] It also leads to the transformation of the Christian. The pope explains that

> The Church's great liturgical tradition teaches us that fruitful participation in the liturgy requires that one be personally conformed to the mystery being celebrated, offering one's life to God in unity with the sacrifice of Christ for the salvation of the whole world. For this reason, the Synod of Bishops asked that the faithful be helped to make their interior dispositions correspond to their gestures and words. Otherwise, however carefully planned and executed our liturgies may be, they would risk falling into a certain ritualism. Hence the need to provide an education in eucharistic faith capable of enabling the faithful to live personally what they celebrate.[26]

---

24. Nichols, *Redeeming Beauty*, 100–1 (my emphasis). In his book, Nichols (89–101) discusses two essays of Joseph Ratzinger, which compare favourably with *Sacramentum Caritatis*, and shows the influence of Hans Urs von Balthasar upon Ratzinger's theology of beauty. See, 'Wounded by the Arrow of Beauty: The Cross and the New "Aesthetics of Faith"' and 'The Face of Christ in Sacred Scripture', in Ratzinger, *On the Way to Jesus Christ*, 13–41. For another recent study on art and Pope Benedict XVI, see Lang, 'The Crisis of Sacred Art and the Sources for its Renewal in the Thought of Pope Benedict XVI', 98–115.

25. Fink, 'Mystagogy'.

26. Pope Benedict XVI, *Sacramentum Caritatis*, no. 64.

This mystagogy should always respect three elements: a) it interprets the rites in the light of the events of our salvation, in accordance with the Church's living tradition; b) a mystagogical catechesis must also be concerned with presenting the meaning of the signs contained in the rites: 'This is particularly important in a highly technological age like our own, which risks losing the ability to appreciate signs and symbols. More than simply conveying information, a mystagogical catechesis should be capable of making the faithful more sensitive to the language of signs and gestures which, together with the word, make up the rite'; and, c) mystagogical catechesis must be concerned with bringing out the significance of the rites for the Christian life in all its dimensions—work and responsibility, thoughts and emotions, activity and repose.[27] Previously, in *The Spirit of the Liturgy*—where considerable attention was given to *participatio actuosa* in its internal[28] and external forms—Joseph Ratzinger referred to the need of a 'true liturgical education' of the laity, leading to their transformation in God:

> True liturgical education cannot consist in learning and experimenting with external activities. Instead one must be led toward the essential *actio* that makes the liturgy what it is, toward the transforming power of God, who wants, through what happens in the liturgy, to transform us and the world. In this respect, liturgical education today, of both priests and laity, is deficient to a deplorable extent. Much remains to be done here.[29]

This *actio*, as we have seen, is the eucharistic prayer, the *oratio* of the Fathers, the essence, and fundamental form and centre of the liturgy. Cardinal Ratzinger also advocated the option of its silent recital—which is still not permitted in the *Missale Romanum* (2002)—but on the pretext that the

---

27.   *Ibid.*
28.   *TSL*, 171–220; see pp. 31–32 above.
29.   *TSL*, 175.

faithful know the contents of this central prayer of the Mass.[30]

In *Sacramentum Caritatis*, Pope Benedict also gives a general definition of *participatio actuosa*, which is none other than the definition which features in the liturgical constitution *Sacrosanctum Concilium* of the Second Vatican Council. It should be noted here that the errors surrounding the notion of 'participation', which emphasize it almost as a purely external thing, including 'creativity' and the notion of what one 'does (externally)' in the liturgy, have not gone unnoticed here. The important 'interior' aspect, emphasized in *Sacramentum Caritatis*, is an important corrective, though it does not ignore those external things which can foster true participation, such as beauty and art:

> The Second Vatican Council rightly emphasized the active, full and fruitful participation of the entire People of God in the eucharistic celebration. Certainly, the renewal carried out in these past decades has made considerable progress towards fulfilling the wishes of the Council Fathers. Yet we must not overlook the fact that some misunderstanding has occasionally arisen concerning the precise meaning of this participation.[31] It should be made clear that the word 'participation' does not refer to mere external activity during the celebration. In fact, the active participation called for by the council must be understood in more substantial terms, on the basis of a greater awareness of the mystery being

30. *TSL*, 174–75, 214–16; p. 41 above.

31. *Sine dubio renovatio his annis effecta magnum fovit progressum in illam semitam, quam Patres conciliarii exoptaverant. At non est obliviscendum quaedam dubia aliquando orta esse circa ipsum huius participationis sensum.* Problems relating to what *participatio actuosa* is—in itself an honest admission that certain things have not gone well—are commented upon here. We saw earlier, for instance, the necessity of the 'hermeneutic of continuity' against rupture, and the pope's comments on the reception of Vatican II at the beginning of his pontificate. We should also bear in mind the other liturgical changes which Pope Benedict has brought about for the total picture of the renewal, and of what needs to be corrected.

celebrated and its relationship to daily life. The conciliar Constitution *Sacrosanctum Concilium* encouraged the faithful to take part in the eucharistic liturgy not 'as strangers or silent spectators,' but as
participants 'in the sacred action, conscious of what
they are doing, actively and devoutly'. This exhortation has lost none of its force. The council went
on to say that the faithful 'should be instructed by
God's word, and nourished at the table of the Lord's
Body. They should give thanks to God. Offering the
immaculate Victim, not only through the hands of
the priest but also together with him, they should
learn to make an offering of themselves. Through
Christ, the Mediator, they should be drawn day
by day into ever more perfect union with God and
each other'.[32]

Furthermore, Pope Benedict noted that the beauty and the
harmony of the liturgy finds 'eloquent expression in the
order by which everyone is called to participate actively',
entailing that the distinct hierarchical roles in the liturgy
are to be acknowledged. Again critique is given over faulty
conceptions of *participatio actuosa*:

The active participation of the laity does not benefit
from the confusion arising from an inability to distinguish, within the Church's communion, the different functions proper to each one. There is a particular need for clarity with regard to the specific
functions of the priest. He alone, and no other, as
the tradition of the Church attests, presides over the
entire eucharistic celebration, from the initial greeting to the final blessing. In virtue of his reception of
Holy Orders, he represents Jesus Christ, the head of

---

32.   Pope Benedict XVI, *Sacramentum Caritatis*, no. 52 and n. 155–57:
      the footnotes there refer to The Second Vatican Council, *The Con-
      stitution on the Sacred Liturgy Sacrosanctum Concilium*, 4 December
      1963, nos 14–20, 30ff., and 48ff., and Congregation for Divine Worship
      and the Discipline of the Sacraments, *Instruction Redemptionis Sac-
      ramentum*, 25 March 2004, nos 36–42.

the Church, and, in a specific way, also the Church herself.[33]

Mention is then made of the ministry of the bishop and the deacon, and 'other ministries of liturgical service which can be carried out in a praiseworthy manner by religious and properly trained laity.'[34] Concerning the 'personal conditions' for the *participatio actuosa* of the faithful, the 'spirit of conversion' is mentioned. *Participatio actuosa* in the eucharistic liturgy 'can hardly be expected if one approaches it superficially, without an examination of his or her life'. The proper inner disposition can be foster by 'recollection and silence for at least a few moments before the beginning of the liturgy, by fasting and, when necessary, by sacramental confession'. An active participation in the life and missionary activity of the Church also brings about *participatio actuosa*. Full participation takes place with the reception of Holy Communion. However it is emphasized that—in order to avoid a mere perfunctory reception of Holy Communion—'care must be taken lest they conclude that the mere fact of their being present in church during the liturgy gives them a right or even an obligation to approach the table of the Eucharist. Even in cases where it is not possible to receive sacramental communion, participation at Mass remains necessary, important, meaningful and fruitful.' 'Spiritual communion' is recommended in such instances, which was praised by Pope John Paul II and 'recommended by saints who were masters of the spiritual life'.[35] *Participatio actuosa* in the Holy Eucharist, which Pope Benedict speaks about in a comprehensive fashion, is then widened to include a discussion of 'The eucharistic celebration and inculturation'; 'Participation by Christians who are not Catholic'; 'Participation through the commu-

---

33. Pope Benedict XVI, *Sacramentum Caritatis*, no. 53.

34. *Ibid.*

35. Pope Benedict XVI, *Sacramentum Caritatis*, no. 55, n. 170–71, mentioning St Thomas Aquinas (*ST*, III, q. LXXX, a.1, 2), St Teresa of Avila, and also Pope John Paul II, *Encyclical Letter Ecclesia de Eucharistia*, 17 April 2003.

nications media'; 'Active participation by the sick'; 'Care for prisoners'; and 'Migrants and participation in the Eucharist'.[36]

It is worthwhile pausing here to see how close this is to Joseph Ratzinger's own theology of *participatio actuosa* and his criticisms of misunderstandings. This is especially evident in his response to Pierre-Marie Gy, where he commented on false and superficial interpretation of the fundamental notion of *participatio actuosa*. *Participatio actuosa* cannot consist in assigning exterior activities in the liturgy to all the faithful gathered for the eucharistic celebration: it is something greater requiring a proper liturgical formation and knowledge of the liturgical texts, 'without which the purely exterior activities remain empty and meaningless'.[37] Participation, which makes possible a close union of the whole being, of thought and action, must also be expressed corporally, and that 'succeeding paragraphs of the chapter [which discusses *participatio actuosa* in *The Spirit of the Liturgy*] give a whole series of indications along these lines that are developed on the basis of the great liturgical traditions of East and West and are carried on up to the present.'[38] The 'corporal expression' of participation in the liturgy is also emphasized in *Sacramentum Caritatis*. (External) reverence for the eucharist, and 'an increased sense of the mystery of God present among us', is actually an indication—and a consequence—of the effectiveness of eucharistic catechesis:

> This can be expressed in concrete outward signs of reverence for the Eucharist which the process of mystagogy should inculcate in the faithful. I am thinking in general of the importance of gestures and posture, such as kneeling during the central moments of the eucharistic prayer. Amid the legitimate diversity of signs used in the context of differ-

---

36.   *Ibid.*, nos 54, 56–60.

37.   Ratzinger, '*The Spirit of the Liturgy* or Fidelity to the Council', 98; Ratzinger, *TSL*, 175, 215.

38.   Ratzinger, '*The Spirit of the Liturgy* or Fidelity to the Council', 98.

ent cultures, everyone should be able to experience and express the awareness that at each celebration we stand before the infinite majesty of God, who comes to us in the lowliness of the sacramental signs.[39]

This is comparable to what Joseph Ratzinger said in *The Spirit of the Liturgy* in regards to 'training the body' in the direction of the future, risen life with Christ:

> This training is an essential part of everyday life, but it has to find its inner support in the liturgy, in the liturgy's 'orientation' toward the risen Christ … it is a way of learning to accept the other in his otherness, a training for love, a training to help us accept the Wholly Other, God, to be shaped and used by him. The body has a place within the divine worship of the Word made flesh, and it is expressed liturgically in a certain discipline of the body, in gestures that have developed out of the liturgy's inner demands and that make the essence of the liturgy, as it were, bodily visible. These gestures may vary in their details from culture to culture, but in their essential forms they are part of that culture of faith which has grown out of Christian cult. They form, therefore, a common language that crosses the borders of the different cultures.[40]

We should emphasize here that the Eucharist is, of course, the *Mysterium Fidei*, and the liturgy, in itself, can teach us in more than one way. The 'mystery' of the Eucharist, indeed the 'mystery' of the liturgy, has not been forgotten in this document. The titles of the three main sections of *Sacramentum Caritatis* are, the *Mysterium Credendum*, *Mysterium Celebrandum*, and *Mysterium Vivendum*. The opening sentences of the first part of *Sacramentum Caritatis* are equally noteworthy:

> 'The mystery of faith!' [*Mysterium Fidei*] With these words, spoken immediately after the words of con-

---

39.   Pope Benedict XVI, *Sacramentum Caritatis*, no. 65.
40.   *TSL*, 176–77.

secration, the priest proclaims the mystery being
celebrated and expresses his wonder before the substantial change [*substantiali ... conversione*] of bread
and wine into the body and blood of the Lord Jesus,
a reality which surpasses all human understanding.
The Eucharist is a 'mystery of faith' par excellence:
'the sum and summary of our faith.'[41]

The frequent absence of the awareness of the concept of
'mystery' in celebrations of the modern liturgy, is something which people rightfully complain about, and is a
matter which Pope Benedict clearly wants to emphasize.

Returning back to gestures, *Sacramentum Caritatis*
includes an appreciation of the anthropological dimensions
of the liturgy, something emphasized by the pope in his
theological writings: 'By its very nature the liturgy operates on different levels of communication which enable it
to engage the whole human person. The simplicity of its
gestures and the sobriety of its orderly sequence of signs
communicate and inspire more than any contrived and
inappropriate additions.'[42] We can enter into the mystery
of the liturgy by celebrating it well. In fact Pope Benedict—
citing the *Propositiones* from the Synod—indicates that, 'the
best catechesis on the Eucharist is the Eucharist itself, well
celebrated'.[43] This refers to the close connection between
participatio actuosa and the *ars celebrandi*, which Pope Benedict proposes as another key liturgical concept, the 'proper
celebration of the rite itself':

The *ars celebrandi* is the best way to ensure their
[that is, the People of God's] *actuosa participatio*.
The *ars celebrandi* is the fruit of faithful adherence
to the liturgical norms in all their richness; indeed,
for two thousand years this way of celebrating has
sustained the faith life of all believers, called to take

---

41.   Pope Benedict XVI, *Sacramentum Caritatis*, no. 6, citing *CCC*, no.
      1327.

42.   Pope Benedict XVI, *Sacramentum Caritatis*, no. 40: cf. *TSL*, 58.

43.   *Ibid.*, no. 64.

part in the celebration as the People of God, a royal priesthood, a holy nation.[44]

The *ars celebrandi* necessarily entails a specific responsibility on the part of those who have received the sacrament of Holy Orders, and they must regard the liturgy as their first duty, above all the diocesan bishop, who is 'the moderator, promoter, and guardian' of the liturgical life of his diocese. He has to maintain unity and harmony in his area of responsibility. He is to see that the clergy and laity 'grasp ever more deeply the genuine meaning of the rites and liturgical texts, and thereby be led to an active and fruitful celebration of the Eucharist'. Pope Benedict asks that 'the liturgies which the Bishop celebrates in his cathedral are carried out with complete respect for the *ars celebrandi*, so that they can be considered an example for the entire diocese'. In other words, the bishop plays a central role in promoting the liturgy of his diocese, and also by his personal celebration of the liturgy.[45]

The *ars celebrandi* also leads to valuing the liturgical norms, fostering 'a sense of the sacred and the use of outward signs which help to cultivate this sense, such as, for example, the harmony of the rite, the liturgical vestments, the furnishings and the sacred space', and when priests and 'liturgical leaders' (*pastoralis liturgicae curatores*) make known current liturgical norms.[46] 'A sense of the sacred', says Pope Benedict XVI, is one the most important elements of the liturgy which needs to be reclaimed, and it must begin with the clergy and the actual celebration of the liturgy. The implementation of official texts has clearly been a problem. Liturgical norms in many churches are either 'unknown' or ignored, and experimentation still takes place. Joseph Ratzinger's views on this subject remain valid, when he speaks of

---

44. Pope Benedict XVI, *Sacramentum Caritatis*, no. 38.
45. *Ibid.*, no. 39.
46. Pope Benedict XVI, *Sacramentum Caritatis*, no. 40.

> ... the attitude of a considerable portion of the lit-
> urgists who continually bombard us, on the con-
> trary, with newly proposed texts and forms and
> who have thereby contributed not a little, in divers
> places, to a certain anarchy in the liturgical domain
> [which] constitutes the principal obstacle to a gen-
> eral and positive reception of the missal of Paul VI.
> The liturgy is often so different from one parish to
> another, that the common missal is scarcely visible
> anymore.[47]

Sacramentum Caritatis contains an honest admission concerning ignorance about what the official texts themselves
contain: 'Perhaps we take it for granted that our ecclesial
communities already know and appreciate these resources,
but this is not always the case [*sed saepe non ita accidit*].
These texts contain riches which have preserved and
expressed the faith and experience of the People of God
over its two-thousand-year history.'[48] Here Pope Benedict is
also trying to demonstrate that there is a 'bridge' between
the missal of 1970—in its 2002 revised version—and the
liturgical tradition, pointing out that the new missal contains ancient treasures which should not be ignored. This is
not to say that—as I pointed out earlier—that there are no
problems with the implementation of the liturgical wishes
of the Second Vatican Council, or the postconciliar missal
and liturgy. Here we see an attempt, as at the beginning of
Sacramentum Caritatis, and elsewhere—in the *IGMR* 2002
for example—at 'harmonization' and 'reconciliation' of
the perceived—or otherwise—division between the liturgical tradition and the new missal. This is the application
or 'implementation' of the 'hermeneutic of continuity' (or
'reform') against the 'hermeneutic of rupture'. Once more
Pope Benedict stresses the importance of external elements
in the *ars celebrandi*: 'equally important for a correct *ars celebrandi* is an attentiveness to the various kinds of language

---

47. Ratzinger, '*The Spirit of the Liturgy* or Fidelity to the Council',
     98–99.

48. Pope Benedict XVI, *Sacramentum Caritatis*, no. 40.

that the liturgy employs: words and music, gestures and silence, movement, the liturgical colours of the vestments.'[49]

In another section of *Sacramentum Caritatis*, Pope Benedict examines 'the structure of the eucharistic celebration'. Continuity with the liturgical past is further emphasized in relation to the structure of the Eucharist, 'which require[s] special attention at the present time, if we are to remain faithful to the underlying intention of the liturgical renewal called for by the Second Vatican Council, in continuity with the great ecclesial tradition (*cunctam praeclaram magnamque Ecclesiae producens traditionem*).'[50] Pope Benedict first emphasizes the inherent unity of the rite of Mass. Quoting the Second Vatican Council's Constitution on the Liturgy and *IGMR* (2002), the pope indicates that the liturgy of the word and the eucharistic liturgy, with the rites of introduction and conclusion, 'are so closely interconnected that they form but one single act of worship.'[51] Their bond is an intrinsic bond: 'From listening to the Word of God, faith is born or strengthened (cf. Rom 10:17); in the Eucharist the Word made flesh gives himself to us as our spiritual food.' The reading and proclamation of the Word of God 'leads to the Eucharist as to its own connatural end.'[52] This is to counter the impression that is sometimes given that the readings at Mass almost constitute a separate service. Although we may distinguish between the various parts of the Mass, for example, 'the liturgy of the Word' (previously referred to as the 'Mass of the Catechumens') and the 'liturgy of the Eucharist' ('the Mass of the Faithful') the Mass is one divine service.

Concerning the 'liturgy of the Word' in itself, the pope emphasizes the care and preparation that is necessary for its proclamation, and that we should never forget that

---

49. *Ibid.*: we have already mentioned art and music, which is also connected to the concept of the *ars celebrandi*.

50. Pope Benedict XVI, *Sacramentum Caritatis*, no. 43.

51. *IGMR*, no. 28; The Second Vatican Council, *The Constitution on the Sacred Liturgy Sacrosanctum Concilium*, 4 December 1963, no. 56.

52. Pope Benedict XVI, *Sacramentum Caritatis*, no. 44.

'when the sacred scriptures are read in the Church, God himself speaks to his people, and Christ, present in his own word, proclaims the Gospel'.[53] If the word is to be properly understood, it to be listened to—and accepted—'in a spirit of communion with the Church'. Christ does not speak in the past, 'but in the present, even as he is present in the liturgical action.' Studying the scriptures is also recommended, enabling us to 'better... appreciate, celebrate and live the Eucharist', and the faithful should be led to appreciate the riches of sacred scripture, which includes *lectio divina*, and the divine office.[54] Pope Benedict then discusses the homily. He is quite blunt about this: 'Given the importance of the Word of God, the quality of homilies needs to be improved.' It is part of the liturgical action, and is meant 'to foster a deeper understanding of the Word of God, so that it can bear fruit in the lives of the faithful.' Although the homily should be preached in such as way that it is closely related to 'the proclamation of the Word of God to the sacramental celebration and the life of the community', to provide the vital nourishment the Church needs from God's word, it is interesting to note that the homily can be based on other sources of spiritual nourishment too. The impression is frequently given today that the homily must be based strictly upon the readings of the Mass. This is simply not the case. The preaching of the doctrinal content of the faith is something which is sorely lacking today. As Pope Benedict himself explains,

> The catechetical and paraenetic aim of the homily should not be forgotten. During the course of the liturgical year it is appropriate to offer the faithful, prudently and on the basis of the three-year lectionary, 'thematic' homilies treating the great themes of the Christian faith, on the basis of what has been authoritatively proposed by the Magisterium in the four 'pillars' of the *Catechism of the Catholic Church* and the recent *Compendium*, namely: the profession

---

53.   Citing *IGMR*, no. 29.
54.   Pope Benedict XVI, *Sacramentum Caritatis*, no. 45.

of faith, the celebration of the Christian mystery, life
in Christ and Christian prayer.[55]

The pope's comments on the 'presentation of the gifts'
(*donorum oblationem*)—mainly referred in *IGMR* (2002) as
praeparatio donorum (the 'preparation of the gifts')—are also
significant, and clearly offer an important corrective in the
light of liturgical tradition, to a certain extent. This section
of the Mass is often played-down, and is perceived as a sort
of 'corridor', in order not to give the impression that it is a
'mini' eucharistic prayer, which partly anticipates Christ's
sacrifice (though this has a long history in liturgical tradition), which is apparent in the eucharistic prayer itself after
the consecration. However is not a simple matter of just
putting bread and wine on the altar. The 'presentation of
the gifts' is actually related to the eucharistic prayer, in that
the bread and wine are brought to God, and are ultimately
transubstantiated into the Body and Blood of Christ, and
offered in sacrifice to God the Father in the eucharistic
prayer. As Pope Benedict XVI himself explains, the 'presentation of the gifts',

> … is not to be viewed simply as a kind of 'interval'
> between the liturgy of the word and the liturgy of
> the Eucharist. To do so would tend to weaken, at
> the least, the sense of a single rite made up of two
> interrelated parts. This humble and simple gesture
> is actually very significant: in the bread and wine
> that we bring to the altar, all creation is taken up
> by Christ the redeemer to be transformed and pre-
> sented to the Father. In this way we also bring to the
> altar all the pain and suffering of the world, in the
> certainty that everything has value in God's eyes.
> The authentic meaning of this gesture can be clearly
> expressed without the need for undue emphasis
> or complexity. It enables us to appreciate how God
> invites man to participate in bringing to fulfilment
> his handiwork, and in so doing, gives human labour
> its authentic meaning, since, through the celebra-

---

55.   *Ibid.*, no. 46.

tion of the Eucharist, it is united to the redemptive sacrifice of Christ.[56]

Pope Benedict then comments on the eucharistic prayer itself, 'the centre and summit of the entire celebration'.[57] Again, we see the 'hermeneutic of continuity' at work:

> Its importance deserves to be adequately empha-sized. The different eucharistic prayers contained in the missal have been handed down to us by the Church's living tradition (*a viva Ecclesiae Traditione*) and are noteworthy for their inexhaustible theologi-cal and spiritual richness. The faithful need to be enabled to appreciate that richness.[58]

The importance and value of the 'sign of peace' (*ritus pacis*) is also given due emphasis by Pope Benedict, as well as the necessity to avoid an 'exaggerated' interpretation of this rite, which is clearly evident:

> We can … understand the emotion so often felt dur-ing the sign of peace at a liturgical celebration. Even so, during the Synod of Bishops there was discus-sion about the appropriateness of greater restraint in this gesture, which can be exaggerated and cause a certain distraction in the assembly just before the reception of Communion. It should be kept in mind that nothing is lost when the sign of peace is marked by a sobriety which preserves the proper spirit of the celebration, as, for example, when it is restricted to one's immediate neighbours.[59]

With this in mind, Pope Benedict has even suggested that the 'competent curial offices' study the possibility of mov-ing the sign of peace—'taking into account ancient and

---

56. Pope Benedict XVI, *Sacramentum Caritatis*, no. 47: this correlates with Cardinal Ratzinger's explanation of the silence in the 'prepa-ration of the gifts', and perhaps gives the gesture a significance which he thought was not entirely clear in the newer *Missale Romanum*. See *TSL*, 210–11, 213 and p. 65, n. 53 above.

57. *IGMR*, no. 78.

58. Pope Benedict XVI, *Sacramentum Caritatis*, no. 48.

59. *Ibid.*, no. 49.

venerable customs and the wishes expressed by the Synod Fathers' — to another place, such as before the presentation of the gifts. Time will tell if this becomes a reality, but it is interesting to see here, that the new *Ordo Missae* is not necessarily set in 'tablets of stone'. It, too, ought to be subject to organic development and change, if necessary.[60] Pope Benedict also suggested that new, 'duly approved' texts be provided for the prayer over the people and the final blessing, in order to emphasis that the *Ite, missa est* — the dismissal at the very end of Mass — refers to the 'sending out' of the People of God and missionary nature of the Church. This, in fact, has now been done, in the 2008 corrected version of the *Missale Romanum* (2002).[61]

Another paragraph in this section of *Sacramentum Caritatis* refers to the distribution and reception of Holy Communion. Sometimes 'communion' is merely thought of in terms of 'community'. However it is also –as the pope has emphasized in his theological writings—a very personal act, a personal encounter with the Lord Jesus. Pope Benedict asks everyone, 'especially ordained ministers and those who, after adequate preparation and in cases of genuine need, are authorized to exercise the ministry of distributing the Eucharist, to make every effort to ensure that this simple act preserves its importance as a personal encounter with the Lord Jesus in the sacrament.' Reverence for the Blessed Sacrament, and the faith and love which all Catholics ought to have for Our Lord under the eucharistic species, is emphatically underlined: 'All Christian communities are to observe the current norms faithfully, seeing in them an expression of the faith and love with which we all must regard this sublime sacrament.' Thanksgiving after Holy Communion is not to be neglected, even a period of silence 'besides the singing of an appropriate hymn', and in particular cases—such as when non-Catholics are

---

60. Pope Benedict XVI, *Sacramentum Caritatis*, no. 49, n. 150. For further discussion of this, see Dobszay, *The Restoration and Organic Development of the Roman Rite*, 226–27.

61. Pope Benedict XVI, *Sacramentum Caritatis*, no. 51.

present at Mass—it is emphasized that 'there is a need to find a brief and clear way to remind those present of the meaning of sacramental communion and the conditions required for its reception.'[62]

Reception of the Eucharist includes adoration. The relationship between the celebration of the Eucharist and adoration is therefore also underlined in *Sacramentum Caritatis*. This was very much focused against the error, which spread in the Church not long after the council, that the Holy Eucharist 'was not given to be looked at, but to be eaten'. This did much damage in Europe, especially in formerly Catholic countries. Receiving the Holy Eucharist 'means adoring him whom we receive. Only in this way do we become one with him, and are given, as it were, a foretaste of the beauty of the heavenly liturgy'. Adoration of the Holy Eucharist also occurs outside of Mass, and this, and other forms of eucharistic devotion are encouraged, including processions of the Blessed Sacrament, especially on *Corpus Christi*, and the Forty Hours devotion. Attention was also given to the position of the tabernacle in churches, which 'contributes to the recognition of Christ's Real Presence in the Blessed Sacrament'. Here, once more, Pope Benedict 'repeats himself', as if to constantly underline fundamental truths concerning the Holy Eucharist. We find similar thoughts expressed by the pope in *The Spirit of the Liturgy*.[63]

Another important aspect of Pope Benedict's liturgical theology also features in *Sacramentum Caritatis*, which sums up many of the aspects which we have already examined: 'spiritual worship'—*logiké latreía*. This theme may be seen in *The Spirit of the Liturgy*, and was also discussed during the synod. This concept, from St Paul's Letter to the Romans (12:1), again shows the anthropological dimension of the Eucharist—which is not to be confused with

---

62. *Ibid.*, no. 50: nos 61 and 63 concern issues relating to 'large-scale concelebrations' and 'Eucharistic celebrations in small groups'.

63. Pope Benedict XVI, *Sacramentum Caritatis*, nos 65–69; *TSL*, 85–91; and pp. 18–19 above.

'anthropocentrism' — and touches upon the Holy Eucharist and its relation to the Christian life: 'I appeal to you therefore, my brothers, by the mercies of God, to present your bodies as a living sacrifice, holy and acceptable to God, which is your spiritual worship'. Our Lord promised that those who ate the Eucharistic Bread would have eternal life (Jn 6:51). 'Eternal life' begins even now — here again is the eschatological dimension of the Eucharist — due to the transformation effected in us by the gift of the Eucharist. 'He who eats me will live because of me' (Jn 6:57): these words help us realize that 'believing' and 'celebrating' the mystery of the Eucharist has an innate power, bringing about new life in us and the form of our Christian existence. The pope explains that

> By receiving the body and blood of Jesus Christ we become sharers in the divine life in an ever more adult and conscious way. Here too, we can apply Saint Augustine's words, in his *Confessions*, about the eternal *Logos* as the food of our souls ... 'I am the food of grown men; grow and you shall feed upon me; nor shall you change me, like the food of your flesh, into yourself, but you shall be changed into me' [*Confessions* VII, 10, 16]. It is not the eucharistic food that is changed into us, but rather we who are mysteriously transformed by it. Christ nourishes us by uniting us to himself; 'he draws us into himself.' Here the eucharistic celebration appears in all its power as the source and summit of the Church's life, since it expresses at once both the origin and the fulfilment of the new and definitive worship of God, the *logiké latreia*. Saint Paul's exhortation to the Romans in this regard is a concise description of how the Eucharist makes our whole life a spiritual worship pleasing to God [and indicates that] the new worship appears as a total self-offering made in communion with the whole Church. The Apostle's insistence on the offering of our bodies emphasizes the concrete human reality of a worship which is anything but disincarnate ... the Eucharist, as the

sacrifice of Christ, is also the sacrifice of the Church, and thus of all the faithful.[64]

This is much more in *Sacramentum Caritatis* that could be discussed here, including the 'Eucharist and moral transformation'—which is connected with spiritual worship—and the importance which Pope Benedict attaches to the observance of Sunday, or *iuxta dominicam viventes*, another prominent theme in his writings and his Magisterium.[65] However we will limit ourselves by looking at two final themes. Eschatology, a prominent theme in the theology of Cardinal Ratzinger, is, as we have seen, no less a prominent theme in *Sacramentum Caritatis*. Joseph Ratzinger was an expert in eschatology and taught the subject for about twenty years.[66] In the first part of *Sacramentum Caritatis*, Pope Benedict discussed eschatology in relation to the Eucharist. The sacraments are part of the Church's pilgrimage through history, towards the full manifestation of the victory of the risen Christ. The liturgy, in particular, and the sacraments, give us 'a real foretaste' of the eschatological fulfilment for which every human being and all creation are destined (cf. Rom 8:19ff.):

> Man is created for that true and eternal happiness which only God's love can give. But our wounded freedom would go astray were it not already able

---

64. Pope Benedict XVI, *Sacramentum Caritatis*, nos 63, 94; Ratzinger, *God is Near Us*, 77–78; TSL, 45–47, 56–58, 175: 'Becoming contemporary with the Pasch of Christ in the liturgy of the Church is... in fact an anthropological reality... It is meant to be indeed a *logikē latreia*, the 'logicizing' of my existence, my contemporaneity with the self-giving of Christ ... The liturgy [has] a bearing on everyday life, on me in my personal existence ... that ... our bodily existence on earth becomes "a living sacrifice" united to the sacrifice of Christ (cf. Rom 12: 1)' (op cit.); see pp. 9–10 above. On the relationship between the Eucharist/liturgy and the cosmos, see Pope Benedict XVI, *Sacramentum Caritatis*, no. 92; TSL, 28–34.

65. Pope Benedict XVI, *Sacramentum Caritatis*, nos 72–76, 82; TSL, 92–111; Ratzinger, *A New Song for the Lord*, 59–77; Pope Benedict XVI, *Heart of the Christian Life*, 11–17, 99–104.

66. See Ratzinger, *Eschatology: Death and Eternal Life*.

> to experience something of that future fulfilment.
> Moreover, to move forward in the right direction,
> we all need to be guided towards our final goal.
> That goal is Christ himself, the Lord who conquered
> sin and death, and who makes himself present to
> us in a special way in the eucharistic celebration ...
> The eucharistic banquet, by disclosing its powerful
> eschatological dimension, comes to the aid of our
> freedom as we continue our journey.[67]

The coming of Jesus responded to an expectation present
in the people of Israel, and in the whole of humanity and
creation, inaugurating the eschatological age and gathering 'the community of the covenant'. He called twelve
apostles—which is a parallel to the twelve tribes of Israel—
and commanded them to celebrate the memorial before his
redemptive passion (*ante suam Passionem redemptricem*).
In this Jesus wished to transfer to his community—the
Church—'the task of being, within history, the sign and
instrument of the eschatological gathering that had its origin in him'. As a consequence, every eucharistic celebration
'sacramentally accomplishes the eschatological gathering
of the People of God. For us, the eucharistic banquet is a
real foretaste of the final banquet foretold by the prophets
(cf. Is 25:6–9) and described in the New Testament as "the
marriage-feast of the Lamb" (Apoc 19:7–9), to be celebrated
in the joy of the communion of saints.'[68] In this discussion
of eschatology and the Eucharist, the pope emphasizes the
importance of praying for the dead, because, by celebrating
the memorial of our salvation, our hope is strengthened in
the resurrection of the body, and the possibility of meeting
each other again, face to face, and marked with the sign of
faith:

> In this context, I wish, together with the Synod
> Fathers, to remind all the faithful of the importance
> of prayers for the dead, especially the offering of

---

67.   Pope Benedict XVI, *Sacramentum Caritatis*, no. 30.
68.   *Ibid.*, no. 31.

Mass for them, so that, once purified, they can come
to the beatific vision of God.[69]

Offering masses for the dead is forgotten in some places,
and the emphasis which the pope places on this, not only
corrects this particular error, but also the errors in the
eschatology of a good number of theologians who seek
to diminish the reality of the bodily resurrection and the
separation from the body—as well as the existence of—the
immortal soul after death, which Joseph Ratzinger discussed elsewhere in greater detail.[70]

Lastly, Pope Benedict refers in *Sacramentum Caritatis* to
Pope John Paul II's appellation of the Blessed Virgin Mary
as 'Woman of the Eucharist', and devoted a section of the
document to 'the eucharist and the Virgin Mary'.[71] Here I
shall confine myself to one particular, but profound point
which the pope makes in relation to Mary and the liturgy.
The liturgy is reflected in her and serves as a model for all
celebrations of the liturgy, again emphasising the theological concept of beauty: 'She [Mary] is the *tota pulchra*, the
all-beautiful, for in her the radiance of God's glory shines
forth. The beauty of the heavenly liturgy, which must be
reflected in our own assemblies, is faithfully mirrored in
her.' [72]

Other references to the liturgy in Pope Benedict XVI's Magisterium

Although Pope Benedict's *Sacramentum Caritatis* has a very
full—though not exhaustive—and systematic discussion
of the liturgy, the pope has taken other occasions in his

---

69. Pope Benedict XVI, *Sacramentum Caritatis*, no. 32: *Hoc in prospectu,
     simul cum Patribus synodalibus, velimus memorare omnibus fidelibus
     pondus orationum suffragii pro defunctis, praesertim celebrationis sanc-
     tarum Missarum pro iis, ut purificati ad beatificam Dei contemplationem
     pervenire possint.*

70. Ratzinger, *Eschatology: Death and Eternal Life, passim*, esp. 104–214.

71. Pope Benedict XVI, *Sacramentum Caritatis*, nos 33, 97–99.

72. *Ibid.*, no. 96.

Magisterium—such as his homilies and, particularly his General Audiences—to highlight its importance, or particular aspects of it. Here we shall indicate a few of these interventions,[73] noting that themes which he discussed in *Sacramentum Caritatis*—and in his theological writings—re-appear. In fact one is led to say that his discussion of liturgy has, at times, a 'mystagogical' character. Pope Benedict's interventions concerning the liturgy give a further indication of the centrality of the liturgy in his pontificate.

Most of Pope Benedict's regular General Audiences have been devoted to a particular theme, and here I shall examine some of his references to the liturgy in his discussions centring around the Church Fathers, St Paul and several saints. We have already seen from our examination of *The Spirit of the Liturgy* that the Church Fathers have had a great influence upon the liturgical theology of Pope Benedict. In his audience on 6 June 2007,[74] Pope Benedict spoke about St Cyprian, a third-century African bishop and martyr. St Cyprian wrote numerous treatises and letters, which were always connected to pastoral ministry, the 'Church' being his favourite subject. Pope Benedict drew attention to St Cyprian's teaching on prayer, centred on *The Treatise on the Lord's Prayer*, the Our Father. In the Our Father the Christian is presented with the proper way to pray. This prayer is presented in the plural in order that the person who prays it, might not pray for himself alone. Our prayer, according to Cyprian, 'is public and common; and when we pray, we pray not for one, but for the whole people, because we, the whole people, are one'.[75] The ecclesiological dimension to this is obvious, as it was to Pope Benedict, who also taught ecclesiology with eschatology. However

---

73. I discuss Pope Benedict's motu proprio *Summorum Pontificum* in the next chapter as this, with *Sacramentum Caritatis*, have particular importance in Pope Benedict's vision of and approach to the liturgy.

74. Pope Benedict XVI, 'General Audience', 6 June 2007, in Pope Benedict XVI, *The Fathers*, 51–56.

75. *Ibid.*, 54, citing St Cyprian, *De Dom. Orat.*, 8.

Pope Benedict makes an astute liturgical observation here, considering that the Our Father has a central place in the Catholic liturgy: 'Thus, personal and *liturgical prayer seem to be strongly bound*. Their unity stems for the fact that they respond to the same Word of God.' Indeed Cyprian also spoke about prayer during the liturgy:

> Moreover, when we meet together with the brethren in one place, and celebrate the divine sacrifices with God's priest, we ought to be mindful of modesty and discipline—not to throw abroad our prayers indiscriminately, with unsubdued voices, not to cast to God with tumultuous wordiness a petition that ought to be commended to God by modesty; for God is the hearer, not of the voice, but of the heart.[76]

Pope Benedict believes that 'Today, too, these words [of Cyprian] still apply and help us to celebrate the Holy Liturgy well', which undoubtedly highlights the importance of the central, inner dimension of *participatio actuosa*, and that personal prayer is not excluded from the liturgy.[77]

Pope Benedict's General Audience on 28 November 2007 dealt with St Ephrem, the Syrian, born in Nisibis in 306. Ephrem—a deacon—had a particular gift for combining poetry with theology—or rather producing theology in poetical form—including hymns, and employed a variety of paradoxes and symbols. Pope Benedict drew attention to the liturgical aspects of Ephrem's hymns, emphasising their catechetical element:

> Ephrem gives his poetry and liturgical hymns a didactic and catechetical genre: they are theological hymns yet at the same time suitable for recitation or liturgical song. On the occasion of liturgical feasts, Ephrem made use of these hymns to spread Church doctrine. Time has proven them to be an extremely

---

76.   Pope Benedict XVI, 'General Audience', 6 June 2007, in Pope Benedict XVI, *The Fathers*, 55, citing St Cyprian, *De Dom. Orat.*, 3–4.

77.   Pope Benedict XVI, 'General Audience', 6 June 2007, in Pope Benedict XVI, *The Fathers*, 55.

effective catechetical instrument for the Christian community.[78]

In one of Ephrem's hymns, Pope Benedict notes that Ephrem 'effectively links Adam (in Paradise) to Christ (in the Eucharist)':[79]

> It was by closing with the sword of the cherub that the path to the tree of life was closed. But for the peoples, the Lord of this tree gave himself as food in his (eucharistic) oblation. The trees of the Garden of Eden were given as food to the first Adam. For us, the Gardener in person made himself food for our souls. Indeed, we had all left Paradise together with Adam, who left it behind him. Now that the sword has been removed here below (on the Cross), replaced by the spear, we can return to him.[80]

Concerning another hymn of Ephrem, in relation to the Eucharist, Pope Benedict explains that

> To speak of the Eucharist, Ephrem used two images, embers or burning coal and the pearl. The burning coal theme was taken from the Prophet Isaiah [Is. 6:6]. It is the image of one of the seraphim who picks up a burning coal with tongs and simply touches the lips of the Prophet with it in order to purify them: the Christian, on the other hand, touches and consumes the Burning Coal which is Christ himself.[81]

The pope is indebted in a particular way to the theology of Pseudo-Dionysius the Areopagite, and discussed this in another General Audience (14 May 2008). Here we can see a reflection of the pope's theological writings:

---

78. Pope Benedict XVI, 'General Audience', 28 November 2007, in Pope Benedict XVI, *The Fathers*, 161.

79. *Ibid.*, 159.

80. Pope Benedict XVI, 'General Audience', 28 November 2007, in Pope Benedict XVI, *The Fathers*, 159–60, citing St Ephrem the Syrian, *Hymn* 49: 9–11.

81. Pope Benedict XVI, 'General Audience', 28 November 2007, in Pope Benedict XVI, *The Fathers*, 160, citing St Ephrem, Hymn *De Fide* 10: 8–10.

All creation speaks of God and is praise of God. Since the creature is praise of God, Pseudo-Diony-sius' theology became a liturgical theology: God is found above all in praising him, not only in reflec-tion; and the liturgy is not something made by us, something invented in order to have a religious experience for a certain period of time; it is singing with the choir of creatures and entering into cos-mic reality itself. And in this very way the liturgy, apparently only ecclesiastical, becomes expansive and great, it becomes our union with the language of all creatures. He says: God cannot be spoken of in an abstract way; speaking of God is always—he says using a Greek word—a *hymnein*, singing for God with the great hymn of the creatures which is reflected and made concrete in liturgical praise... Thus, a great and mysterious theology also becomes very concrete, both in the interpretation of the lit-urgy and in the discourse on Jesus Christ.[82]

More recently Pope Benedict has spoken about the exam-ple and the lives of the saints in his General Audiences. He has also highlighted the important role of the liturgy in their lives, particularly in his discourses concerning SS. Gertrude the Great and Matilda of Hackeborn, who were both mystics, sisters, as well as nuns, in the thirteenth cen-tury. Here we see echoes of *Sacramentum Caritatis* and the relationship between liturgy and life. Commenting on St Matilda's life, Pope Benedict indicates that

> This Saint had a striking capacity for living the vari-ous elements of the liturgy, even the simplest, and bringing it into the daily life of the convent. Some of her images, expressions and applications are at times distant from our sensibility today, but, if we were to consider monastic life and her task as mis-tress and choir mistress, we should grasp her rare ability as a teacher and educator who, starting from the liturgy, helped her sisters to live intensely every moment of monastic life. Matilda gave an empha-

---

82. Pope Benedict XVI, 'General Audience',14 May 2008.

sis in liturgical prayer to the canonical hours, to the celebrations of Holy Mass and, especially, to Holy Communion.[83]

Pope Benedict makes a particularly important point about the life of St Matilda in the context of participation in the liturgy, and the liturgy as 'a school of spirituality', something which for us, today, can, and should be, a reality:

> Dear friends, personal and liturgical prayer, especially the Liturgy of the Hours and Holy Mass are at the root of St Matilda of Hackeborn's spiritual experience. In letting herself be guided by sacred scripture and nourished by the Bread of the Eucharist, she followed a path of close union with the Lord, ever in full fidelity to the Church. This is also a strong invitation to us to intensify our friendship with the Lord, especially through daily prayer and attentive, faithful and active participation in Holy Mass. The Liturgy is a great school of spirituality.[84]

Concerning St Gertrude—who is well known for her *Revelations*—the pope notes that, from a certain moment,

> her life of intimate communion with the Lord was intensified, especially in the most important liturgical seasons Advent-Christmas, Lent-Easter, the feasts of Our Lady even when illness prevented her from going to the choir. *This was the same liturgical humus as that of Matilda,* her teacher; but Gertrude describes it with simpler, more linear images, symbols and terms that are more realistic and her references to the Bible, to the Fathers and to the Benedictine world are more direct.[85]

In his General Audiences, between 2 July 2008 and 4 February 2009, in the Year of St Paul, Pope Benedict devoted a series of catecheses on St Paul. One of the lengthiest of these focused again on a central theme of his liturgical theology,

---

83. Pope Benedict XVI, 'General Audience', 29 September 2010.

84. *Ibid.*

85. Pope Benedict XVI, 'General Audience', 6 October 2010 (my emphasis).

which has direct parallels with *The Spirit of the Liturgy* and *Sacramentum Caritatis*. This theme is 'spiritual worship' (*logiké latreía*) present in St Paul's Letter to the Romans (3: 25; 12: 1; 15:15ff.).[86] We have already examined this in some detail, so here I shall briefly refer to the pope's commentary on Rom 12, 1 to illustrate how similar this is with his other statements on 'spiritual worship': 'I appeal to you therefore, brethren, by the mercies of God, to present your bodies as a living sacrifice, holy and acceptable to God, which is your spiritual worship'. St Paul refers to the *life* of the Christian, though sacrifice normally requires the *death* of a victim. He describes, explains Pope Benedict, the sacrifice of a Christian's life—the honouring of God in one's life—in three adjectives: 'The first "living" expresses vitality. The second "holy" recalls the Pauline idea of holiness not linked to places or objects but to Christians themselves. The third "acceptable to God" recalls perhaps the recurrent biblical expression of sacrifice "a pleasing odour" (cf. Lv 1: 13, 17; 23: 18; 26: 31, and so on)'. This new way of living is 'spiritual worship'. The pope then discusses what the original Greek phrase actually means, thereby beginning to make a connection between daily life with the liturgy, with particular reference to the ancient Roman Canon or the first eucharistic prayer:

> Commentators on this text well know that the Greek expression (*ten logiken latreían*) is not easy to translate. The Latin Bible translates it as: *rationabile obsequium*. The actual word *rationabile* appears in the first eucharistic prayer of the Roman Canon: in it the faithful pray that God will accept this offering as *rationabile* ... In any case it is not a matter of less real worship or even worship that is only metaphorical but rather of a more concrete and realistic worship, a worship in which the human being him-

---

86. Pope Benedict XVI, 'General Audience', 7 January 2009, in Pope Benedict XVI, *Paul of Tarsus*, 127–36.

self, in his totality as a being endowed with reason, becomes adoration, glorification of the living God.[87]

In St Paul we see a further stage in the development of the notion of sacrifice since the Old Testament, a renewed sacrifice, where the whole man is offered to God instead of 'the flesh of bulls' (cf. Ps 49:12–14). However this should not be misunderstood in a new moralistic sense: 'In this way, worship with animals would be replaced by moralism: man himself would do everything on his own with his moral strength. And this was certainly not St Paul's intention.' In this 'reasonable worship', St Paul 'presumes that we are all "one in Christ Jesus" (Gal 3: 28), that we died in Baptism (cf. Rom 1) and that we now live with Christ, for Christ, in Christ'. 'In this union', explains the pope, 'and only in this way we are able to become in him and with him "a living sacrifice", to offer "true worship"'. The sacrificed animals of the past could not replace the human beings they were supposed to represent, the 'gift of self':

> In his gift of himself to the Father and to us, Jesus Christ is not a substitute but truly bears within him the human being, our sins and our desire; he really represents us, he takes us upon himself. In communion with Christ, realized in faith and in the sacraments, despite all our inadequacies we truly become a living sacrifice: "true worship" is achieved.[88]

This combination of elements forms the background of the Roman Canon, during which we pray that the offering become *rationabile* for spiritual worship to be made. The Church, conscious that Christ and his true sacrifice become present in the Mass, also prays that 'the community celebrating may truly be united with Christ and transformed; she prays that we may become what we cannot be with our own efforts: a "rational" offering that is acceptable to God', thus giving a correct interpretation of St Paul's words. Pope

---

87. Pope Benedict XVI, 'General Audience', 7 January 2009, in Pope Benedict XVI, *Paul of Tarsus*, 129–31.

88. *Ibid.*, 131–34.

Benedict cites St Augustine's[89] explanation for this from the tenth chapter of the *City of God*:

> This is the sacrifice of Christians: we, being many, are one body in Christ ... The whole redeemed city, that is to say, the congregation or community of the saints, is offered to God as our sacrifice through the great High Priest, who offered Himself.[90]

On a good number of occasions, Pope Benedict has spoken about liturgies and devotions to Our Lord in the Blessed Sacrament, including those outside of Mass, such as eucharistic adoration and processions. These are matters which—as we have seen—the pope has not only written about in the past: he has also defended these liturgies and devotions as true developments of the Church's liturgical tradition.[91] The solemnity of Corpus Christi is a feast where the pope—and his predecessors—have drawn particular attention to the worship of the Blessed Sacrament. From the examples which could be cited here, we refer, in particular, to Pope Benedict's homily in front of the Basilica of Saint John Lateran on 7 June 2007. In this homily the pope frequently referred to *Sacramentum Caritatis*, as well as the readings of the Mass. However he also quoted no less than three times from a particular liturgical text, and gave commentary upon it, namely the sequence of the Mass, the *Lauda Sion salvatorem*, which encapsulates the feast of Corpus Christi:

> We have just sung the sequence: '*Dogma datur christianis,/ quod in carnem transit panis,/ et vinum in sanguinem*—this [is] the truth each Christian learns,/ bread into his flesh he turns, to his precious blood the wine'. Today we reaffirm with great joy our faith in the Eucharist, the Mystery that constitutes the

---

89. St Augustine of Hippo is one of Pope Benedict's favourite Church Fathers.

90. Pope Benedict XVI, 'General Audience', 7 January 2009, in Pope Benedict XVI, *Paul of Tarsus*, 134–35, citing St Augustine, *City of God*, 10, 6).

91. See pp. 18–19 above.

> heart of the Church… *Corpus Christi*… is a unique feast and constitutes an important encounter of faith and praise for every Christian community … It is a feast that was established in order to publicly adore, praise and thank the Lord, who continues 'to love us "to the end", even to offering us his body and his blood' [*Sacramentum Caritatis*, no. 1].[92]

At the culminating point of the sequence, is sung *Ecce panis Angelorum, factus cibus viatorum: vere panis filiorum*: 'Lo! The angel's food is given, to the pilgrim who has striven; see the children's bread from heaven'. The pope comments that '… by God's grace we are the children. The Eucharist is the food reserved for those who in Baptism were delivered from slavery and have become sons; it is the food that sustained them on the long journey of the exodus through the desert of human existence'.[93] The feast of Corpus Christi,

> …wants to make the Lord's knocking audible, despite the hardness of our interior hearing. Jesus knocks at the door of our heart and asks to enter not only for the space of a day but for ever. Let us welcome him joyfully, raising to him with one voice the invocation of the Liturgy: 'very bread, Good Shepherd, tend us,/ Jesu, of your love befriend us …/You who all things can and know,/ who on earth such food bestow,/ grant us with your saints, though lowest,/ where the heavn'ly feast you show,/ fellow heirs and guests to be.' Amen![94]

During his homily for the Chrism Mass, on Holy Thursday in 2008, the pope provided a commentary on the second eucharistic prayer of the *Missale Romanum* (2002), focusing on the words, *astare coram te et tibi ministrare*: 'to stand

---

92. Pope Benedict XVI, 'Homily on the Solemnity of Corpus Christi', 7 June 2007, in Pope Benedict XVI, *Heart of the Christian Life*, 93; cf. Pope Benedict XVI, *Encyclical Letter Deus caritas est*, 25 December 2005, no. 17 on love and the Eucharist.

93. Pope Benedict XVI, 'Homily on the Solemnity of Corpus Christi', 7 June 2007, in Pope Benedict XVI, *Heart of the Christian Life*, 95.

94. *Ibid.*, 97.

and minister in the name of the Lord', which come from the Book of Deuteronomy (18: 5, 7). These words relate to the priestly ministry, and relate to the question 'what does it mean to be a priest of Jesus Christ?': the identity of the priest was a topic of some discussion after the Second Vatican Council.[95] The words *astare coram te et tibi ministrare*, which follow the consecration, 'points to being before the Lord present, that is, [they indicate] the Eucharist as the centre of priestly life.' However they are also an expression of vigilance, following on from the Lenten hymn in the Office of Readings [that is, in the *Liturgia Horarum*], *arctius perstemus in custodia: we* must be even more intensely alert. The priest 'must keep the world awake for God. He must be the one who remains standing: upright before the trends of time. Upright in truth. Upright in the commitment for good'.[96] 'To serve' (*ministrare*) has, in the pope's words, 'an essentially ritualistic meaning' in the Old Testament, and has been brought over into Christian worship. Here Pope Benedict then explores the centrality of the liturgy in the life of the priest and the faithful, laying particular emphasis on the *ars celebrandi* and the liturgy as the 'School of Christ', and of the saints down the ages:

> What the priest does at that moment, in the eucharistic celebration, is to serve, to fulfil a service to God and a service to humanity. The cult [that is, worship] that Christ rendered to the Father was the giving of himself to the end for humanity. Into this cult, this service, the priest must insert himself. Thus, the word 'serve' contains many dimensions. In the first place, part of it is certainly *the correct celebration of the liturgy* and of the sacraments in general, accomplished through interior participation [*partecipazione interiore*]. We must learn to increasingly understand the sacred liturgy in all its essence, to develop a living familiarity with it, so that it becomes the

---

95.   Pope Benedict XVI, 'Homily for the Chrism Mass', 20 March 2008, in Pope Benedict XVI, *Heart of the Christian Life*, 105–6.

96.   *Ibid.*, 106–7.

soul of our daily life. It is then that we celebrate in the correct way; it is then that the *ars celebrandi*, the art of celebrating, emerges by itself. In this art there must be nothing artificial. If the liturgy is the central duty of the priest, this also means that prayer must be a primary reality, to be learned ever anew and ever more deeply at the school of Christ and of the saints of all ages.[97]

The connection between the altar—where the priest performs his central duty—the earthly with the heavenly liturgy, and eschatology, apparent in the Book of the Apocalypse of St John, is related in a homily the pope gave during the dedication of a new altar in the cathedral of Albano in Italy:

> In the Roman liturgy, when the priest has made the offering of the bread and the wine, he bows to the altar and prays quietly: 'Lord God, we ask you to receive us and be pleased with the sacrifice we offer you with humble and contrite hearts'. In this way, together with the whole assembly of the faithful, he prepares to enter into the heart of the Eucharistic Mystery, into the heart of that heavenly liturgy to which the Second Reading from Revelation refers. St John presents an Angel who offers 'much incense to mingle with the prayers of all the saints upon the golden altar before the throne' of God (cf. Apoc 8: 3). The altar of the sacrifice becomes in a certain way the meeting point between Heaven and earth; the centre, we might say, of the One Church that is heavenly yet at the same time a pilgrim on this earth where, amidst the persecutions of the world and the consolations of God, disciples of the Lord proclaim his Passion and his death until he comes in glory. Indeed, every eucharistic celebration already anticipates Christ's triumph over sin and over the world and in the mystery shows the radiance of the Church, 'the spotless spouse of the spotless Lamb.

---

97. Pope Benedict XVI, 'Homily for the Chrism Mass', 20 March 2008, in Pope Benedict XVI, *Heart of the Christian Life*, 107–8.

It is she whom Christ loved and for whom he delivered himself up that he might sanctify her'.[98]

The pope's concerns with the liturgy in the Church, and
viewing the liturgy in the light of the hermeneutic of continuity, is once more apparent in a message sent to the
Italian Episcopal Conference gathered for a plenary session in Assisi (4 November 2010). Though it is addressed
to a particular group of bishops, its contents have certainly
implications for the wider Catholic Church. A significant
part of the message touches upon the liturgy, and the pope
has centred this on the life and example of St Francis of
Assisi, the patron saint of Italy. The pope makes obvious
parallels between the Church in the thirteenth century and
the situation of the Church today, after the Second Vatican Council. However it also reveals the reverence that we
ought to have for the older liturgy and its 'continuity' and
'relevance' for today, and not view it simply as an historical
relic. The pope refers to the adoption of the breviary of the
papal chapel by St Francis and his friars:

> … thanks to the work of Pope Innocent III—the one
> from whom the Poverello of Assisi obtained the first
> canonical recognition—the Church undertook a
> profound liturgical reform. An eminent expression
> of this is the Fourth Lateran Council (1215), which
> counts among its fruits the 'Breviary.' *This book of
> prayer includes in itself the richness of theological reflec-
> tion and of the praying experience of the previous mil-
> lennium.* Adopting it, St Francis and his friars made
> their own the liturgical prayer of the Supreme Pon-
> tiff. In this way, the saint listened to and meditated
> assiduously on the Word of God, to make it his own
> and then transmit it in the prayers of which he was
> author, as well as generally into all his writings.[99]

---

98.   Pope Benedict XVI, 'Homily at the Eucharistic Celebration and
      Dedication of the New Altar in the Cathedral of Albano', 21 Sep-
      tember 2008; cf. The Second Vatican Council, *Dogmatic Constitu-
      tion on the Church Lumen Gentium*, 21 November 1964, nos 6, 8.

99.   Pope Benedict XVI, 'Message to the Italian Bishops' Plenary Ses-
      sion', 4 November 2010: I have made alterations to this translation

The Fourth Lateran Council itself had inserted into the profession of faith the term 'transubstantiation', affirming the Real Presence of Christ in the Eucharistic Sacrifice: 'From attendance at Mass and reception, with devotion, of Holy Communion, springs the evangelical life of St Francis and his vocation to follow the way of the Crucified Christ.' St Francis had also a profound respect for priests, and he instructed his friars 'to respect them always and in every case, "because of the Most High Son of God. I do not see anything else physically in this world, but his Most Holy Body and Blood which they alone consecrate and they alone administer to others (*Franciscan Sources*, no. 113)."' This reverence for the Eucharist, and the liturgy, remains relevant today:

> The genuine believer, in every age, experiences in the liturgy the presence, the primacy and the work of God. It is *veritatis splendor* [*Sacramentum Caritatis*, no. 35], [a] nuptial event, [a] foretaste of the new and definitive city and participation in it; it is [a] link [between] creation and redemption, open[ing] a heaven above the earth of men, [a] passage from the world to God; it is Easter, in the cross and in the resurrection of Jesus Christ; it is the soul of Christian life.[100]

Pope Benedict then spoke about the forthcoming new Italian translation of the third typical edition of the *Missale Romanum* (2002), emphasising the necessity of the new translation and the 'obedience to faith'; and that the liturgy is something which demands respect, and is not something that can merely be altered at will:

> The correspondence of the prayer of the Church (*lex orandi*) with the rule of the faith (*lex credendi*) molds the thought and feelings of the Christian community, giving shape to the Church, [the] Body

---

where appropriate. On the work of Pope Innocent III concerning the breviary and the Franciscans, and the period after Lateran IV, see Van Dijk, *Sources of the Modern Roman Liturgy*, vol. 1, 40–41.

100. *Ibid.*

of Christ and temple of the Spirit. No human word
can do without time, even when, as in the case of
the liturgy, it constitutes a window that open[s]
beyond time. Hence, to give voice to a perennially
valid reality calls for the wise balance of continuity
and novelty [*novità*], of tradition and actualization.
The missal itself is placed within this process. Every
true reformer, in fact, is obedient to faith. He does
not move arbitrarily, nor does he arrogate to himself
any discretion about the rite; he is not the owner but
the guardian of the treasure instituted by the Lord
and entrusted to us. The whole Church is present in
every liturgy: to adhere to its form is the condition
of the authenticity of what is celebrated.[101]

The liturgy also acts as a source of Christian formation: in
other words, it is also didactic. Pope Benedict exhorts the
Italian bishops

to appreciate the liturgy as [a] perennial source of
education in the good life of the Gospel. The latter introduces the person to the encounter with
Jesus Christ, who with words and deeds constantly
builds the Church, forming her in the depths of listening, of fraternity and of mission. The rites are
eloquent by virtue of their intrinsic rationality and
teach a conscious, active and fruitful participation
[cf. *Sacrosanctum Concilium*, no. 11].[102]

The connection between the 'Word of God' and liturgy
received further attention by Pope Benedict XVI, in his
post-synodal exhortation *Verbum Domini* (30 September
2010), especially in the section entitled 'The Liturgy, privileged setting for the Word of God' (nos 52–71).[103] I want
to highlight just a few matters discussed by the pope, in
these last extracts from his Magisterium. The liturgy is

---

101. Pope Benedict XVI, 'Message to the Italian Bishops' Plenary Ses-
    sion', 4 November 2010.

102. *Ibid.*

103. Pope Benedict XVI, *Post-synodal Exhortation Verbum Domini*, 30
    September 2010.

'the privileged setting', 'in which God speaks to us in the midst of our lives; he speaks today to his people, who hear and respond. Every liturgical action is by its very nature steeped in sacred scripture.' The readings and psalms are taken from sacred scripture, and the petitions, prayers and liturgical hymns receive their inspiration and substance from it. The liturgical actions and signs draw their meaning from sacred scripture. The Church has always been aware that in the liturgical action 'the Word of God is accompanied by the interior working of the Holy Spirit who makes it effective in the hearts of the faithful', and strengthens their unity and fosters their gifts. Therefore in order to understand the Word of God 'we need to appreciate and experience the essential meaning and value of the liturgical action. *A faith-filled understanding of sacred scripture must always refer back to the liturgy*, in which the Word of God is celebrated as a timely and living word'. This 'expansion' of God's Word in time,

> ... takes place above all in the eucharistic celebration and in the Liturgy of the Hours. At the centre of everything the paschal mystery shines forth, and around it radiate all the mysteries of Christ and the history of salvation which become sacramentally present.[104]

There is a close bond between sacred scripture and the sacred liturgy, and Pope Benedict notes that this profound unity of word and Eucharist 'is grounded in the witness of scripture (cf. Jn 6; Lk 24), attested to by the Fathers of the Church, and reaffirmed by the Second Vatican Council.' Here Pope Benedict cites St Jerome, among other sources:

> The flesh of the Lord is true food and his blood true drink; this is the true good that is reserved for us in this present life, to nourish ourselves with his flesh and drink his blood, not only in the Eucharist but also in reading sacred scripture. Indeed, true food

---

104. *Ibid.*, no. 52.

and true drink is the Word of God which we derive
from the scriptures.[105]

Jesus' discourse on the bread in the Gospel of St John (6:
22–69), speaks of 'the gift of God, which Moses obtained for
his people with the manna in the desert, which is really the
Torah, the life-giving Word of God (cf. Ps 119; Pr 9:5).' This
is brought to fulfilment in Jesus: 'The bread of God is that
which comes down from heaven and gives life to the world
… I am the bread of life ' (Jn 6: 33–35). Here Pope Benedict
XVI cites the work of a theologian, which indicates once
more, in an unmistakable manner, how the pope's own
theology has influenced his Magisterium and, to a certain
extent, been appropriated by it: that theologian is Joseph
Ratzinger: 'Here "the law has become a person. When we
encounter Jesus, we feed on the living God himself, so to
speak; we truly eat 'bread from heaven'"'.[106] The mystery
of the Eucharist 'reveals the true manna, the true bread of
heaven. It is God's *Logos* made flesh, who gave himself up
for us in the paschal mystery.' The Word of God and the
Eucharist are so deeply bound that one cannot understand
one without the other. Pope Benedict explains this:

> the Word of God sacramentally takes flesh in the
> event of the Eucharist. The Eucharist opens us to
> an understanding of scripture, just as scripture for
> its part illumines and explains the mystery of the
> Eucharist. Unless we acknowledge the Lord's Real
> Presence in the Eucharist, our understanding of
> scripture remains imperfect.

It is for this reason that—'the Church has honoured the
Word of God and the Eucharistic Mystery with the same
reverence, *although not with the same worship*'.[107] The pope

---

105. *Ibid.* (St Jerome, *Commentarius in Ecclesiasten*, vol. 3, *Patrologia Latina*, 23, 1092A).

106. Pope Benedict XVI, *Post-synodal Exhortation Verbum Domini*, 30 September 2010, no. 54, n. 192, explicitly citing Pope Benedict XVI/ Ratzinger, *Jesus of Nazareth*, 268.

107. Pope Benedict XVI, *Post-synodal Exhortation Verbum Domini*, 30 September 2010, nos 54–55 (citing *Ordo Lectionum Missae*, no.10):

also emphasizes that 'The Synod also clearly reaffirmed a point already laid down by liturgical law, namely that *the readings drawn from sacred scripture may never be replaced by other texts*, however significant the latter maybe from a spiritual or pastoral standpoint'.[108] Referring to the 'sacramentality' of the Word of God, one can understand this by *analogy* with the Real Presence of Christ under the appearances of the consecrated bread and wine (cf. *CCC*, nos 1373–74):

> By approaching the altar and partaking in the eucharistic banquet we truly share in the body and blood of Christ. The proclamation of God's word at the celebration entails an acknowledgment that Christ himself is present, that he speaks to us, and that he wishes to be heard.[109]

Those entrusted with the proclamation of God's word, 'even those not instituted in the ministry of reader, should be truly suitable and carefully trained. This training should be biblical *and liturgical*, as well as technical'.[110] In order to improve the quality of homilies which explain God's Word—a concern Pope Benedict also raised in *Sacramen-*

---

my emphasis.

108. Pope Benedict XVI, *Post-synodal Exhortation Verbum Domini*, 30 September 2010, no. 69. This is a problem in some European countries, in particular.

109. Pope Benedict XVI, *Post-synodal Exhortation Verbum Domini*, 30 September 2010, nos 55–56: Pope Benedict cites St Jerome (no. 56) : 'We are reading the sacred scriptures. For me, the Gospel is the Body of Christ; for me, the holy scriptures are his teaching. And when he says: "whoever does not eat my flesh and drink my blood" (Jn 6: 53), even though these words can also be understood of the [Eucharistic] Mystery, Christ's body and blood are really the word of scripture, God's teaching. When we approach the [Eucharistic] Mystery, if a crumb falls to the ground we are troubled. Yet when we are listening to the Word of God, and God's word and Christ's flesh and blood are being poured into our ears yet we pay no heed, what great peril should we not feel?': *In Psalmum* 147: *Corpus Christianorum Series Latinum*, vol. 78, 337–38.

110. Pope Benedict XVI, *Post-synodal Exhortation Verbum Domini*, 30 September 2010, no. 58 (my emphasis).

tum Caritatis (no. 46)—he has called for a 'Directory on Homiletics' to be compiled.[111]

Verbum Domini also devotes a section to sacred scripture and the 'Liturgy of the Hours' or 'Divine Office'. Pope Benedict says that, 'Above all we should reflect on the profound theological and ecclesial dignity of this prayer', where the Church, exercising the priestly office of Christ offers continuous praise to God a 'sacrifice of praise'. As the public prayer of the Church, the Liturgy of the Hours 'sets forth the Christian ideal of the sanctification of the entire day, marked by the rhythm of hearing the Word of God and praying the psalms'. Those who are charged with the obligation of praying the office, 'should carry out this duty faithfully for the benefit of the whole Church.' The pope also encourages religious communities ('communities of consecrated life'), 'to be exemplary in the celebration of the Liturgy of the Hours, and thus to become a point of reference and an inspiration for the spiritual and pastoral life of the whole Church.' The participation of the entire 'People of God' is also encouraged, particularly the celebration of Lauds and Vespers.[112]

Among the practices which the pope recommends for promoting fuller participation in the liturgy includes silence and moments of recollection in the liturgy: 'The great patristic tradition teaches us that the mysteries of Christ all involve silence'.[113] The suggestion has also been made that the book containing the Word of God should enjoy a visible place of honour in church. However this is to be done 'without prejudice to the central place proper to the tabernacle containing the Blessed Sacrament'.[114] The pope also mentioned liturgical chants, which should be

---

111. *Ibid.*, no. 60.

112. Pope Benedict XVI, *Post-synodal Exhortation Verbum Domini*, 30 September 2010, no. 62.

113. *Ibid.*, no. 66.

114. Pope Benedict XVI, *Post-synodal Exhortation Verbum Domini*, 30 September 2010, no. 68.

'biblically-inspired', and singled out—as in *Sacramentum Caritatis* —the use of Gregorian chant.[115]

The celebration of the papal liturgy under Pope Benedict XVI

It is evident that Pope Benedict clearly intends to lead by *exemplo* as well as by *verbo* in the field of liturgy. One is certainly struck with how Pope Benedict's theology of liturgy and magisterial teaching, is made visible. The papal liturgy—especially in Rome—has noticeably changed. What sort of changes have occurred, and how do they match Pope Benedict's liturgical vision? We can list the following (at least): the prominence of the six large candlesticks on the papal altar(s), with the crucifix and seventh candle in the centre; the redesigning of the 'Altar of the Chair' in St Peter's Basilica; the celebration of Mass *versus Deum* or *ad orientem* in the Sistine Chapel on the feast of the Baptism of the Lord; increased use of kneeling and the distribution of Holy Communion on the tongue during papal masses; the greater use of older vestments from previous pontiffs, or newly commissioned vestments in older styles (newer vestments also being retained), including, copes, mitres, lace albs, and older dalmatics for the deacons; old papal choir dress restored, including the Easter mozzetta and broad stole; the re-instatement of traditional papal clothing for the *Urbi et Orbi*, instead of wearing a cope and mitre; the replacement of the papal staff of Pope Paul VI; the restoration of old papal thrones and steps; the papal 'morse' for copes; the papal *astericus* for some celebrations of the Eucharist, used over the paten; restored use of the cardinal deacons; and a new design for the papal pallium. We can find in Pope Benedict's Magisterium, as well as in the theology which clearly influences it, and in the books of the Roman Rite—the use of the seventh candle for instance[116]—the deeper basis for the visible changes

---

115. *Ibid.*, no.70.
116. Cf. *IGMR*, no. 117.

which we have witnessed in the papal liturgies. We can
summarize the elements behind these changes as follows:
the harmonization of newer and older elements, including
an emphasis on continuity with the past, organic development and the end of 'artificial discontinuities' in growing
fidelity to the Second Vatican Council; emphasis on (the
theology of) beauty and 'the splendour of the liturgy', adoration, and the positioning of the crucifix to emphasize that
Christ is the 'centre' of the liturgy;[117] more emphasis on the
ars celebrandi and the importance of outward signs, also
apparent in the vestments, furnishings, music, art, sacred
vessels and the harmony of the liturgical rites; and emphasising the 'transcendental' elements of the liturgy. In many
ways, one can see that elements mentioned in *Sacramentum Caritatis* are visibly presented, as well as an emphasis
on more traditional elements. One can also speak of the
importance given to the sacred expression of bodily posture during the liturgy—kneeling for Holy Communion,
hands joined, and so on—which, with other elements, such
as clothing, we could call Pope Benedict XVI's 'liturgical
theology of the body'.[118] Papal liturgies, as well as those of
diocesan bishops, are, in a particular way, models for liturgies throughout entire dioceses, and, in the case of papal
liturgies, for the celebration of the Latin liturgy throughout
the world.[119] In a real sense, the changes in the papal liturgies strongly suggest that 'the reform of the reform' has also
begun in a very visible way, 'building upon' and 'developing' recent liturgical practice. One also finds confirmation
of these deeper foundations elsewhere, for instance, in the
opinions and comments made by Mgr Guido Marini, the
papal master of ceremonies, in interviews concerning the

---

117. See *TSL*, 83–84; Ratzinger, '*The Spirit of the Liturgy* or Fidelity to the
     Council', 101; *IGMR*, nos 117, 277, 308.

118. See pp. 31–42 and my discussion on *Sacramentum Caritatis* above.

119. *Caeremoniale Episcoporum*, no. 12; *IGMR*, no. 22.

recent papal liturgies.[120] These changes are gradually having an impact on liturgies in certain parts of the world.[121]

Some conclusions

It now remains in this chapter to make some concluding remarks on the liturgy in Pope Benedict XVI's Magisterium, from the documents we have thus far seen. The evident importance of the liturgy for Pope Benedict cannot be underestimated. His Post-synodal exhortation, *Sacramentum Caritatis*, has a central place as one of the pillars of what we can rightly call 'the liturgical reform of Pope Benedict XVI', based on 'the hermeneutic of continuity', in faithfulness to the Second Vatican Council and the life-giving liturgical tradition of the Church. This renewal has a very important spiritual basis. We should remember that Pope Benedict—after an Ordinary General Assembly of the Synod of Bishops on the Eucharist—wanted to 'offer some basic directions aimed at a renewed commitment to eucharistic enthusiasm and fervour in the Church', to encourage the Christian people to 'deepen their understanding of the relationship between the *Eucharistic Mystery*, the *liturgical action*, and the *new spiritual worship* which derives from the Eucharist as the *sacrament of charity*'. At the same time the

---

120. See the appendix.

121. Other influences may also be apparent. See Schneider, *Dominus Est—It is the Lord!* The Rev. Peter M. J. Stravinskas writes in his forward to this book, concerning reverence for the Holy Eucharist and communion on the tongue, 'One cannot help but wonder if Bishop Schneider's... book did not play a part in the decision of Pope Benedict XVI to return to the traditional mode of communion distribution at his masses, namely, on the tongue to kneeling communicants': *Ibid.*, 8. However see Pope Benedict XVI, *Light of the World*, 158–59: 'The idea behind my current practice of having people kneel to receive communion on the tongue was to send a signal and to underscore the Real Presence [of Christ in the Eucharist] with an exclamation point... Something quite special is going on here! *He* is here, the One before whom we fall on our knees! Pay attention!' (the pope's emphasis). The pope has—happily—developed his thinking on this matter: cf. Ratzinger, *God is Near Us*, 69–71.

pope is 'conscious of the immense patrimony of doctrine and discipline accumulated over the centuries with regard to this sacrament'.[122] Pope Benedict wants to renew 'our eucharistic wonder', 'through the splendour and beauty radiating from the liturgical rite, the efficacious sign of the infinite beauty of the holy mystery of God'.[123] I have demonstrated that the influence of Joseph Ratzinger's theological writings upon the liturgical aspects of the Magisterium of Pope Benedict XVI, is abundantly clearly. The similarities are unmistakable: the theology of beauty and the notion of 'spiritual worship' being particular good examples of this.

We should also note in particular, that if one studies attentively the references given by Pope Benedict in his statements on the liturgy—especially in *Sacramentum Caritatis*—one also sees how indebted he is, not only to the Second Vatican Council, and the views of the Synodal Fathers, but also to the Magisterium of Popes Paul VI and John Paul II. It is quite clear that, particularly in the case of the latter, that Pope Benedict is building upon, and going further than his predecessors—particularly in this theological explanation of the liturgy—which is fairly common in the development of the Church's Magisterium. This 'building upon' and 'going further' (that is, development), which also faces up to newer insights and situations, in the framework of the 'hermeneutic of continuity', places an even greater emphasis, appreciation for, and cognisance of the liturgical heritage of the Church, and that the Church is the same Church before and after Vatican II. One should note here, for example, antecedents in Pope John Paul II's pontificate: the desire to correct abuses, the third edition of the *Missale Romanum* (2002), the emphasis placed upon the theological continuity of the Second Vatican Council with the past. Joseph Ratzinger was very much involved in these matters, as a close collaborator with Pope John Paul II and a prominent member of his Curia. Indeed, Helen Hull Hitch-

---

122. Pope Benedict XVI, *Sacramentum Caritatis*, no. 5.
123. *Ibid.*, no. 97.

cock has rightly observed, and demonstrated, the same points: 'There is, I believe, a rather remarkable similarity in the perspectives of Pope John Paul II and then-Cardinal Ratzinger—and these passages [cited in her article] reveal the strong parallel in their views of the need for a thorough re-evaluation of the postconciliar liturgical reform, and to make necessary corrections, which must grow organically from authentic tradition.'[124] We should also note here the influence, if not the thought of Joseph Ratzinger, in Pope John Paul II's encyclical *Ecclesia de Eucharistia.*[125] Cardinal George Pell of Sydney has gone so far as to say that 'the partnership of Pope John Paul II and Cardinal Ratzinger was one of the most brilliant and effective in papal history as they dialogued with the world of learning and confronted the culture of death. Any future initiatives of Pope Benedict are likely to be in continuity, complementary and not antithetical to the patrimony of his mentor'.[126]

And yet *Sacramentum Caritatis* and the other statements of the pope on the liturgy, important as they undoubtedly are, and the faithful celebration of the new missal, are only one significant part of Pope Benedict's efforts to 'reform the reform', in greater fidelity to the Second Vatican Council and its achievements, as well as to correct errors of interpretation and implementation. We should remind ourselves that Pope Benedict is 'conscious of the immense patrimony of doctrine and *discipline* accumulated over the centuries with regard to this sacrament'.[127] It was quite clear to Pope Benedict that something else needed to be done, something

---

124. Hull Hitchcock, 'Pope Benedict XVI and the "reform of the reform"', 81. For a comparison of both popes in general, see Rowland, *Ratzinger's Faith*, 1, 9–11, 24–5, 32–33, 73–74, 141, 151–54; Pope John Paul II, *Apostolic Letter Spiritus et Sponsa of the Supreme Pontiff John Paul II on the 40th Anniversary of the Constitution of the Sacred Liturgy Sacrosanctum Concilium*, 4 December 2003, nos 6, 7, 12.

125. Baldovin, *Reforming the Liturgy*, 89; Pope John Paul II, *Encyclical Letter Ecclesia de Eucharistia*, 17 April 2003.

126. Cardinal Pell in his preface to Rowland, *Ratzinger's Faith*, xii.

127. Pope Benedict XVI, *Sacramentum Caritatis*, no. 5 (my emphasis).

which many have regarded as quite radical and unthinkable: more prophetic voices in the Church would call this an outstanding and logical development in the field of liturgy. This was to emphasize and to reconcile, where there was liturgical rupture, the continuity of the Church's liturgical tradition in an even more complete manner, for 'the reform of the reform' and to strengthen the Church's eucharistic faith, and continuity with the past. This was done in Pope Benedict's motu proprio *Summorum Pontificum*.

Chapter IV
One Rite, Two Forms:
Summorum Pontificum —
Towards a *Pax Liturgica*,
Part Two

Introduction

One of the most important liturgical reforms of Pope Benedict XVI was the promulgation of the motu proprio, *Summorum Pontificum*, issued on 7 July 2007, and, from 14 September that year, the law of the Church. This document has particular significance in that it affects the very structure of the Roman Rite as well as how one defines it. It is the positive law of the Church, and not an indult or a privilege.[1] Indeed, we should note here that in our detailed examination of *Summorum Pontificum*, it will be necessary to pay particular attention to its canonical/legislative aspects in order to understand its significance in the liturgical, and wider life of the Church. *Summorum Pontificum* relates to the rites of the Roman liturgy promulgated after the Second Vatican Council, and those in general use before that time; it allows greater freedom for priests to celebrate the latter, and more access to this liturgy by the faithful.

---

1. Pope Benedict XVI, *Litterae Apostolicae Motu Proprio Datae 'De Usu Extraordinaria Antiquae Formae Ritus Romani' Benedictus XVI*, 7 July 2007, *AAS* 99 (2007), 777–81: English translation *Summorum Pontificum* (hereafter referred to as 'Pope Benedict XVI, *Summorum Pontificum*'). I have taken account of the changes made to the Latin text—in *AAS*—in the English translation. On the legal status of *Summorum Pontificum*, see Lüdecke, 'Kanonistische Anmerkungen zum Motu Proprio *Summorum Pontificum*', 3–8, 25–7; Weishaupt, *Päpstliche Weichenstellungen*, 19–20.

How does this fit in with Pope Benedict's vision of reforming and renewing the Roman liturgy? Before attempting to answer this question, we need to briefly examine the historical background which led to *Summorum Pontificum*, what the motu proprio itself says, particularly in the light of the pope's accompanying letter to the world's bishops, and Cardinal Ratzinger's own views on the 'old liturgy'.

Background to Summorum Pontificum

After the promulgation of the *Novus Ordo Missae* in 1969 following the Second Vatican Council—a period of great change in the liturgy—there were significant numbers of individuals who still had a certain attachment to the rites in previous use. The older form of the Mass was known as, for example, 'The Tridentine Mass'—an historically inaccurate description—'The Traditional (Latin) Mass' or as 'The Mass of Pope Pius V', because the missal was promulgated by Pope St Pius V in 1570.[2] There are various reasons why individuals and groups were attached to this form of the Mass—rightly or wrongly—including a love of beauty and 'mystery' in this liturgy, which they did not find in the new rites—not to mention years of attending that form of liturgy—the major differences between the old and the new forms of the Mass, and doctrinal reasons: the 'Tridentine' Mass, which had developed over the centuries, was a part of the fabric of Catholicism, and was unambiguously expressed in the rites as a 'sacrifice'. To some, the Mass that was presented after the council appeared as a Protestant form of worship, especially for some Catholics in Protestant countries, such as England and Scotland, who had experienced centuries of persecution. A number of these people—but not all—questioned the legitimacy of the reforms and decrees of the Second Vatican Council, and if its documents were in line with previous Church teachings. Added to this was the terrible confusion which reigned in Church in the 1960s and 1970s, in the area of

---

2.   For this section, see Edwards, *Catholic Traditionalism*.

theology, when priests and religious left their vocations in their thousands. The new liturgy was often interpreted by individual priests in a very subjective level, frequently calling into question the validity of the rites themselves and central dogmas of the Catholic faith, which actually misrepresented what Vatican II taught. Mistakes made in the formulation of the new rites, bad translations of official, Latin texts, even at an official level, also contributed to this, and the impression was often given that the Church's 'pre-Vatican II' past, along with its liturgy, was taboo, if not 'legally' suppressed. The liturgical tradition of the Church seemed to have been broken off, and cast aside.[3] Some individuals, such as Archbishop Marcel Lefebvre, the founder of the 'Priestly Fraternity of St Pius X', refused to accept the new liturgy—even rejecting certain doctrinal teachings of Vatican II—and set up seminaries to ordain priests in order to minister to many of those who preferred the 'Tridentine' Mass. Eventually, after a visitation, the Fraternity was suppressed, and Lefebvre was forbidden to carry out ordinations. He continued to do so, and the Fraternity continued to operate, which led to Lefebvre's suspension *a divinis* under Pope Paul VI in 1976.[4]

Although permission was granted in 1969 and 1971 for older or infirm priests to use a modified version of this 'Tridentine' missal (and breviary), if they found the new rites difficult to use, pastoral provision for its use was made for England and Wales with an indult in 1971. This allowed local bishops to grant permission for this liturgy, with certain modifications made in the 1960s, on specific occasions, and was due to the intervention of Cardinal Heenan, following a petition from prominent individuals, such as

---

3.   For a moving, personal account of the liturgical changes, and their aftermath, see Mosebach, *The Heresy of Formlessness*.

4.   For fuller details of the legal background, including the excommunications in 1988, see Read, 'SSPX Lifting of the Excommunications', 13–21.

Agatha Christie and Graham Greene.[5] In 1984 the 'problem' of the Tridentine Mass was addressed by Pope John Paul II, and an indult *Quattuor Abhinc Annos* was issued by the Congregation for Divine Worship, which allowed *any* bishop in the world to extend permission to celebrate Mass according to the Missal of 1962, after the pope invited the bishops to make a report on the implementation of the reforms after the Second Vatican Council, and problems which were encountered. However permission was granted in restricted terms: for example, parish churches could not ordinarily be used.[6] After the illegal consecration of four bishops by Archbishop Lefebvre in 1988, despite an agreement that had been reached by the Holy See for their reconciliation, the archbishop, Antonio de Castro Mayer, bishop emeritus of Campos—who assisted with the consecrations—and the four newly-ordained bishops, were excommunicated. Pope John Paul II, in a further move for reconciliation, and to care for the pastoral well-being of those attached to the Tridentine Mass, issued the motu proprio *Ecclesia Dei adflicta* (1988). As well as pointing out errors propagated by Archbishop Lefebvre and his followers—not to mention the necessity for the whole Church to reflect on the Church's Magisterium in the light of tradition—the pope asked that 'all the pastors and the other faithful have a new awareness, not only of the lawfulness, but also of the richness for the Church of a diversity of charisms, traditions of spirituality and apostolate, which also constitutes the beauty of unity in variety: of that blended "harmony" which the earthly Church raises up to heaven under the impulse of the Holy Spirit.' To all Catholics who were attached to previous liturgical and disciplinary forms, the pope wished 'to manifest [his] will to facilitate their ecclesial communion by means of the necessary measures to guarantee respect for their

5.   For another indult, from France in 1972, see Sacred Congregation for Divine Worship, *'Unicuique suum ...'*, 48.

6.   Congregation for Divine Worship, *Quattuor Abhinc Annos*, 3 October 1984, *AAS* 76 (1984), 1088–1089.

rightful aspirations', calling on the support of the world's bishops and those engaged in pastoral ministry. The pope set up a pontifical commission — known later as the Pontifical Commission Ecclesia Dei — to facilitate communion to those attached to Archbishop Lefebvre, and asked that 'respect must everywhere be shown for the feelings of all those who are attached to the Latin liturgical tradition, by a wide and generous application of the directives already issued some time ago by the Apostolic See for the use of the Roman Missal according to the typical edition of 1962' (that is, as specified in *Quattuor Abhinc Annos*), which widened the extent to which local bishops could grant permission.[7] As a result the 'Priestly Fraternity of St Peter' was established, along with other religious congregations who, while accepting Vatican II, were permitted to use the *Missale Romanum* of 1962 and other liturgical books. However it must be honestly admitted, that many bishops did not grant 'a wide and generous application' of these directives, as Pope John Paul II had asked.

The text of Summorum Pontificum *and its interpretation*

At this point we come to *Summorum Pontificum* itself, which clearly goes much further than Pope John Paul II's *Ecclesia Dei*.[8] *Summorum Pontificum* begins by recalling the solicitude of the popes 'to ensure that the Church of Christ offers a worthy ritual to the Divine Majesty' and the history of the Roman Rite, down to the third edition of the new *Missale Romanum* under Pope John Paul II. The document recalls recent papal legislation concerning the missal of 1962, and indicates that 'in some regions, no small numbers of faithful adhered and continue to adhere with great love and affection to the earlier liturgical forms'. Having taken account of 'the insistent prayers of these faithful',

---

7.   Pope John Paul II, *Apostolic Letter Ecclesia Dei of the Supreme Pontiff John Paul II given Motu Proprio*, 2 July 1988.

8.   Cf. Crouan, *The History and the Future of the Roman Liturgy*, 213–17.

which his predecessor had long considered, the views expressed by the cardinals at a recent consistory, and having 'reflected deeply upon all aspects of the question, invoked the Holy Spirit', Pope Benedict then established norms, given in twelve articles. The first article marks a fundamental change in what the Roman Rite is. The pope stipulates that the missal promulgated by Pope Paul VI is the 'ordinary expression' of the *lex orandi* of the Catholic Church of the Latin rite, and that the missal of Pope St Pius V, 'reissued by Blessed John XXIII [the missal of 1962]' is the 'extraordinary expression of that same *lex orandi* and must be given due honour for its venerable and ancient usage'.

In other words, there is one Roman Rite (*unici ritus Romani*) with two usages (*duo usus/duae expressiones*), which 'will in no way lead to a division in the Church's *lex credendi*': here we see the application of 'the hermeneutic of continuity'. The missal of 1962, which was 'never abrogated' (*numquam abrogatam*), may be celebrated. This point was reiterated by the pope in his letter to the bishops of the world: 'I would like to draw attention to the fact that this missal was never juridically abrogated and, consequently, in principle, was always permitted'.[9] The legal status of the missal of Pope St Pius V, after the reforms of the Second Vatican Council, was a matter of some controversy, and has now been decided upon by Pope Benedict in *Summorum Pontificum*.[10]

9. Pope Benedict XVI, *Letter to the Bishops on the Occasion of the Publication of the Apostolic Letter "Motu Proprio Data"*, 7 July 2007, 21.

10. For commentaries on this aspect, and on what is meant by 'abrogation' ('the total abolition of a law'), see Bux and Vitiello, *The Motu Proprio of Benedict XVI Summorum Pontificum cura*; Lüdecke, 'Kanonistische Anmerkungen zum Motu Proprio *Summorum Pontificum*', 3–14; Read, '*Motu Proprio Summorum Pontificum*', 9–22; Weishaupt, *Päpstliche Weichenstellungen*, 28–35. Further documentation 'in assoluta fedeltà alla *mens* del Santo Padre', may be found at the website of the Pontifical Commission Ecclesia Dei: http://www.ecclesiadei-pontcommissio.org. Baldovin, and others who have problems accepting that the missal of 1962 'was never juridically abrogated', ought to study this documentation: see Baldovin, *Reforming the Liturgy*, 131.

The pope then substituted the previous legislation—
Quattuor Abhinc Annos and *Ecclesia Dei adflicta*—and laid
down precise rules for the use of the *Missale Romanum* of
1962. Here we should note that *Summorum Pontificum* 'does
not take away personal indults or permissions granted by
the Pontifical Commission Ecclesia Dei, nor those granted
to groups such as various religious communities. This is
an important point, because they may have more extensive
rights in this regard. For them the preconciliar liturgical
uses are not an extraordinary form of the Roman Rite, but
their proper rite'.[11] Here we shall itemize each of these
rules as they appear in the articles of *Summorum Pontificum*,
with canonical commentary for several of them, concerning certain aspects relating to their practical application
and interpretation. This is particularly important because
it helps us to understand what exactly Pope Benedict XVI
has done to change the relationship between the missal of
Pope St Pius V and the liturgy of the Church in the twenty-
first century: [12]

> Art. 2. In masses celebrated without the people, each
> Catholic priest of the Latin Rite, whether secular or
> regular, may use the Roman Missal published by Bl.
> Pope John XXIII in 1962, or the Roman Missal pro-
> mulgated by Pope Paul VI in 1970, and may do so on
> any day with the exception of the Easter Triduum.

It is clear that no liturgies *sine populo* from *both* missals—that
is, the priest with a server, or alone, if no server is avail-

---

11. Read, '*Motu Proprio Summorum Pontificum*'.
12. Fuller, and more detailed commentary is given in Read, '*Motu
     Proprio Summorum Pontificum*'—cf. idem, '*Summorum Pontificum*:
     Questions, Answers, Issues', 32–36; Lüdecke, 'Kanonistische
     Anmerkungen zum Motu Proprio *Summorum Pontificum*', 3–34: I
     am grateful to Shawn Tribe of 'The New Liturgical Movement' blog
     for the use of translations from this article; Weishaupt, *Päpstliche
     Weichenstellungen*, which is probably the most important canonical
     commentary on *Summorum Pontificum* to date. Just before publi-
     cation, the long-awaited official instruction (*Universae Ecclesiae*)
     relating to *Summorum Pontificum* was finally released. Compare the
     following commentary with the 'Addendum'.

able—may be offered during the Easter Triduum, which is entirely consistent with the usage stipulated in both forms of the Roman Rite. This does not, of course, prevent *public* celebrations of the Easter Triduum, in accordance with the stipulations further indicated. These could also be done previously, under the indult *Ecclesia Dei adflicta*. One should also note that canon 906 (1983 code) stipulates that Mass may not be offered without the participation of at least one of the faithful, 'unless there is a good (*iusta*) and reasonable cause for doing so'. This should be interpreted in light of canon 904, which strongly recommends that priests offer Mass daily, which would thus constitute a 'reasonable cause' for saying Mass alone if a server could not be found.[13]

> For such celebrations, with either one missal or the other, the priest has no need for permission from the Apostolic See or from his Ordinary.

This includes priests who are 'religious' (*religiosus*): the pope is clearly aware of the particular canonical circumstances of religious who live under their own ordinaries and superiors. Specific conditions are laid down when *entire* communities belonging to institutes of consecrated life and societies of apostolic life wish frequent, habitual or permanent celebrations (see art. 3). The celebration of the *Missa sine populo* is, except in the case of insurmountable obstacles, to be allowed 'at any legitimate place'. 'Restrictions of the *usus antiquior*[14] to certain places or times by particular law are ... inadmissible'. However one could not celebrate a separate Mass—whether it be in the ordinary or extraordinary form—at the same time as a concelebrated Mass in the ordinary form is being celebrated in the same

---

13. *Contra* Baldovin, *Reforming the Liturgy*, 130, n. 68. Concerning the 'private Mass' and the *usus antiquior*, see, Vijgen, 'Is de H. Mis in de Buitengewone Vorm een "Privé-Mis"?', 208–19; Lüdecke, 'Kanonistische Anmerkungen zum Motu Proprio *Summorum Pontificum*', 14–18; Weishaupt, *Päpstliche Weichenstellungen*, 48–54.

14. This is one of the terms used by the pope to describe the extraordinary form.

church, following canon 902: both forms of the Roman Rite are treated equally.[15]

> Art. 3. Communities of institutes of consecrated life and of societies of apostolic life, of either pontifical or diocesan right, wishing to celebrate Mass in accordance with the edition of the Roman Missal promulgated in 1962, for conventual or 'community' celebration in their oratories, may do so. If an individual community or an entire institute or society wishes to undertake such celebrations often, habitually or permanently, the decision must be taken by the superiors major, in accordance with the law and following their own specific decrees and statutes.
>
> Art. 4. Celebrations of Mass as mentioned above in art. 2 may—observing all the norms of law—also be attended by faithful who, of their own free will, ask to be admitted.

Weishaupt, and other canonists, while emphasizing that the faithful do have a right to attend these masses *sine populo*, and that the priests can communicate their intention to celebrate them, orally or in writing, to the faithful, indicate that they should not be advertised in parish newsletters and on parish websites, to preserve their 'private character' ('Privatcharakter').[16] The faithful, of their own volition, can still ask to participate in these masses (and cf. article 5) and can tell each other about them, and also receive Holy Communion. However, given the generous nature of *Summorum Pontificum*, surely a priest can advertise a Mass *sine populo* in his parish bulletin or website *apart* from the list of scheduled parish masses? Lüdecke comments that there are *no* restrictions on 'advertising' or letting people know about such celebrations. The parish priest must not

---

15. Lüdecke, 'Kanonistische Anmerkungen zum Motu Proprio *Summorum Pontificum*', 14–18; Weishaupt, *Päpstliche Weichenstellungen*, 53–54.

16. Weishaupt, *Päpstliche Weichenstellungen*, 59; cf. Read, '*Motu Proprio Summorum Pontificum*', 17–18.

discriminate against masses according to the old use 'by keeping them secret or scheduling them at times difficultly accessible'.[17]

> Art. 5. § 1 In parishes, where there is a group of faithful who stably adhere to the earlier liturgical tradition, the pastor should willingly accept their requests to celebrate the Mass according to the rite of the Roman Missal published in 1962, and ensure that the welfare of these faithful harmonizes with the ordinary pastoral care of the parish, under the guidance of the bishop in accordance with canon 392, avoiding discord and favouring the unity of the whole Church.

Note the Latin text concerning 'a group': *In paroeciis, ubi coetus fidelium traditioni liturgicae antecedenti adhaerentium stabiliter exsistit* (my emphasis). What constitutes a 'group' (*coetus*) here? Canonical opinion indicates 'at least three people'. Furthermore, 'the revised text [of article 5. § 1] makes it clear that, contrary to the assertions of some, the group does not need to have been 'fighting the good fight' without a break since the 1960's. It simply needs to be 'stable' rather than a one off group assembled for a particular occasion, although this does not preclude permission for a 'one off' request. Equally, the motu proprio does not state, as some have argued, that the stable group must come from within the parish. This is to take §1 in isolation from §5. The phrase 'in parishes' is parallel to 'in churches that are not parish or conventual churches'.[18] The diocesan bishop or (parish) priest cannot establish a higher minimum number.[19] The group need not be actual parishioners

---

17. Lüdecke, 'Kanonistische Anmerkungen zum Motu Proprio *Summorum Pontificum*', op cit., 14–18. When Mass is celebrated in a private chapel the consent of the owner (at least 'tacit' consent) may be necessary: Weishaupt, *Päpstliche Weichenstellungen*, 58.

18. Read, '*Motu Proprio Summorum Pontificum*' and idem, '*Summorum Pontificum*: Questions, Answers, Issues', *passim*; cf. Weishaupt, *Päpstliche Weichenstellungen*, 61, n. 117, and 66–68.

19. Lüdecke, 'Kanonistische Anmerkungen zum Motu Proprio *Summorum Pontificum*', 18–23; Weishaupt, *Päpstliche Weichenstellungen*,

of a parish: a *coetus fidelium* is not the same as *paroeciani* ('parishioners').[20]

> § 2 Celebration in accordance with the missal of Bl. John XXIII may take place on working days; while on Sundays and feast days one such celebration may also be held.

'Note that the document says *una etiam* not *una tantum*. It envisages one Mass on Sundays and holy days, but does not strictly preclude more than one. The wording is concessionary rather than limiting in tone'.[21]

> § 3 For faithful and priests who request it, the pastor should also allow celebrations in this extraordinary form for special circumstances such as marriages, funerals or occasional celebrations, for example, pilgrimages.

> § 4 Priests who use the missal of Bl John XXIII must be qualified to do so and not juridically impeded.

idonei esse—that is, have the basic *minimum* requirements. Celebrants are not expected to have an academic knowledge of Latin: 'The celebrant must be free from any impediment, for example, suspension or excommunication…, or reception of orders without documentation, and so on. He must also be *idoneus*, or 'qualified', that is, have sufficient understanding of the text and rubrics as to be able to celebrate worthily. Common sense will be needed here'.[22]

> § 5 In churches that are not parish or conventual churches, it is the duty of the rector of the church to grant the above permission.

66.

20. Weishaupt, *Päpstliche Weichenstellungen*, 63.

21. Read, '*Motu Proprio Summorum Pontificum*'; Weishaupt, *Päpstliche Weichenstellungen*, 72–76.

22. Read, '*Motu Proprio Summorum Pontificum*'; Lüdecke, 'Kanonistische Anmerkungen zum Motu Proprio *Summorum Pontificum*', 21–22; Weishaupt, *Päpstliche Weichenstellungen*, 77–82.

Art. 6. In Masses celebrated in the presence of the people in accordance with the missal of Bl. John XXIII, the readings may be given in the vernacular, using editions recognized by the Apostolic See.

Approved translations of the readings in the missal of 1962 seem to be intended here rather than the lectionary of 1970, though further clarification appears to be necessary in regard to the text used.[23]

Art. 7. If a group of lay faithful, as mentioned in art. 5 § 1, has not obtained satisfaction to their requests from the pastor, they should inform the diocesan bishop. The bishop is strongly requested to satisfy their wishes. If he does not want to arrange[24] for such celebration to take place, the matter should be referred to the Pontifical Commission Ecclesia Dei.

Art. 8. A bishop who, desirous of satisfying such requests, but who for various reasons is unable to do so, may refer the problem to the Commission Ecclesia Dei to obtain counsel and assistance.

Art. 9. § 1 The pastor, having attentively examined all aspects, may also grant permission to use the earlier ritual for the administration of the sacraments of Baptism, Marriage, Penance, and the Anointing of the Sick, if the good of souls would seem to require it.

§ 2 Ordinaries are given the right to celebrate the sacrament of Confirmation using the earlier Roman Pontifical, if the good of souls would seem to require it.

'No mention is made of sacramentals, but this is possibly because the 1614 *Rituale Romanum* was never imposed as mandatory, and the lesser is seen as included in the greater concession and the former ritual may be used for baptisms, weddings, funerals, and so on.'[25]

---

23.   Weishaupt, *Päpstliche Weichenstellungen*, 84–86.

24.   *Si ille ad huiusmodi celebrationem providere* non vult… (my emphasis).

25.   Read, '*Motu Proprio Summorum Pontificum*'.

§ 3 Clerics ordained *in sacris constitutis* may use the Roman Breviary promulgated by Bl. John XXIII in 1962.

Clerici. This means that all clerics, without distinction, can use the *Breviarium Romanum* of 1962 (*Ubi lex non distinguit, nos non distinguere debemus*): bishops, priests and deacons, including clerics of consecrated life ('religious') when following their institute's directives concerning the praying of the *Breviarium Romanum* in choir, otherwise when they recite (that is, fulfil) it outside choir. Strictly speaking the canonical obligation of clerics to fulfil the daily recitation of the entire *Breviarium Romanum* concerns clerics who belong to institutes of consecrated life or societies of apostolic life—for example, the Priestly Fraternity of St Peter—whose constitutions or statutes indicate that the *Breviarium Romanum* is the breviary to be used. For other clerics, who choose to use this breviary instead of the *Liturgia Horarum*, promulgated after the Second Vatican Council, they are only obliged to recite Matins, Lauds, one little hour, Vespers and Compline. There is nothing to prevent clerics who wish to celebrate this breviary communally.[26]

> Art. 10. The ordinary of a particular place, if he feels it appropriate, may erect a personal parish in accordance with can. 518 for celebrations following the ancient form of the Roman Rite,[27] or appoint a chaplain, while observing all the norms of law.

CIC 1983, c. 518 refers to the canonical establishment of a parish for those of a particular rite, language and nationality: but these categories are not exhaustive. Those who prefer the *usus antiquior* can also be grouped together.[28]

---

26. Weishaupt, *Päpstliche Weichenstellungen*, 99–109; Read, '*Motu Proprio Summorum Pontificum*'; Note that permanent deacons are obliged to recite that part of the office determined by the episcopal conference: *Ibid.* and *CIC*, c. 276, §2, 3º.

27. *iuxta formam antiquiorum ritus Romani.*

28. Weishaupt, *Päpstliche Weichenstellungen*, 110–12.

Art. 11. The Pontifical Commission Ecclesia Dei, erected by John Paul II in 1988, continues to exercise its function. Said Commission will have the form, duties and norms that the Roman Pontiff wishes to assign it.

Art. 12. This Commission, apart from the powers it enjoys, will exercise the authority of the Holy See, supervising the observance and application of these dispositions.

For articles 11 and 12, concerning the Pontifical Commission Ecclesia Dei, one should now refer to Pope Benedict XVI's apostolic letter, *Motu Proprio Ecclesiae Unitatem* (2 July 2009).[29] The commission Ecclesia Dei is now joined with the Congregation for the Doctrine of the Faith and will collaborate with the Congregation in efforts to bring about full communion between the Priestly Fraternity of St Pius X and the Catholic Church. It also deals with future queries concerning the motu proprio, and other liturgical issues. The prefect of the Congregation is the president of the commission Ecclesia Dei.[30] Certain legislation which is contrary to *Summorum Pontificum* is now abrogated (repealed), which includes the restrictions upon the celebration of the *usus antiquior* in *Ecclesia Dei adflicta* (1988).[31]

The pope has allowed the freedom of every priest in the Latin Rite to offer the Mass according to the 1962 missal privately, but also publicly for the pastoral needs of the

---

29. Pope Benedict XVI, *Apostolic Letter, Motu Proprio Ecclesiae Unitatem*, 2 July 2009, concerning the Pontifical Commission Ecclesia Dei.

30. Weishaupt, *Päpstliche Weichenstellungen*, 116–18. An article on the restructuring of the Pontifical Commission Ecclesia Dei by Mgr Gordon Read in the *Newsletter of the Canon Law Society of Great Britain and Ireland* is forthcoming. I would like to thank Mgr Read for allowing me to read an advanced copy of this.

31. *Quaecumque vero a Nobis hisce Litteris Apostolicis Motu Proprio* [i.e. *Summorum Pontificum*] *datis decreta sunt, ea omnia firma ac rata esse et a die decima quarta Septembris huius anni, in festo Exaltationis Sanctae Crucis, servari iubemus, contrariis quibuslibet rebus non obstantibus*: Pope Benedict XVI, *Summorum Pontificum*; Weishaupt, *Päpstliche Weichenstellungen*, 120–23.

faithful, who may freely attend these masses. The setting up of parishes to celebrate the *usus antiquior* by the bishops, is another way to facilitate this. But—and this is also significant—parish priests, rather than the bishops, are the first point of contact for those laity whom wish to avail themselves of this form of the Roman liturgy, which should be harmonized with existing parish liturgies. The bishops retain their authority concerning the liturgy in their dioceses. They can intervene if problems arise for parish priests 'in full harmony, however, with all that has been laid down by the new norms of the motu proprio'.[32] The bishops may issue 'annotations and instructions for the implementation' of *Summorum Pontificum*, but they may not add 'new mandatory content'. 'Applications' for the traditional liturgy are 'not petitions of grace or favour ... Parish priests as well as diocesan bishops are legally held to meet this request'.[33] The stigma that often accompanied people who attended these masses in the past, with the creation of a 'ghetto mentality' is effectively removed with the normalization and regularization of the *usus antiquior* as a form of the Roman Rite. Funerals, pilgrimages and the celebration of the sacraments in the older forms are also provided for, and the possibility of clerics ordained *in sacris constitutis* to use the *Breviarium Romanum* of 1962. Undoubtedly other issues of the interpretation of the motu proprio will arise, which can be dealt with by the competent office of the Holy See, most probably by the Pontifical Commission Ecclesia Dei.[34]

The pope explains, more fully, the reasons behind this fundamental change in the Roman Rite in his accompanying letter to *Summorum Pontificum*, addressed to the world's

---

32. Pope Benedict XVI, *Letter to the Bishops on the Occasion of the Publication of the Apostolic Letter "Motu Proprio Data"*, 7 July 2007, 26–7.

33. Lüdecke, 'Kanonistische Anmerkungen zum Motu Proprio *Summorum Pontificum'*, 25–7.

34. See n. 30 above.

bishops.[35] Though this document is not legislation, it helps to indicate the mind of the legislator—the pope—and is therefore very useful in interpreting *Summorum Pontificum*.[36] It became clear after the liturgical changes of the Second Vatican Council that there were 'a good number of people' who were still strongly attached to the previous liturgy, which was familiar to them since their childhood, especially 'where the Liturgical Movement had provided many people with a notable liturgical formation and a deep, personal familiarity' with these rites. Apart from the division brought about by Archbishop Lefebvre's movement, many people, while accepting Vatican II, and who were faithful to the pope and the bishops, also desired 'to recover the form of sacred liturgy that was dear to them'. Deformations in the celebration of the new liturgy were also 'hard to bear', a painful period which the pope also bore witness to. Significantly, the pope also recognized that, as well as people from an older generation, 'it has clearly been demonstrated that young persons too have discovered this liturgical form, felt its attraction and found in it a form of encounter with the Mystery of the Most Holy Eucharist, particularly suited to them.' In addition to wanting to heal divisions and bring about 'interior reconciliation at the heart of the Church'—the 'positive' motivation for Pope Benedict's motu proprio, indeed a keynote for his entire pontificate—and to facilitate other pastoral needs, the pope commented that Pope John Paul II's *Ecclesia Dei adflicta* only appealed in a general way to the bishops to be generous in responding to the 'legitimate aspirations' of the faithful who wanted the older rites. It did not contain 'detailed prescriptions', and hence the pope wanted to free

35. For the following see Pope Benedict XVI, *Letter to the Bishops on the Occasion of the Publication of the Apostolic Letter "Motu Proprio Data"*, 7 July 2007, 20–7; Pope Benedict XVI, 'Interview of the Holy Father Benedict XVI during the Flight to France', 12 September 2008; Pope Benedict XVI, 'Meeting with French Episcopal Conference Address of His Holiness Benedict XVI', 14 September 2008.

36. Read, '*Motu Proprio Summorum Pontificum*'.

the bishops from constantly having to make case-by-case decisions, by giving more concrete juridical norms. Concerning opposition to the document, Pope Benedict says explicitly that 'there is the fear that the document detracts from the authority of the Second Vatican Council, [and that] one of whose essential decisions—the liturgical reform—is being called into question. This fear is unfounded.' The *Novus Ordo* remains the 'ordinary' form of the Roman Rite.

Of great importance is the fact that Pope Benedict goes even further than normalising the *usus antiquior*: he wants both usages of the Roman Rite to enrich each other. *Summorum Pontificum*, then, clearly affects the entire Church and not just particular individuals. The *usus antiquior*, then, is clearly not 'extraordinary' in the sense that it only concerns just a small group or ought to be rarely celebrated. It is for the *whole* Church. *Extraordinarius* is not to be interpreted in the same way as, for example, in the case of 'extraordinary ministers of the Holy Eucharist', who aid with the distribution of Holy Communion when it is absolutely necessary, in certain defined circumstances. This would be to narrow the interpretation of *Summorum Pontificum* and to contradict the clear intention of the legislator.[37] This enrichment of the liturgical life of the Church—the celebration of the *usus antiquior* with the ordinary form—can be seen to be part of Pope Benedict XVI's solution for the problems encountered with the *Novus Ordo* and the implementation of the liturgical reforms after the Second Vatican Council. The mutual enrichment of both forms of the Roman Rite may include the alteration of liturgical texts in the future by the Apostolic See. However, on a practical level—as far as those who celebrate the ordinary form are concerned—one must obviously work within current rubrics of the new missal, as well as availing oneself of frequent celebrations of the *usus antiquior*. This includes the following: legitimate rubrical interpretation; the implementation of the aspirations, and theology expressed in *Sacramentum Caritatis*;

---

37. For further discussion of *extraordinarius*, see Weishaupt, *Päpstliche Weichenstellungen*, 42–45.

using the newer translations of the vernacular version of the missal, when these are promulgated; more use of the ancient Roman Canon; *ad orientem* celebrations; the use of Latin and Gregorian chant; and following the standards set by recent papal liturgies, to give only a few examples. Recourse to the *usus antiquior* concerning the interpretation of rubrics in the ordinary form which are unclear, or where rubrics are absent, is also quite legitimate. Elements in the new missal which also demonstrate 'liturgical continuity' with the older liturgy, should also be given due emphasis, and also lawful customs within the liturgical tradition of the Church, while avoiding the kind of 'creativity' that characterizes a good number of 'contemporary' liturgies. These elements are part of, and not to be separated from the *usus antiquior*, as a tree can only grow, and flourish, when firmly joined to its roots.[38] Once more we see that older liturgical usages, now regularized in conjunction with newer forms, are to play an important role in Pope Benedict's overall vision for the Roman liturgy, effectively working towards a 'reform of the reform', and a greater emphasis of, as Aidan Nichols puts it—in relation to Joseph Ratzinger's views on the older liturgy—'a liturgical life able to express the precious truths the older liturgy housed'.[39] This truly is 'a challenging reform'[40] for those who are exclusively attached to either the 1962 or to the 1970 (2002) missal. The pope indicates that more recently canonized saints and newer prefaces—aside from the possibility of vernacular readings and recent changes to the prayers for the Jews on Good Friday—'can and should be inserted in the old

---

38. McNamara (professor of liturgy at the Regina Apostolorum University), 'Both Hands at Elevation of the Host'; cf. Elliott, *Ceremonies of the Liturgical Year*; idem, *Ceremonies of the Modern Roman Rite*. Interesting examples where older rubrics are used to interpret the ordinary form of the Roman Rite may be found in *Caeremoniale Episcoporum*, nos 90–91, n. 72–75; nos 106–8, n. 79–81.

39. Nichols, *The Thought of Pope Benedict XVI*, 234.

40. I borrowed this phrase from the title of Archbishop Piero Marini's book, *A Challenging Reform*.

missal'.[41] Those attached to the older forms are also asked to accept the 'holiness' of the new missal and are not to discount its celebration. It is to be hoped that these moves will help lead towards a greater 'peace' and reconciliation in the Church, and a *pax liturgica*, after a long period of liturgical problems in the Church. The influence of the 'new' over the 'old', in the long run, can also have a positive effect, not in only recognising that important insights have been gained in the last forty years—that could have been more prudently implemented—but that the notion of *participatio actuosa*, for example, and other doctrinal aspects of *Sacrosanctum Concilium*, and statements of Pope Benedict XVI's Magisterium, are equally applicable to the *usus antiquior*, and, as we shall see, have roots that go deeper than the Second Vatican Council.[42] Indeed Pope Benedict himself noted—when he was prefect of the Congregation for the Doctrine of the Faith—that 'it is important to observe the essential criteria of the Constitution on the Liturgy [*Sacrosanctum Concilium*] also when one celebrates according to the old missal'.[43]

This brings us to the question of the pope's specific views on what we now call the *usus antiquior* before his pontificate. The-then Cardinal Ratzinger, who was very much involved with this issue—and the situation with the Society of St Pius X—as Prefect for the Congregation for the Doctrine of the Faith, had always a certain fondness for the 'Tridentine liturgy', and while he did not favour its exclusive use—and was critical of proponents of this view—he occasionally celebrated it for specific occasions after 1988. Although Joseph Ratzinger can argue—and rightly so—that his liturgical principles have remained constant, they have certainly developed and been 'enriched' over time,

---

41. Pope Benedict XVI, *Letter to the Bishops on the Occasion of the Publication of the Apostolic Letter "Motu Proprio Data"*, 7 July 2007, 24: cf. n. 60 below.

42. See n. 59 below.

43. Ratzinger, 'Ten Years of the Motu Proprio *Ecclesia Dei*' (24 October 1998).

but more especially his views on 'liturgical practices'. His views on the 'Tridentine' Mass have also evolved, in that he became more in favour of its continued celebration and value in the church.[44] In *The Feast of Faith* (1981), Cardinal Ratzinger voiced his concerns concerning the continuity between the more recent *Missale Romanum* with previous editions, and that this ought to be made more visible. The older liturgy should be permitted for those that wanted it for a period of time. What was good in the older liturgy could be used in the newer liturgy.[45] He also connected here the idea of the organic development of the liturgy, his desire for a 'reform of the reform' of the new liturgical rites, and continuity in the Church. In 2001, twenty years later, he expressed the view that 'I was from the beginning in favour of the freedom to continue using the old missal for a very simple reason: people were already beginning to talk about making a break with the preconciliar... and obsolete type of Church, and a new and conciliar type of Church ... It seems to me essential, the basic step, to recognize that both missals [that is, the *Missale Romanum* of 1962 and 1970] are missals of the Church, and belong to the Church which remains the same as ever ... And in order to emphasize that there is no essential break, that there is continuity in the Church ... it seems to me indispensable to continue to offer the opportunity to celebrate according to the old missal, as a sign of the enduring identity of the Church'. The older rites could also serve the whole Church as a 'corrective' to current liturgical practice.[46] These rites ought to be linked to the newer forms, as growth on a venerable old tree, but one which retains the appearances of youth. There was therefore no contradiction between Joseph Ratzinger's

---

44. See Rowlands, *Ratzinger's Faith*, 12, 123–45, and Ratzinger, *Milestones: Memoirs 1927–1977*, 122–24, 146–49 which also mentions some of his earlier criticisms of 'Baroque tendencies' in the liturgy, and their context: cf. *TSL*, 146.

45. Ratzinger, *The Feast of Faith*, 74 n. 9, 85–87.

46. Ratzinger, 'Assessment and Future Prospects', 148–49; idem, 'Ten Years of the Motu Proprio *Ecclesia Dei*' (24 October 1998).

calls for 'the reform of the reform', organic development, and his support for the older liturgies. Here we can, and should, cite a passage from Joseph Ratzinger's autobiography (to 1977), which, again, summarises, and gives a coherent synthesis of his views on the new missal, its positive elements and deficiencies and the notion of organic development, within the broader, historical context of the liturgy. This also includes his suggestion of the 'impression' of rupture ('breach') given by the presentation of the new missal and the prohibition of the previous missal (1962), noting—significantly—that Pope St Pius V, in promulgating his *Missale Romanum* for the Latin Church did not abolish previous missals that had been in existence for two hundred years :

> In this case [that is, the Missal of Pope St Pius V] we cannot speak of the prohibition of a previous missal that had formerly been approved as valid. The prohibition of the missal [of Pope St Pius V after Vatican II]... a missal that had known continuous growth over the centuries... introduced a breach into the history of the liturgy whose consequences could only be tragic. It was reasonable and right of the council [of Vatican II] to order a revision of the missal... But more than this now happened: the old building was demolished, and another was built, to be sure largely using materials from the previous one and even using the old building plans. There is no doubt that this new missal in many respects brought with it a real improvement and enrichment; but setting it as a new construction over against what had grown historically, forbidding the results of this historical growth, thereby makes the liturgy appear to be no longer a living development but the product of erudite work and juridical authority; this has caused us enormous harm... A renewal of liturgical awareness, a liturgical reconciliation that again recognizes the unity of the history of the liturgy and that understands Vatican II not as a breach, but as

a stage of development: these things are urgently needed for the life of the Church.'[47]

We can see here that many of the ideas expressed by Cardinal Ratzinger in relation to what we now know as the *usus antiquior*, have been implemented by him as pope, including the idea of 'one Roman Rite with two forms' and 'liturgical reconciliation'. This, together with other stipulations in the motu proprio, and aspects of Pope Benedict's explanatory letter, also bear some relation to suggestions previously proposed by other scholars and liturgists.[48]

Some reactions to Summorum Pontificum

It is, of course, impossible to discuss here absolutely everything that has been said about *Summorum Pontificum*. But, to conclude this section, I want to make a few comments on several views—some of which differ considerably—expressed by four authors: Bishop Marc Aillet, Laurence Paul Hemming (with László Dobszay), and John F. Baldovic—as I think that this can help us come to a better understanding of certain aspects of *Summorum Pontificum*. In 2010 there appeared an English translation of a very interesting and useful analysis of *Summorum Pontificum* by Bishop Marc Aillet of Bayonne, which can be read with great profit.[49] Aillet now celebrates the 'old' and the 'new' Mass, and has praiseworthy comments concerning the old. His efforts to implement *Summorum Pontificum* are to be highly commended. But we should be aware, however—without undermining the very positive aspects, and suggestions made in this book—that Aillet's examination of the motu proprio is really not so much a detailed analy-

---

47. Ratzinger, *Milestones: Memoirs 1927–1977*, 147–48.

48. Ratzinger, 'Assessment and Future Prospects', 148–50; idem, 'Ten Years of the Motu Proprio *Ecclesia Dei*' (24 October 1998); Gamber, *The Reform of the Roman Liturgy*, 91–95, 113–14; Dobszay, *The Bugnini Liturgy and the Reform of the Reform*, 176–79; Kocik, *The Reform of the Reform*, 92; Nichols, 'Salutary Dissatisfaction', 203–4; Folsom, 'Roman Rite or Roman Rites?', 58–81.

49. Aillet, *The Old Mass and the New*.

sis of this document, nor the *usus antiquior*. Aillet focuses
on the improved celebration of the Roman Missal promulgated after Vatican II. He explains that the intention of
his book 'is not to praise the earlier missal, but rather to
attribute full value to the principles of liturgical reform
and to highlight the theological and spiritual treasures
of the new missal'.[50] The latter is praiseworthy, including
his analysis of *Sacramentum Caritatis*. The improvement of
the celebration of the newer liturgy is certainly one of the
important intentions of *Summorum Pontificum*. However
Aillet's emphasis on this aspect tends to give a one-sided
interpretation of the motu proprio, where both uses of the
Roman Rite, which are of equal value, form the one Roman
Rite. Bishop Aillet also suggests that, 'the aim of the motu
proprio is not to advocate either a general return to the old
missal or the use of the two missals indiscriminately in the
ordinary life of our ecclesial communities. In *essence, then,
this motu proprio makes no change in the present situation*'[51] —
and that — 'The motu proprio *Summorum Pontificum*... does
not aim to *reestablish* the old missal — which has in any case
never been abrogated and ought never to have been forbidden. But it is trying to invite pastors and faithful to take
another look at the way they celebrate the liturgy according to the ordinary [newer] form of the Roman Rite: this is
what is really at stake'.[52] One would agree that the pope has
not imposed the older missal universally above the newer
missal, and that it was never abrogated, as well as advocating a re-think about how the ordinary form is celebrated.
But to say that nothing has (really) changed regarding the
older form of Mass — especially as its legal status was curtailed, and even disputed — after *Summorum Pontificum*, is
not the case. The pope has certainly said — as Bishop Aillet
pointed out — that 'the new missal will certainly remain the
ordinary form of the Roman Rite, not only on account of

---

50.   Aillet, *The Old Mass and the New*, 13.

51.   *Ibid.*, 19–20 (my emphasis).

52.   Aillet, *The Old Mass and the New*, 91 (Aillet's emphasis).

the juridical norms, but also because of the actual situation of the communities of the faithful'.[53] But this does not mean that the pope is necessarily satisfied with the lack of 'a certain degree of liturgical formation and some knowledge of the Latin language' in parish communities, which, he indicates, is a presupposition for use of the older missal. The point is, as we have seen,[54] that Pope Benedict XVI—at this present stage in the history of the Church—not only wants the older *usus antiquior* to influence the newer liturgy, in greater fidelity to the Second Vatican Council, but also, in a reconciliatory act, wishes to preserve and develop the older liturgy in its own right, while safeguarding the newer missal and the positive aspects of the recent liturgical reforms. *Summorum Pontificum*, which affects the entire Church, reconciles, in a more tangible manner than previously, the recent liturgy to the more ancient liturgy, emphasising 'continuity' between them both. While there is no 'rupture' but 'progress' in liturgical history, the pope is certainly aware that (dis)ruptures occurred after the recent liturgical reforms, which need to be repaired. My examination of *Summorum Pontificum* has made these things abundantly clear. A passage from Pope Benedict's explanatory letter to the bishops also underlines this:

> Let us generously open our hearts and make room for everything that the faith itself allows. There is no contradiction between the two editions of the Roman Missal. In the history of the liturgy there is growth and progress, but no rupture. What earlier generations held as sacred, remains sacred and great for us too, and it cannot be all of a sudden entirely forbidden or even considered harmful. It behoves all of us to preserve the riches which have

---

53. *Ibid.*, 20, citing Pope Benedict XVI, *Letter to the Bishops on the Occasion of the Publication of the Apostolic Letter "Motu Proprio Data"*, 7 July 2007, 24.

54. See pp. 153–57.

developed in the Church's faith and prayer, and to give them their proper place.[55]

Perhaps more controversial is Aillet's citation of the comparison made of both the 'Pauline' and the 'Pian' missals by Dom François Cassingena-Trévedy, placed in the context of the mutual enrichment of both missals.[56] Dom François, as related by Bishop Aillet, indicated that 'if the Tridentine liturgy is related on the whole to an Antiochene and Dionysian tradition that lends it an essentially "transcendent and hierarchical" tone, one "of mysteries", the liturgy as restored under Paul VI moved more toward the pole of a "social, ministerial" ecclesiology, "that of community", of an Augustinian type'. Both these 'genealogical lines' are 'equally traditional', and both worthy of consideration, two ethoses of celebration, 'one belonging to the sphere of *absolute liturgy*, and the other to that of liturgy *related to the world*'. That being so, then both ethoses ought to become acquainted with each other and to enrich each other with their specific character. According to Aillet, 'Benedict XVI seems to appropriate this interesting suggestion'.[57] I would suggest that great caution be exercised when proposing, let alone entirely accepting, such a theological comparison of both missals. Pope Benedict XVI certainly called for the mutual enrichment of both missals, and Aillet's analysis of Cassingena-Trévedy's comparison, has a certain appeal, on the surface. However it has to be questioned whether Pope Benedict really had in mind the 'social, ministerial' ecclesiology, 'that of community', of an Augustinian type and liturgy 'related to the world'. He had expressed views—particularly in his theological writings—on the failures present in the implementation and formulation of the *Novus Ordo*, and what we might call an excessive

---

55. Pope Benedict XVI, *Letter to the Bishops on the Occasion of the Publication of the Apostolic Letter "Motu Proprio Data"*, 7 July 2007, 25–26.

56. Cassingena-Trévedy, *Te Igitur*, 73–82, cited in Aillet, *The Old Mass and the New*, 48–50.

57. *Ibid.*

'communal self-centredness' in the liturgy, to the detriment of a liturgy focused *ad Deum*.[58] One might also call into question the narrowness of defining the newer liturgy in apparently horizontal terms, in Aillet's presentation of Cassingena-Trévedy's views, and if such a vision is purely Augustinian: though it has to be admitted that an excessive interaction between priest and congregation is a problem which frequently occurs with the newer liturgy, especially *versus populum* celebrations. However that the liturgy has a 'communal' aspect—properly understood, and in context—where everybody has a specific role, according to their state of life and ministry, is undeniable. *Participatio actuosa* of worshippers is also an essential component of the liturgy. The Holy Eucharist 'builds up' the Body of Christ, the Church, and facilitates, and strengthens, *communio* between the members of that one body, transforming them into Christ. As I indicated above, *participatio actuosa* is *also* apparent in the *usus antiquor*, thanks to the positive influences of the Liturgical Movement before the council and documents of the Magisterium. Perhaps this needs to be encouraged with greater vigour in the celebration of the *usus antiquior*.[59] Nevertheless Aillet's particular suggestion for the mutual enrichment of both missals is, however, certainly worthy of further reflection by theologians and liturgists. They should study both missals of the Roman Rite in the context of the writings of the Church

---

58. See especially my analysis of Gy's critique of Joseph Ratzinger in chapter two of the present book and chapter one *passim*. One would also question if the ecclesiology in both missals is fundamentally different, while not denying that advances have certainly been made in the area of ecclesiology both before and after the Second Vatican Council, which are also present in the conciliar documents.

59. See Ratzinger, *On the Way to Jesus Christ*, 107–28; Ratzinger, *Pilgrim Fellowship of Faith*, 60–122; Pope Benedict XVI, *Letter to the Bishops on the Occasion of the Publication of the Apostolic Letter "Motu Proprio Data"*, 7 July 2007, 21–2; Pope Pius XII, *Encyclical Letter Mediator Dei*, 20 November 1947; Sacred Congregation of Rites, *Instruction De Sacra Musica et Sacra Liturgica*, 3 September 1958; cf. Dobszay, *The Restoration and Organic Development of the Roman Rite*, 54–55.

Fathers, notable theologians, spiritual writers and saints concerning the liturgy, and above all the Magisterium of the Church, before proposing just *how* one goes about the enrichment of both missals, beyond, for example, the addition of saints in the calendar and increasing the prefaces in the *usus antiquior.*[60]

Another good example of a possible enrichment of the *usus antiquior* is the readings. It might be advocated that the new lectionary be allowed *ad libitum* for masses in the *usus antiquior.* Indeed it had been a permitted option—perhaps relatively little used—in the period between *Ecclesia Dei* and *Summorum Pontificum.*[61] This idea—which amounts to the wider use of sacred scripture in the *usus antiquior*—should not be dismissed as a future possibility, despite criticisms of the new lectionary, for instance by Klaus Gamber (d. 1989), a liturgist whom the pope greatly admired as a 'Father' of a new Liturgical Movement.[62] However the value, as well as the antiquity of the current arrangement of readings and texts from sacred scripture—let alone their correlation with the *Breviarium Romanum*—in the *usus antiquior* should, at

---

60. Permission for this, among other things, *had* previously been given by the Pontifical Commission Ecclesia Dei, but little used. Some of these permissions—including the use of the prefaces in the Pauline *Missale Romanum*—have recently been overturned: see Anon., 'More Decisions of the Ecclesia Dei Commission'; Kollmorgen, 'Important Clarifications from Ecclesia Dei'. Pope Benedict's comments on increasing the feast days and prefaces in his letter to the bishops, indicate, however, that this will be done at a later stage, perhaps in the near future; 'The Ecclesia Dei Commission, in contact with various bodies devoted to the *usus antiquior*, will study the practical possibilities in this regard': Pope Benedict XVI, *Letter to the Bishops on the Occasion of the Publication of the Apostolic Letter "Motu Proprio Data"*, 7 July 2007, 24.

61. Mayer, 'Concerning the Apostolic Letter *Ecclesia Dei*': but see the previous footnote.

62. The Second Vatican Council, *The Constitution on the Sacred Liturgy Sacrosanctum Concilium*, 4 December 1963, no. 51. For an assessment of the life and work of Klaus Gamber, see Hauke, 'Klaus Gamber: Father of the "New Liturgical Movement"', 24–69.

the same time, also be acknowledged. Bishop Aillet makes some pertinent comments on this subject:

> Doubtless the old missal opened the treasures of the Bible less generously [than the new liturgy], but the repetition of the Sunday texts during the week did perhaps allow the faithful to assimilate the word more completely, and, above all, the songs of the Mass—introit, gradual ... [and so on] always [*sic*] drawn from scripture ... constituted a commentary of scripture by scripture. There was a whole liturgical catechism there, the impact of which should not be underestimated and which has been preserved in the *Graduale Romanum*, which Pope Pius X had restored precisely in order to facilitate a better participation of the faithful.[63]

Laurence Paul Hemming wrote a fascinating and scholarly book called *Worship as a Revelation*, where he gives much food for thought about the theological and philosophical background of the liturgy, and the liturgy 'past, present, and future'.[64] To a certain extent he is indebted for the development of his view on the liturgy—and in pinpointing where things went wrong in the past—to László Dobszay, a Hungarian scholar whose liturgical studies, especially those concerning Church music and texts, the future direction of the liturgy, and organic development, are becoming better known.[65] Hemming has also dwelt upon *Summorum Pontificum*, and has the following to say:

> What the motu proprio *Summorum Pontificum* of 2007 does is make possible in the ordinary life of the Church that the 'rupture' proposed by adherents of the 'spirit of the council' can only be healed through the Church's sacred activity of prayer and administration of the sacraments. What Benedict announces [in his accompanying letter to *Summo*-

---

63. Aillet, *The Old Mass and the New*, 58–59.

64. Hemming, *Worship as a Revelation*.

65. Dobszay, *The Bugnini-Liturgy and the Reform of the Reform*; idem, *The Restoration and Organic Development of the Roman Rite*.

> *rum Pontificum*] as a 'fact' – that there is no rupture
> between the two forms of the rite will then become
> an actual truth, one which will have effects in every
> aspect of the Church's life.[66]

What Hemming says contains more than a grain of truth, in that ruptures from the Church's liturgical tradition have been, and are still clearly evident in the Church. However one must point to the 'reality' that both uses of the Roman Rite have been 'liturgically reconciled' by the Holy See— some might argue that the continuity of the old and new rites have merely been 'underlined'—and in a striking manner in *Summorum Pontificum*. A period of growth and consolidation is certainly necessary to repair 'ruptures' from the liturgical tradition in the Church by the 'application' of the reconciliatory measures of Pope Benedict, which includes the gradual re-development of the *Novus Ordo*. We should add that the Church's faith has not been altered by the Second Vatican Council. Thus, in the pope's words, the 'two expressions [the extraordinary and ordinary forms of the Roman Rite] of the Church's *lex orandi* [law of prayer] will in no way lead to a division in the Church's *lex credendi* [law of belief].'[67] We should also recall here the connection between the *lex orandi* and the *lex credendi* with the celebration of the Holy Eucharist, as emphasized in *Sacramentum Caritatis*.[68] However Hemming's preference for the *Missale Romanum* of 1884 and the *Breviarium Romanum* of 1623, instead of those from 1961/62—as mandated in *Summorum Pontificum*—and analysis of the liturgical reforms from Pope St Pius X to Blessed John XXIII, is certainly more contentious. For example, Hemming says that,

> The successive reforms of the breviary from 1911
> to 1970 *have left us with a liturgy of the hours that is
> barely recognizable* when compared to the breviaries
> of 1568 and 1623 (and even that of 1568 had been

---

66. Hemming, *Worship as a Revelation*, 153.
67. Pope Benedict XVI, *Summorum Pontificum*, art. 1.
68. Pope Benedict XVI, *Sacramentum Caritatis*, no. 34.

simplified and truncated by Paul IV, both as pope
and as Cardinal Carafa) and St Pius V. [69]

One might certainly agree with his analysis when comparing the breviaries of 1961 (or earlier) and 1970—where a
huge difference is noticeable between both of them[70]—and
that certain changes made from the pontificate of Pope
St Pius X to that of Blessed John XXIII were regrettable:
and that some were even contrary to what we may call
'received liturgical tradition' and its proper development.
One could cite, for instance, the excision of the daily recital
of psalms 148 to 150 at Lauds, which was a very ancient
practice.[71] Nevertheless it is evident that the liturgical
books promulgated under Blessed John XXIII remain in

---

69.   Hemming, *Worship as a Revelation*, 159 (my emphasis).

70.   I would also add here that one should recognize that the 'Liturgy
      of the Hours'/'The Divine Office' (*Liturgia Horarum*), most cer-
      tainly, has excellent aspects: for example, the extended readings
      from the writings of the Fathers, doctors and saints of the Church
      in the Office of Readings.

71.   Space does not permit an extensive discussion here on the ques-
      tion of the re-arrangement of the psalter by Pope St Pius X in 1911,
      which Hemming regards as the most important 'disturbance and
      loss' of the breviary: Hemming, *Worship as a Revelation*, 159. I
      would argue that—from a general perspective—the redistribution
      of the psalms or 'spreading out' of the traditional psalter by St Pius
      X, was a positive development, breathing new life into the psalter,
      and that its arrangement had a great respect for the cultus of the
      saints and the liturgical seasons of the Church. It brought about
      the weekly recitation of the psalter, which, hitherto, was a rarity,
      and was overshadowed by the sanctoral. I do think that St Pius X
      was correct not to burden the clergy with an even lengthier hybrid
      office on saints days, for instance mixing the offices of the saints
      with the existing—venerable but mainly dormant—psalms from
      the pre-Pius X psalter for Matins. While Hemming also makes
      many valuable points and criticisms about the reform of St Pius X,
      as does Alcuin Reid, I am inclined to agree mainly with the latter's
      assessment of this. While Reid says that 'the abolition of ancient
      elements of the received tradition was to the detriment of the
      Roman breviary', he also points out that, 'this break with tradition
      was not so great as to be complete: the structure of the breviary
      remained the same, the texts of the offices themselves were not
      completely recast, and the redistribution of the psalter followed

'organic continuity' with the breviary of St Pius V, and its ancient roots, and are *substantially* an organic development of the latter. This has been clearly recognized by Pope Benedict XVI in *Summorum Pontificum*:

> Many ... Roman pontiffs, in the course of the centuries, showed particular solicitude in ensuring that the sacred liturgy accomplished this task [that is, to bear fruit in the spiritual lives of the faithful] more effectively. Outstanding among them is St Pius V ... 'It was towards this same goal that succeeding Roman pontiffs directed their energies during the subsequent centuries in order to ensure that the rites and liturgical books were brought up to date and when necessary clarified. From the beginning of this century [that is, the twentieth century], they undertook a more general reform.' Thus our predecessors Clement VIII, Urban VIII, St Pius X, Benedict XV, Pius XII and Blessed John XXIII all played a part.[72]

Alcuin Reid, on the reform of the rubrics under Blessed John XXIII, says, 'All in all, it was a pastoral reform in line with those of preceding years that respected objective liturgical tradition'.[73] Indeed it is noteworthy that in Dobszay's recent book, *The Restoration and Organic Development of the Roman Liturgy*—edited and introduced by Hemming—that the liturgical books of 1962 are used there as a starting point

---

traditional and not purely Gallican lines': Reid, *The Organic Development of the Liturgy*, 67.

72. Pope Benedict XVI, *Summorum Pontificum*, 11–13: Pope Benedict XVI cites Pope John Paul II, *Apostolic Letter Vicesimus quintus annus*, 4 December 1988, no. 3.

73. Reid, *The Organic Development of the Liturgy*, 275. I should add here that I am in agreement with the general principle Reid states concerning 'contemporary pastoral needs': 'Such needs can certainly be a valid component of organic development. If pastoral considerations were excluded, the living organism that is the liturgy would be reduced to an archaism rambling throughout history. However, were pastoral needs to be a sole or overriding principle of reform, the objective traditional organism that is the liturgy would be subjected to the mercy of each passing age': *Ibid.*, 67.

for his proposed future organic development of the Roman Rite, which seeks fidelity to liturgical tradition and the Second Vatican Council. Anything of value that was lost in the passage of time, or misunderstood, perhaps ought to be re-evaluated.[74] While one may not agree entirely with Professor Dobszay's view of liturgical developments before and after the Second Vatican Council—though, happily, his views converge with mine (quite independently) on quite a few issues—his writings, especially *The Restoration and Organic Development of the Roman Liturgy*, merit careful study by those seriously interested in the possible future development of the liturgy.

John L. Baldovin in *Reforming the Liturgy*, has a number of problems with *Summorum Pontificum*. They are a good illustration that its aims, and intended effects upon the liturgy, have not yet been fully grasped by a number of liturgists. He comments, for example, that the motu proprio does not specifically indicate that ordinations can be performed according to the old Roman pontifical, and that 'their omission seems significant'.[75] However he overlooks the fact that ordinations according to the 'pre-Vatican II form', have been performed since the new rites were promulgated, by the Society of St Pius X, and subsequently by those 'traditionalist' orders/societies in peace and communion with the Holy See: the orders of the latter are lawfully conferred, as well as valid. However the actual reason as to *why* Baldovin believes that ordination was omitted, may be found in his comments on the sacrament of Confirmation. It was, according to Baldovin, 'mainly for historical and ecumenical reasons [that] Paul VI made a somewhat radical decision to change the traditional form of the sacrament ... The difference between the forms by which this sacrament is administered *is difficult to reconcile with the assertion of Benedict XVI that we now have one Roman Rite with "two uses"'*. He also believes that 'considering the

---

74. Dobszay, *The Restoration and Organic Development of the Roman Rite*, 263.

75. Baldovin, *Reforming the Liturgy*, 130.

pre- and post-Vatican II Roman liturgies as "uses" certainly stretches the meaning of the term'.[76] Whether one agrees or not with 'historical and ecumenical' reasons as justification to change the form of Confirmation, this sacrament has *also* been celebrated in the old form between the liturgical changes and *Summorum Pontificum*. A problem before *Summorum Pontificum* was written—which was surely reflected upon—was, 'can one have two 'Roman Rites' existing side-by-side?'. The answer is surely 'no'—but certainly two versions or 'uses' of the rite, or variant formulas within one rite, most certainly can exist: this is obvious from the history of the Roman Rite. It may, or may not be, unusual, but surely one could not have theological objections to two variant forms of the conferral of Confirmation co-existing within the same rite if these—sanctioned by the Church—essentially signify what is validly conferred? The pope, can, if he has the power to change the wording of the form of certain sacraments—with the caveats above—surely permit more than one form within a given rite, especially 'if the good of souls would seem to require it'?[77] And surely he can also sanction two uses of the same rite? In fact the bringing into existence of two uses in the one Roman Rite by Pope Benedict was a good solution.[78] We have already mentioned that Baldovin has problems with the decision of Pope Benedict XVI, in respect of the former liturgy having never been abrogated.[79]

Baldovin also believes that the pope should have made it clear that those who wish to adopt the missal of 1962 'should

---

76. *Ibid.*, 130–31 (my emphasis). The forms are, for the ordinary form: *N. accipe signaculum Doni Spiritus Sancti.* In the extraordinary form: *N. Signo te signo Cru+cis et confirmo te Chrismate salutis. In nomine Pa+tris, et Fi+lii, et Spiritus + Sancti.*

77. Pope Benedict used these words in *Summorum Pontificum*, concerning the use of the older texts: Pope Benedict XVI, *Summorum Pontificum*, art. 9 § 2.

78. See n. 48 above for antecedents to this idea. Clearly the legal position of other uses in the Roman Rite, such as the Premonstratensian use, also merits consideration.

79. See n. 10 above.

be clear about their allegiance to Church teaching, in this case Vatican II', despite the pope describing as 'unfounded' the fear that *Summorum Pontificum* detracts from Vatican II's authority and calls into question the liturgical reform.[80] Reconciliation is an important theme in Pope Benedict's papacy. However the purpose of the motu proprio is not only to assist with bringing about the *reconciliation* of those who are not in full communion with the Church and use the older rites, which has already borne some early fruit: one could cite, for example, the reconciliation of the 'Transalpine Redemptorists' in Scotland and New Zealand—now called 'The Sons of the Most Holy Redeemer'—and the beginning of formal discussion of points of disagreement between the Holy See and the Society of St Pius X in October 2009.[81] Pope Benedict reminds the bishops that 'Many people who clearly accepted the binding character of the Second Vatican Council, and were faithful to the pope and the bishops, nonetheless also desired to recover the form of the sacred liturgy that was dear to them', and that this liturgy has attracted many young people.[82] Furthermore, Baldovin, in saying that 'except for a tiny minority the future of Roman Catholic liturgy does not lie with the pre-Vatican II rites', once more demonstrates that he does not fully comprehend what has been happening—gradually—to the liturgy during Pope Benedict's pontificate, nor the purpose of *Summorum Pontificum*, which I have outlined in this book.[83] The 'hermeneutic of continuity', which Pope Benedict XVI has emphasized, does not appear to be an

---

80. Baldovin, *Reforming the Liturgy*, 132; Pope Benedict XVI, *Letter to the Bishops on the Occasion of the Publication of the Apostolic Letter "Motu Proprio Data"*, 20–1.

81. I should add here that Baldovin's accusation that the late Michael Davis, Alcuin Reid—both known to the author—and the monks of Fontgombault and Le Barroux are 'extreme traditionalists' is, quite simply, not the case: Baldovin, *Reforming the Liturgy*, 134.

82. Pope Benedict XVI, *Letter to the Bishops on the Occasion of the Publication of the Apostolic Letter "Motu Proprio Data"*, 22, 23.

83. Baldovin, *Reforming the Liturgy*, 133.

important part of Baldovin's book. Baldovin has also not come fully to terms with the valid criticisms of many scholars concerning the reform of the liturgy after the council, though he has certainly made a noble effort to understand them. There may well be further efforts by the Holy See to minimize any danger of perceiving the newer liturgical rites as a 'rupture' from the past, while again emphasising the development of the liturgy, in parallel and continuity with the living liturgical tradition of the Church, of which the *IGMR* speaks so eloquently.[84] In the last section of this book, I will make some further, final comments on the important changes in the Roman liturgy and Pope Benedict's Magisterium, including *Summorum Pontificum.*

---

84.   *IGMR*, nos 1–15.

Conclusion

The pontificate of Pope Benedict XVI can be said to be a momentous 'event' in the modern history of the Church, which is noteworthy after the lengthy, and historic papacy of the great Pope John Paul II. This is seen in a particular way in the considerable attention which Pope Benedict devotes to the liturgy. Indeed we are blessed with a pope who is profoundly conscious of the liturgy's importance in the life of the universal Church. In this present book, I have sought to uncover Pope Benedict XVI's liturgical theology, and, by doing so, provide the means to understanding what has thus far taken place in the Catholic liturgy in recent years. A significant part of it has therefore focused on the writings of Pope Benedict as a theologian. We have seen that his 'theology of the liturgy', especially *The Spirit of the Liturgy*, can lead to a deeper appreciation of what the liturgy actually *is*. Pope Benedict's writings, as with those of St Bonaventure, for instance, and the Church Fathers, are not only beneficial for theologians. The widespread distribution and translation of Pope Benedict's works testifies to their usefulness to the lives of all Christians who seek to fellow in the footsteps of the Lord Jesus Christ, true God and true man, within the community he founded, the *Ecclesia Catholica*, and beyond. In this respect they could, at least, also be described as a kind of 'mystagogia', a 'mystical theology' and 'food' for the spiritual life, as well as providing a 'logos' (an 'account') of the liturgy. Pope Benedict's liturgical writings are also a response to what we may describe as the widespread 'liturgical decadence' of the last forty years, with the hope that a 'new liturgical movement' would be born in the Church, which can revitalize the liturgy and point towards it true nature, with a renewed understanding of it.[1] We have also seen that the liturgical issues discussed by the-then Cardinal Joseph Ratzinger, are still relevant for ascertaining the true nature of the liturgy and its proper celebration, including the antiquity of *versus Deum/ad orientem* liturgies. This is illustrated very well in his dialogue with Pierre-Marie Gy, which reveals prevailing liturgical trends in many quarters, and how the discussion of the liturgy can bring to the forefront serious issues which are stake in this, including the real intentions of the Fathers of the Second Vatican Council, and the correct interpretation of the council. This is reflected, to a great extent, in the celebration of the liturgy and in how one defines the liturgy, and the Church, because the latter truly 'subsists as liturgy and in the liturgy'.[2] The Church has great need of the work of good, solid liturgists who not only have a command of the liturgical sources, but have a real 'feeling' and great respect for what the liturgy is, and the theology of the liturgy. Such *periti* are essential for the 'New Liturgical Movement'. Although Pope Benedict proposes—with his characteristic humility—that Klaus Gamber is indeed, 'Father' of this movement, such movements tend to have several 'Fathers'. Pope Benedict is surely one of them.[3]

The transcendence of the sacred liturgy, its 'otherness', its greatness, and sacredness, are themes in Pope Benedict's liturgical theology which have great relevance for us today in an increasingly secularized world, and are important elements which feature in his description of 'what the liturgy is'. Pope Benedict/Joseph Ratzinger, in *The Spirit of the Liturgy*, has unpacked these themes and given them a newer emphasis and demonstrated their perennial vitality. His theology of liturgy is one which sees authentic liturgy as growing organically, and is based on the best sources of Catholic theology, namely the sacred scriptures and patris-

---

1.   *TSL*, 8–9.
2.   Ratzinger, *God is Near Us*, 121.
3.   Hauke, 'Klaus Gamber: Father of the "New Liturgical Movement"', 24–69.

tics, in fidelity to the Magisterium. In this Pope Benedict is also indebted to the influence of a number of theologians and liturgists of the 'old' Liturgical Movement including, among others, Hans Urs von Balthasar, Henri de Lubac, Odo Casel, and Romano Guardini.[4] From this rich 'logos' of the liturgy in Pope Benedict's theology, and his Magisterium, I want to conclude this book by highlighting a few central points, as well as make some general comments and reflections.

For Pope Benedict, in his liturgical theology, man is privileged to share in the divine liturgy of heaven on earth because of the incarnation of the *Logos*, Jesus Christ. Man is created for worship (*homo adorans, homo liturgicus*).[5] Therefore our lives, as with the liturgy, are 'orientated' towards God. This was surely one of the aims of the old Liturgical Movement, namely, to immerse the lives of the faithful in the celebration of the liturgy, to deepen worship 'in spirit and in truth', and to make the liturgy a fundamental basis in their spiritual relationship with God. This has clearly practical consequences for our understanding and celebration of the liturgy, including the arrangement and decoration of churches, the orientation of altars, and the focus of worship during the liturgy, sacred music—the love song of the Church to its Creator *Per Christum Dominum nostrum*—and art work. It is noteworthy that Pope Benedict has a profound understanding of the Eastern theology of the icon and that this is something which we ought to rediscover and suitably apply in the Western Church. Indeed it could be said that Pope Benedict has assisted with laying the foundations for a renewed understanding of sacred images, a sort of 'westernized' theology of the icon. This theology, together with the renewed understanding of the Fathers, can greatly assist with the renewal of Western liturgical theology. Pope

---

4.   For example Nichols, *Redeeming Beauty*, 94; *TSL*, 7–8, 86; Ratzinger, *Pilgrim Fellowship of Faith*, 114–20.

5.   See George, '*Sacrosanctum Concilium* Anniversary Address: The Foundations of Liturgical Reform', 49–50.

Benedict's contribution in this regard, should not be under-estimated.[6]

Gesture, which has undoubtedly suffered at the hands of many so-called 'liturgical reformers', is also given due emphasis because of the 'incarnational' or christological understanding which Pope Benedict has of the liturgy: the Son of God, Our Lord Jesus Christ had a human body, offered in the supreme act of worship on the cross for our salvation. Therefore, the body, too, has a place in worship, particularly gestures such as the sign of the cross, and kneeling, which are conformed to our inner spiritual dispositions. The inner and outer aspects of worship combine to form a more credible explanation of the theology of *participatio actuosa*, as found in the documents of the Magisterium, more notably in *Sacrosanctum Concilium* of the Second Vatican Council. Here Pope Benedict has made an important contribution, particularly with his emphasis on St Paul's concept of *logikē latreia*, of divine worship in accordance with *logos*, as the most appropriate way of expressing the essential form of Christian liturgy. It is through the liturgy—in its anthropological reality—that our existence is 'logicized' (*logikē latreia*) with the self-giving of Christ, which has a bearing on everyday life.[7]

Among the central, indeed fundamental truths concerning the liturgy, which is re-affirmed by Pope Benedict, is that the liturgy is centred on God. It is not a self-celebration of ourselves, based on what *we* do, a feast of self-affirmation and self-seeking worship.[8] It is something in which we, gathered together as members of Christ's body, the Church, are privileged to participate. The liturgy's cosmic grandeur and transcendence embraces heaven and earth, uniting and forming the Church ('The Eucharist makes the Church'), linking it to, and applying the salvific fruits of the sacrificial work of our redeemer, Jesus Christ, the *Logos*

---

6.   *TSL, passim.*

7.   *Ibid.,* 45–49, 175.

8.   *TSL,* 22–3, 125, 175; Ratzinger, *A New Song for the Lord,* 32.

incarnatus. The liturgy on earth—particularly the Eucharist—is a reflection and foretaste of the heavenly liturgy to which it is united. One could say that this is mirrored in the beautiful antiphon *O Sacrum convivium*, composed by St Thomas Aquinas.[9] The ecclesiological, as well as cosmological and eschatological aspects of Ratzinger's theology of liturgy, are particularly noteworthy. The Church, in her liturgy, is led by, and gathered around 'the lamb that was slain' (Apoc 5:12), who reigns over the universe. We journey towards him in the liturgy, where past, present and future are present, and proclaim his coming again in glory. The theology of Pope Benedict is at pains to point out that the eucharistic liturgy cannot be described as a 'simple communal meal' around a table, for at the foundation of the liturgy is the sacrificial death of Christ on the cross and the whole paschal mystery, to which the liturgy gives us access as contemporaries, in union with the Church throughout the ages: 'Here is the real heart and true grandeur of the Eucharist, which is more, much more than a meal'.[10] 'Sacrifice' is an essential theme of Joseph Ratzinger's theology of liturgy, and a failure to understand the sacrificial nature of the Mass and its connection to the supreme sacrifice of love by Christ on the cross, distorts the essence of the Mass making Christian worship 'null and void'.[11] The liturgical worship of the Eucharist also flows out into ordinary daily life, and in other aspects of the liturgical and devotional life of the Church, including the adoration and veneration of the Eucharist outside Mass, especially the inheritance of the Middle Ages, and the *sancta sanctorum*: the tabernacle in our churches, which has truly taken the place of the

---

9. *O sacrum convivium, in quo Christus sumitur: recolitur memoria passionis eius: mens impletur gratia: et futurae gloriae nobis pignus datur, alleluia*: Magnificat antiphon for Second Vespers of Corpus Christi.

10. *TSL*, 45–59.

11. *Ibid.*, 54–55.

'Holy of Holies' of former times, the Ark of the Covenant, the eucharistic presence of God among us.[12]

Regarding the 'rite' of the liturgy—especially the Eucharist—such as the Roman Rite, there is, in the great liturgical families, a certain uniformity, but '*unity* in diversity', with organic growth and lawful development. This has no place for the kind of creativity and spontaneity which is destructive of liturgy and does not respect the tradition of the liturgy. Liturgy is a 'form of apostolic tradition', which must be respected by clergy and laity alike.[13] It is therefore inappropriate to classify the organic development of the liturgy as 'the living faith of the dead', where traditionalism is 'the dead faith of the living'.[14] Such polemics are unhelpful and betray an inaccurate understanding of organic development.

When comparing Pope Benedict's liturgical theology with his Magisterium, we have seen how the former has been extremely important for understanding the latter, while being conscious of the distinction which must also be made between them. We cannot understand what has happened with the liturgy during Pope Benedict's pontificate without reference to his liturgical theology, which has also directly influenced his Magisterium. Time and time again the themes which we read in Joseph Ratzinger's liturgical writings appear in Pope Benedict's Magisterium. This is no mere coincidence, and is particularly evident in Pope Benedict's *citation* from his own book, *Jesus of Nazareth*— a non-magisterial work—in his Post-synodal exhortation *Verbum Domini*, his discussion of 'spiritual worship'—the *logikē latreia*—his 'theology of images' and the 'theology of beauty' ('the splendour of the liturgy'/*veritatis splendour*),

---

12. *TSL*, 85–91; Ratzinger, *God is Near Us*, 74–113; idem, *The Feast of Faith*, 127–37.

13. *TSL*, 166–69; Ratzinger, *The Feast of Faith*, 61–68: and see n. 21 below.

14. Baldovin, *Reforming the Liturgy*, 56–57, citing Jaroslav Pelikan.

with its roots in the writings of Hans Urs von Balthasar.[15] The inner and exterior elements of the liturgy—which are both spiritual—including the *ars celebrandi*, the cosmological and eschatological aspects, a proper understanding of *participatio actuosa*, a reassertion of the identity of the Catholic priesthood, and traditional Catholic teaching concerning the Eucharist, are also prominent in the pope's magisterial teachings on the liturgy. The influence of Pope Benedict's theology in his Magisterium should not be negatively viewed as the implementation of his private opinions in the Magisterium, but rather the use of his talents, in his office as the supreme pastor of the Church, in expressing the central ideas and concepts concerning the nature of the liturgy and its celebration. The pope's desire, and that of the synod of bishops on the Holy Eucharist, for 'a mystagogical catechesis, which would lead the faithful to understand more deeply the mysteries being celebrated', is crucial, especially for a 'New Liturgical Movement' in the Church as well as the re-vitalisation of liturgical celebrations.[16] This is closely connected with the *logikē latreia* and the pope's references to the liturgy as 'a school of prayer' in several of his General Audiences, where the lives of the saints are 're-presented' as models of Christian living for the faithful. Pope Benedict's wish that the Christian faithful be educated in, and imbued with, what we can truly call 'the spirit of the liturgy', highlights the centrality of the liturgy in the life of the Catholic Church, a liturgy which is, by definition, oriented on the worship of God (*ad Deum*),

---

15. Pope Benedict XVI, *Post-synodal Exhortation Verbum Domini*, 30 September 2010, no. 54, n. 192; Pope Benedict XVI/Ratzinger, *Jesus of Nazareth*, 268; Nichols, *Redeeming Beauty*, 53–69, 94; Ratzinger, *On the Way to Jesus Christ*, 36–37.

16. Pope Benedict XVI, *Sacramentum Caritatis*, nos 52, 64, 65: 'the best catechesis on the Eucharist is the Eucharist itself, celebrated well' (no. 64).

and not man, but capable of uniting and transforming man.[17]

The actual celebration of the papal liturgies, as well as the pope's written Magisterium, particularly *Sacramentum Caritatis* and *Summorum Pontificum*—the two key pillars of Pope Benedict's 'liturgical reform'—are important steps towards changing the unsatisfactory elements in the current liturgical climate in the Church. While this includes a greater appreciation of the liturgical forms which have developed naturally in the course of the Church's history, it also includes recognition of the fruits of the liturgical changes after the Second Vatican Council, seeking to foster them, and place them in their proper context. The 'theology of beauty' in *Sacramentum Caritatis*, for example, acts as an important corrective to the sterile misinterpretation of the 'noble simplicity' which we have witnessed in liturgical celebrations and in the re-ordering—or rather disordering—of many churches. The liturgy is anything but 'simple'. It is a complex and rich spiritual mine, that is never exhausted, just as the cosmos is complex. And yet through Christ, we have access to the liturgy. For Pope Benedict, then, the liturgy, the 'summit toward which the activity of the Church is directed',[18] plays a clear role in the proper implementation and reception of the Second Vatican Council. Indeed, if one were to speak of 'development' in the liturgical thought of Pope Benedict, between his theological writings as a cardinal and his Magisterium, a particular example would be his own application of the 'hermeneutic of reform' or 'the hermeneutic of continuity'

---

17.   I would like to draw attention here to an old 'classic' of liturgical spirituality which deserves more widespread attention: von Hildebrand, *Liturgy and Personality*. Von Hildebrand, a great philosopher and spiritual author, had a profound understanding of continuity in the liturgy and its organic, and classical elements. Blessed Columba Marmion's writings, including *Christ in His Mysteries*, are also to be recommended. They are deeply imbued with a liturgical spirituality and theology.

18.   The Second Vatican Council, *The Constitution on the Sacred Liturgy Sacrosanctum Concilium*, 4 December 1963, no.10.

in the sphere of liturgy as the utilization and theological development of the notions of 'the reform of the reform' and organic development. It is a pivotal concept in understanding the celebration and interpretation of the liturgy in Pope Benedict's pontificate, where the ecclesiological element is paramount: that is, in continuity with and development of the Church's liturgical tradition. Pope Benedict's connection of the *ars celebrandi* with *participatio actuosa*— the former also acting as an important catalyst to promote the latter—is also noteworthy.

It is clearly apparent that, as with Joseph Ratzinger's commitment to the Second Vatican Council, Pope Benedict also remains committed to it. Yet it is refreshing that he— as with Pope John Paul II—is honest in not shying away from criticism of the reception and implementation of the council. Mistakes in the field of liturgy should, where evident, be humbly recognized and corrected. Efforts to produce improved and more faithful translations of the missal—begun under Pope John Paul II—some changes to the *Missale Romanum* (2002)—mainly in the *IGRM*—and *Sacramentum Caritatis* and *Summorum Pontificum*, strongly indicate that the liturgical 'reform programme' of Pope Benedict is not only a question of correcting abuses, which includes the promotion of good practice. The healing of the sad and multifaceted divisions which arose in the Church after the Second Vatican Council and the liturgical reforms, and attempts to bring reconciliation 'at the heart of the Church', is also a prominent feature of Pope Benedict's liturgical reform programme. Indeed reconciliation is an important theme for his whole pontificate. Pope Benedict is frequently prepared to go 'the extra mile', without compromising Catholic doctrinal teaching. This is also evident with his efforts to promote Christian Unity.[19] However he is also aware—and this is quite significant considering the extent of liturgical change after the Second Vatican Council—of the profound respect that the pope and Mag-

---

19. Pope Benedict XVI, *Apostolic Constitution Anglicanorum Coetibus*, 4 November 2009.

isterium must also have for the liturgy as something which is received as part of the living tradition of the Church. Papal authority is not limitless:

> The Pope is not an absolute monarch whose thoughts and desires are law. On the contrary: the Pope's ministry is a guarantee of obedience to Christ and to his Word. He must not proclaim his own ideas, but rather constantly bind himself and the Church to obedience to God's Word, in the face of every attempt to adapt it or water it down, and every form of opportunism.[20]

In the current liturgical reform, it is astounding, and perhaps inconceivable to some, that Pope Benedict XVI has mandated that the single Roman Rite consist of two uses, the 'ordinary form' and the 'extraordinary form' (*usus antiquior*), which was never abrogated. However this was clearly a courageous move which challenges everyone in the Church to think again about the liturgy. The maintenance of the ordinary form together with the extraordinary form, not only acknowledges, in broad terms, the validity of the *instauranda et fovenda*[21] of the sacred liturgy as decreed by the Second Vatican Council; the extraordinary form can also act as a reminder that the liturgy has living roots. As a signpost, the *usus antiquior* can indicate the origin, as well as the 'way' of the liturgy, namely, that liturgy

---

20.   Pope Benedict XVI, 'Mass of the Possession of the Chair of the Bishop of Rome, Homily', 7 May 2005; *TSL*, 165–66; Ratzinger, 'The Spirit of the Liturgy or Fidelity to the Council', 99; cf. Ratzinger, *God is Near Us*, 66–73; idem, *The Feast of Faith*, 79–95. For one recent assessment of Pope Paul VI's prudential judgement and the revision of the liturgy, see Rowland, *Ratzinger's Faith*, 127–28: though the present author is inclined to extend more sympathy to this pope, who suffered a great deal in the aftermath of Vatican II, despite, perhaps, showing too much trust in the liturgical experts, especially in making the liturgy more appealing or 'in tune' to modern man.

21.   I.E. 'restoration and promotion': The Second Vatican Council, *The Constitution on the Sacred Liturgy Sacrosanctum Concilium*, 4 December 1963, no. 14.

must be in tune with the melody of the liturgical tradition. Although it is nowhere explicitly expressed by Pope Benedict XVI—at least in his Magisterium—one could also say that the extraordinary form can act as a corrective to the ordinary form, concerning those elements of the liturgical tradition which, in one way of another, were not given proper emphasis. In this way, too, the ordinary form can be enriched by the extraordinary form.[22] The *usus antiquior* will certainly help to strengthen the use, as well as help to ensure the survival of Latin and Gregorian chant in the Roman liturgy.

It is true, of course, that canonical and theological questions concerning the effects of *Summorum Pontificum* may be legitimately explored, in fidelity to the Magisterium. Nevertheless it is regrettable, though not entirely unsurprising, that some commentators on this motu proprio are still stuck in the erroneous mindset of 'the Church *then*' (before Vatican II) and 'the Church *now*' (post Vatican II), failing to take sufficient account of continuity in doctrine and the old axiom *lex credendi, lex orandi*, as if the 'two churches' have a completely different ecclesiology.[23] This citation from *Summorum Pontificum* answers these critics convincingly, who believe that this document is a step backwards:

> Since time immemorial it has been necessary—
> as it is also for the future—to maintain the prin-
> ciple according to which 'each particular Church
> must concur with the universal Church, not only
> as regards the doctrine of the faith and the sacra-

---

22.   Pope Benedict XVI, *Letter to the Bishops on the Occasion of the Publication of the Apostolic Letter "Motu Proprio Data"*, 7 July 2007. For the pope on 'liturgy: no rupture', see pp. 187–88 below.

23.   See Bovens, 'Chronique inachevée des publications autour de la Lettre apostolique en forme de Motu proprio "Summorum Pontificum" de Benoît XVI", 529–36; de Jong, 'Enkele overpeinzingen naar aanleiding van de buitengewone misorde'. Useful bibliographical information—by no means complete—may be found in Haunerland, 'Ein Ritus in zwei Ausdrucksformen? Hintergründe und Perspektiven zur Liturgiefeier nach dem Motu proprio "Summorum Pontificum"', 179–203.

mental signs, but also as regards the usages universally accepted by uninterrupted apostolic tradition, which must be observed not only to avoid
errors but also to transmit the integrity of the faith,
because the Church's law of prayer [*lex orandi*] corresponds to her law of faith [*lex credendi*]' ... These
two expressions of the Church's *lex orandi* [that is,
the ordinary and extraordinary forms of the Roman
Rite] will in no way lead to a division in the Church's
lex credendi. They are, in fact two usages of the one
Roman Rite.[24]

The experience of the last forty years strongly suggests
that liturgists ignore the traditional theology of the Holy
Eucharist at *our* peril, and that many of them should be
more open minded with the reforms and rediscovery of
the essence of the sacred liturgy as promoted by Pope Benedict.

The desire that the extraordinary form of the Roman
Rite, the *usus antiquior*, and the ordinary form, should
influence each other, is certainly another step towards a
'reform of the reform', even though the phrase itself is not
invoked. The new *Compendium Eucharisticum*, in a graphic
way illustrates the parity between both uses, and how each
use of the Roman Rite can influence and, all things considered, complement each other. The *Compendium* draws
texts from both uses in presenting the Church's doctrine
on the Holy Eucharist, underlining, once again, the importance of *lex orandi, lex credendi*, and the liturgy as part of
the Church's tradition. Cardinal Cañizares Llovera, the
prefect for the Congregation for Divine Worship and the
Discipline of the Sacraments indicates, in his preface to this
important book, that the missal promulgated by Pope St
Pius V, as edited by Blessed John XXIII, *uti extraordinaria
expressio legis orandi Ecclesiae et ob venerabile et antiquum eius*

---

24. Pope Benedict XVI, *Summorum Pontificum*, *op. cit.*, which cites
     IGMR, no. 397.

usum debito gaudet honore.[25] The proper celebration of the *Missale Romanum* (2002), in line with liturgical tradition and parallel to it—which is underlined by the celebration of the *usus antiquior*—may, in certain aspects, give new, prudent growth to the *usus antiquior*, in the increase of prefaces and feast days, for example, and how one is to understand this use of the Roman Rite in the context of the Church's teaching on the Eucharist and the liturgy, including the Second Vatican Council. This would, in itself, also suggest that there is 'no rupture' in the liturgy, as Pope Benedict has indicated, while—together with the 'hermeneutic of continuity'—he clearly recognizes that there have been 'ruptures' in the implementation of the liturgy and the Second Vatican Council.[26] By maintaining both ordinary and extraordinary forms of the Roman Rite, Pope Benedict effectively 'liturgically reconciles' both the newer and older forms of the Roman liturgy, correcting rupture where it actually occurred or is perceived to have occurred. Again, though Pope Benedict does not say it explicitly in *Summorum Pontificum*, one cannot help but also think that the restoration—or rather acknowledgement—of the legal status of the *usus antiquior*, is another recognition of the fact that all has not gone well with the formulation and implementation of the liturgy after the Second Vatican Council. The pain caused in the years after the council due to unwarranted liturgical innovations, at least, was acknowledged by the pope in his letter to the bishops.[27]

---

25. Congregation for Divine Worship and the Discipline of the Sacraments, *Compendium Eucharisticum*, 6. For the *Ordo Missae* from the missal of 1962 and the office for the feast of Corpus Christi from the *Breviarium Romanum* (1961), see *Ibid.*, 205–40, 289–359.

26. Pope Benedict XVI, *Letter to the Bishops on the Occasion of the Publication of the Apostolic Letter "Motu Proprio Data"*, 7 July 2007, 21–2, 25–6; Pope Benedict XVI, *Sacramentum Caritatis*, nos 3, 52: Pope Benedict XVI, 'Address of His Holiness Benedict XVI to the Roman Curia Offering them His Christmas Greetings', 22 December 2005: cf. Ratzinger, 'The Spirit of the Liturgy or Fidelity to the Council', 99.

27. See the previous note.

Here, as with other matters, I do not believe that Pope Benedict has changed his views concerning the newer *Missale Romanum*, especially when he spoke in the past, as Cardinal Ratzinger, about what we may conveniently describe as an 'artificiality' present in the creation of the newer rites.[28] Cardinal Ratzinger also spoke about the discontinuities of the implementation of the Second Vatican Council and faults in the process of producing the newer liturgical texts, while holding to the validity and lawfulness of the newer texts and their celebration.[29] In his recent interview—not magisterial—with Peter Seewald, Pope Benedict effectively reiterated what he had said in *The Spirit of the Liturgy*, and elsewhere, concerning the basic 'immutability' of liturgical rites:

> [The liturgy] is not about our doing something, about our demonstrating our creativity ... Liturgy is precisely not a show, a piece of theatre, a spectacle. Rather, it gets its life from the Other. This has to become evident, too. This is why the fact that the ecclesial form has been given in advance is so important. It can be reformed in matters of detail, but cannot be reinvented every time by the community. It is not a question, as I said, of self-production. The point is to go out of and beyond ourselves to him, and to let ourselves be touched by him. In this sense, it's not just the expression of this form that's important, but also its communality. This form can exist in different rites, but it must always contain that element which precedes us, that comes from the whole of the Church's faith, from the whole of her tradition, from the whole of her life, and does not just spring from the fashion of the moment.[30]

The celebration of both usages of the Roman Rite may well, over time, be an important factor in also bringing about

---

28. From Ratzinger's preface to Gamber, *The Reform of the Roman Liturgy*, end-cover.

29. Ratzinger, '*The Spirit of the Liturgy* or Fidelity to the Council', 99; cf. Ratzinger, *God is Near Us*, 66–73; idem, *The Feast of Faith*, 79–95.

30. Pope Benedict XVI, *Light of the World*, 156–57.

further changes—and any realignment of texts with liturgical tradition that is necessary—to the newer, ordinary form of the Roman Missal, beyond improved translations and alignment with traditional liturgical usages, such as celebrating the Mass *ad orientem*. The evident increase in the celebration of the *usus antiquior* will be of great benefit to the liturgical life of the Church, including improved celebrations of the *novus ordo* as well as recognising the spiritual riches of the liturgy, which is the inheritance of every Catholic today, especially those young people who has never experienced the *usus antiquior*. An openness of heart on all sides, as well as mind, is an important element on the part of all in the Church, in accepting what Pope Benedict has said and done concerning the Church's liturgy. His desire for a healthy attitude to and recognition of those elements which are *nova et vetera* in the liturgy, is summed up in his explanatory letter concerning *Summorum Pontificum*, which also has relevance for the adequate discovery of 'the sense of the sacred'. The text is given here once more for convenience:

> Let us generously open our hearts and make room for everything that the faith itself allows. There is no contradiction between the two editions of the Roman Missal. In the history of the liturgy there is growth and progress, but no rupture. What earlier generations held as sacred, remains sacred and great for us too, and it cannot be all of a sudden entirely forbidden or even considered harmful. It behoves all of us to preserve the riches which have developed in the Church's faith and prayer, and to give them their proper place.[31]

---

31. Pope Benedict XVI, *Letter to the Bishops on the Occasion of the Publication of the Apostolic Letter "Motu Proprio Data"*, 7 July 2007, 25–6. Cf. Pope Benedict XVI, *Sacramentum Caritatis*, no. 40: 'The *ars celebrandi* should foster a sense of the sacred [*sensui sacro*] and the use of outward signs which help to cultivate this sense, such as, for example, the harmony of the rite, the liturgical vestments, the furnishings and the sacred space.'

We can favourably compare this with what Pope Paul VI said in his apostolic constitution *Missale Romanum*:

> The Roman Missal, promulgated in 1570 by our predecessor, St Pius V, by decree of the Council of Trent, has been received by all as one of the numerous and admirable fruits which the holy Council has spread throughout the entire Church of Christ. For four centuries, not only has it furnished the priests of the Latin Rite with the norms for the celebration of the Eucharistic Sacrifice, but also the saintly heralds of the Gospel have carried it almost to the entire world. Furthermore, innumerable holy men have abundantly nourished their piety towards God by its readings from sacred scripture or by its prayers, whose general arrangement goes back, in essence, to St Gregory the Great. [32]

As I said in the introduction, I believe that 'the reform of the reform', as implemented by Pope Benedict in his Magisterium, and as indicated in his theological writings, *with* the reverent celebration of the missal of Pope Paul VI *and* the 'extraordinary form of the Roman Rite' (*usus antiquior*), is the way forward for the Church in the field of liturgy. It is interesting to see how individuals and groups who hold various opinions concerning 'the reform of the reform' and those who adhere solely to the traditional liturgy, have been brought together, not only in dialogue about the liturgy, but also in celebrating the liturgy together, thanks to *Summorum Pontificum*. For those individuals and others, including myself, it is evident that the hermeneutic of continuity, together with the other constituents of Pope Benedict XVI's liturgical reform, provides the necessary means to restoring the sacred liturgy. Undoubtedly, much has already been achieved by the pope, at a reasonable, but cautious pace. However if any reader is (still) not convinced that we are witnessing a liturgical 'reform' under Pope Benedict XVI, then he or she would be wise to read the following words of

---

32.   Pope Paul VI, *Apostolic Constitution Missale Romanum*, 3 April 1969.

Cardinal Raymond Burke, the prefect of the Supreme Tribunal of the Apostolic Signatura:

> I think also of the tireless work of our Holy Father to carry out a reform of the postconciliar liturgical reform, conforming the celebration of the sacred liturgy to the perennial teaching of the Church as it was presented anew at the Second Vatican Ecumenical Council, so that in every liturgical action we may see more clearly the action of Christ Himself who unites heaven and earth, even now, in preparation for his final coming, when he will inaugurate [a] 'new heaven and a new earth', when we will all celebrate the fullness of life and love in the liturgy in the heavenly Jerusalem. The cardinal today is called, in a special way, to assist the successor of Saint Peter, in handing on, in an unbroken organic line, what Christ himself has given us in the Church, his Eucharistic Sacrifice, 'the font and highest expression of the whole Christian life.' The right order of sacred worship in the Church is the condition of the possibility of the right order of her teaching and the right order of her conduct.[33]

What the distant future for the development of the liturgy will be—in other words, what would eventually happen as a result of the implementation of Pope Benedict XVI's liturgical reform—cannot possibly be predicted with absolute certainty. The pope's efforts in the field of liturgy will hopefully, in time, bring about the *pax liturgica* which the Latin Church solely needs, united before the altar of the Lord. It is preferable that this occur *ad orientem/Deum*, as we really do need to retreat from the idea that *versus populum* celebration is *a priori* the 'characteristic fruit of Vatican II's liturgical renewal'.[34] However the *pax liturgica* will not happen overnight: though Pope Benedict, as a good shepherd, would rather that people were persuaded than 'compelled' towards this. The full significance of what has

---

33. Burke, 'Cardinal Burke's Homily at [the] Solemn Mass of Thanksgiving on the Occasion of the Ordinary Public Consistory'.

34. *TSL*, 77.

occurred in the Roman liturgy, thus far in Pope Benedict's pontificate, has still to be fully appreciated. It is important to be faithful to the 'theology of the liturgy' as presented by the Second Vatican Council, in the same way that Pope Benedict is faithful. Whether this includes a revision of any of the 'prudential judgments' of this pastoral and ecumenical council, in disciplinary matters, as is evident from the history of the ecumenical councils, remains to be seen: though Joseph Ratzinger/Pope Benedict XVI has not called for this, but for the correct interpretation and implementation of the council. Some liturgical scholars—including László Dobszay—have made suggestions worthy of serious consideration, which sees the traditional liturgy as a basis for a future liturgy with the best elements from the *Novus Ordo*, in fidelity with the Second Vatican Council. It is surely to be hoped that both uses of the Roman Rite will grow more together in an organic harmony that is rooted in the living liturgical tradition of the Church. Whether this will actually mean that 'one' form of the Roman Rite will be organically developed, under the authority of the Holy See and—above all—under the guidance of the Holy Spirit, or that the two uses as at present will remain in place, is something which is known to God alone, at least at the present time. Above all we must hope, and pray, that the Church may grow in its fidelity to her divine master, for an increase in fervour for the Holy Eucharist, with a new 'movement' for an increased understanding of the liturgy in the Church, built upon the rock of the organic, new and yet ever old liturgical tradition, for the worship of God. This 'New Liturgical Movement', which has clearly begun in the Church, and is growing in momentum, will help with the rediscovery of the legacy of the Second Vatican Council.[35] The good Lord has provided the Church in the twenty-first century with a shepherd who, by his theological writings, Magisterium and personal example, can help us on this journey, and to remedy the defects. Pope

---

35.   Ratzinger, *Milestones: Memoirs 1927–1977*, 149.

Benedict XVI's contribution to the study of the liturgy and its celebration, will undoubtedly enrich future generations of Catholics in the same way as it enriches us today. It remains for us to accompany Pope Benedict in this liturgical quest as *cooperatores veritatis*.[36]

---

36.   The pope's motto, 'co-workers of the truth'.

Appendix
Some Interviews with
Mgr Guido Marini,
Papal Master of Ceremonies

A) *Interview in Il Riformista [2008]*[1]

(Interview with Paolo Rodari)

'The very first reaction was great surprise and great fear. Then I felt a certain trepidation the night before beginning my service, and I also very much felt the separation from my diocese and my city, my sister and her family, from so many friends, from the places where I have exercised my priesthood in a special way: the [Genoese] curia, the seminary, the cathedral. At the same time, however, I felt much honoured to be called by the Holy Father to perform the service of Master of Liturgical Celebrations. The possibility I have been given to be near the Holy Father, I have felt immediately to be a true grace for my priesthood.'

---

1. Translation and further details available from http://www.newliturgicalmovement.org/2008/03/interview-with-msgr-guido-marini-papal.html; accessed 8 December 2010. I am most grateful to Shawn Tribe for his permission to use the following excerpts from Mgr Marini's interviews, which appeared in 'The New Liturgical Movement' blog, and to the translators. The translations are a little crude in places, and the texts are slightly repetitive; however they convey a great deal about the pope's 'vision of the liturgy' and how this is manifested in a practical sphere. I have made corrections and adjustments to the texts where this was absolutely necessary. At the time of publication, a collection of conferences given by Mgr Marini has been published: Marini, *Liturgical Reflections of a Papal Master of Ceremonies*.

Monsignor Guido Marini, Genoese, forty-two years old, thus describes to the Riformista *his arrival, last October, at the Vatican to assume the post of Master of the Liturgical Celebrations of the Pope. An appointment which allows him to work in close contact with Benedict XVI.*

'That which I have perceived at the beginning of my new assignment [he tells] I have found to be confirmed exactly every time I have had the grace to encounter the Holy Father. These encounters have been and are always for me a cause of great joy and great emotion. I would never have thought, having been an attentive reader and appreciator of Cardinal Ratzinger, that one day I would have the grace to be as close to him as I am now. And then, every time, together with the profound reverence which the figure of the pope inspires in me, I experience his serene, gentle, fine and delicate manner of dealing with people which fills my heart with joy and which invites me to exert myself with all my energy to collaborate with generosity, humility and fidelity in the exercise of his Magisterium in the liturgical sphere, as far as pertains to my competences.'

'Lex orandi lex credendi'
The office of Master of the Liturgical Celebrations of the pope is important because, if it is true that lex orandi lex credendi (the Church believes in that which She prays [Rodari's translation]), then to direct the papal ceremonies with rigour and faithfulness to the norms is a help to the faith of the entire Church.

'The liturgy of the Church [explains Marini] with its words, gestures, silences, chants and music causes us to live with singular efficacy the different moments of the history of salvation in such a way that we become really participant in them and transform ourselves ever more into authentic disciples of the Lord, walking again in our lives along the [footsteps] of him who has died and risen for our salvation. The liturgical celebration, if it is truly participated in, induces to this transformation which is the history of

holiness.' And a help in this 'transformation' can be that
'repositioning' of the cross in the centre of the altar, which
has been carried out in the papal liturgies, as a residue
[Rodari's word] of the old 'orientation towards [the] orient' of churches: towards the rising Sun, he who is coming.
'The position of the Cross at the centre of the altar'—says
Marini—'indicates the centrality of the Crucified in the
eucharistic celebration and the precise interior orientation
which the entire congregation is called to have during the
eucharistic liturgy: one does not look at each other, but
one looks to him who has been born, has died and is risen
for us, the saviour. From the Lord comes salvation, he is
the Orient, the Sun which rises to whom we all must turn
our gaze, from whom we all must receive the gift of grace.
The question of liturgical orientation, and also the practical manner in which it takes shape, is of great importance,
because through it is conveyed a fundamental fact, at once
theological and anthropological, ecclesiological and relevant for the personal spirituality.'

'Continuity'
A 'repositioning', that of the cross, exposes how the liturgical practices of the past must also live today. 'The liturgy
of the Church'—says Marini—'as incidentally all her life,
is made of continuity: I would speak of development in
continuity. This means that the Church proceeds on her
way through history without losing sight of her own roots
and her own living tradition: this can require, in some
cases ... the recovering of precious and important elements which have been lost, forgotten along the way and
which the passing of time has rendered less shining in
their authentic significance. When that happens it is not
a return to the past, but a true and enlightened progress
in the liturgical field.' And in this progress it is impossible not to mention the motu proprio *Summorum Pontificum*:
'Considering attentively the motu proprio, as well as the
letter addressed by the pope to the bishops of the world,
a twofold precise understanding emerges. First of all, that

of facilitating the accomplishing of 'a reconciliation in the bosom of the Church'; and in this sense, as has been said, the motu proprio is a most beautiful act of love towards the unity of the Church. In second place, and this is a fact which must not be forgotten, that [*sic* understanding] of favouring a reciprocal enrichment between the two forms of the Roman Rite: in such a way, for instance, that in the celebration according to the Missal of Paul VI (ordinary form of the Roman Rite) "can become manifest, more powerfully than has been the case hitherto, the sacrality which attracts many people to the ancient usage".' [...]

B) *Interview given in L'Osservatore Romano [2008]*[2]

(Interview with Gianluca Biccini)

From 29 June onwards the pallium worn by Benedict XVI for the solemn liturgical celebrations changes. The one which the Pope will use for the Mass of Saints Peter and Paul will be of the shape of a closed circle, with two end pieces that hang down in the middle of the chest and the back. The cut will be wider and longer, whereas the red colour of the crosses which adorn it will be preserved. 'This is the development of the Latin form of the pallium used up to John Paul II', says the Master of Papal Liturgical Celebrations, Monsignor Guido Marini, explaining [the] historical and liturgical reasons for the new insignia in this interview to *L'Osservatore Romano*.

What are the elements of continuity and innovation compared to the past?

---

2.   Available from http://www.newliturgicalmovement.org/2008/06/
      development-in-continuity-full. html; accessed 8 December 2010.

In light of careful studies, regarding the development of the pallium over the centuries, it seems that we can say that the long pallium crossed over the left shoulder and was not worn in the West as from the ninth century onwards. Indeed, the painting in the Sacred Cave of Subiaco, dating back to c.1219 and representing Pope Innocent III with this type of pallium, seems to be a deliberate archaism. In this sense the use of the new pallium intends to meet two requirements: first of all to emphasize more strongly the continuous [organic] development which in an arch of more than twelve centuries, this liturgical vestment continued to have; in second place the practical [requirement], because the pallium used by Benedict XVI since the beginning of his pontificate ... has led to several annoying problems from this point of view.

There remain differences between the papal pallium and the one which the pontiff imposes on the archbishops?

The difference remains even in the current pallium. What will be worn by Benedict XVI from the solemnity of Saints Peter and Paul onwards takes the form of the pallium used up to John Paul II, albeit in a larger and longer cut, and with the colour red for the crosses. The different form of the papal pallium vis-à-vis the one of the metropolitans highlights the diversity of jurisdiction which is signified by the pallium.

A few months ago the pastoral staff that the pope uses in [liturgical] celebrations has changed. What are the reasons for this choice?

The golden pastoral staff in the shape of a Greek cross—which belonged to Blessed Pius IX and was used for the first time by Benedict XVI in the celebration of Palm Sunday this year—is now used constantly by the pontiff, who has thus decided to replace the silver one surmounted by a crucifix, introduced by Paul VI and also used by John Paul I, John Paul II and by himself. This choice does not mean simply a return to the old way, but attests to a development in continuity, a rootedness in tradition that allows you to proceed in an orderly manner on the way of history. This pastoral staff, called 'ferula', corresponds in fact in a more faithful way to the form of [the] papal pastoral staff typical of Roman tradition, which has always been in the shape of a cross without crucifix, at least since the pastoral staff began to be used by the Roman pontiffs. And then we must not forget also an element of practicality: the ferula of Pius IX is lighter and easier to handle than the pastoral staff introduced by Paul VI.[3]

And the pastoral staff made by Lello Scorzelli for Pope Montini in the mid-sixties?

It remains available to the papal sacristy, along with so many objects that belonged to the predecessors of Benedict XVI.

Can we say the same for the choice of vestments worn by the Pope in the various celebrations?

In this case, it must also be said that the liturgical vestments chosen, as well as some details of the rite, intend to emphasize the continuity of the liturgical celebration of today with that which has characterized the life of the Church in the past. The hermeneutic of continuity is always the precise criterion by which to interpret the Church's journey in the time. This also applies to the liturgy. A pope cites the popes who preceded him in his documents, in order to indicate continuity in the Magisterium of the Church. In the same way, in the liturgical sphere, a pope also uses liturgical vestments and sacred objects of the popes who preceded him to indicate the same continuity with the *lex*

---

3.   Pope Benedict now uses a ferula that was specially made for him.

orandi. But I would like to point out that the pope does not always use old liturgical vestments. He often wears modern ones. The important thing is not so much antiquity or modernity, but beauty and dignity, important components of every liturgical celebration.

An example would be the visits [of the pope] in Italy and outside Italy, where the papal vestments are prepared by the local churches.

Of course. Just think of the visit to the United States or to that in Italy, first to Genoa and then to Salento. In both cases it was the diocese who prepared the liturgical vestments of the Pope, in agreement with the Office of Liturgical Celebrations of the supreme pontiff. In the variety of styles and with attention to characteristic local elements, the criterion adopted was that of beauty and dignity, typical dimensions of the sacred action which takes place in the eucharistic celebration.

At this point could you indicate to us some particular liturgical aspect of the next international voyage [to Australia]?

I can say that the time of preparation was very fruitful and the collaboration found in Australia very cordial and ready. Pope Benedict XVI will meet once more young people from all over the world and we all pray that once again this meeting may be the cause of great grace for all, an opportunity to come to know with more intensity the face of Jesus and the face of the Church, a spur for a prompt and generous response to the Lord's call. The hope is also that the liturgical celebrations, prepared with care and really participated in, because they are lived from the heart, may be privileged occasions for the reception of this grace.

What can you tell us about the high papal throne, used on occasions like the consistory, and about the cross which has been returned to the centre of the altar?

The so-called throne, used in special circumstances, is simply meant to highlight the liturgical presidency of the pope, the successor of Peter and vicar of Christ. As for the position of the cross at the centre of the altar, it indicates the centrality of the crucified [Lord] in the eucharistic celebration and the correct orientation which the whole assembly is called to have during the Liturgy of the Eucharist: one does not look at each other, but we look to Him who was born, died and rose again for us, the saviour. From the Lord comes salvation, He is the East (Orient), the rising Sun to whom we must all turn our gaze, from whom we must all receive the gift of grace. The issue of liturgical orientation within the eucharistic celebration, and also the practical way in which this takes shape, has great importance because with it is conveyed a fundamental fact which is at the same time theological and anthropological, ecclesiological and concerning the personal spirituality.

Is this also the criterion to understand the decision to celebrate at the ancient altar of the Sistine Chapel, on the occasion of the Feast of the Baptism of the Lord?

Exactly. In circumstances where the celebration takes place in this way, this is not about turning the back to the faithful, but rather about orientating oneself together with the faithful towards the Lord. From this point of view 'the door is not closed to the assembly', but 'the door is opened to the assembly', leading it to the Lord. Particular circumstances can be found in which, because of the artistic circumstances of the sacred place and its unique beauty and harmony, it becomes desirable to celebrate at the old altar, where among other things the correct orientation of the liturgical celebration is preserved. This should not be surprising: it suffices to go into St Peter's in the morning and to see how many priests celebrate according to the ordinary rite which resulted from the liturgical reform, but on traditional altars and therefore oriented as the one of the Sistine Chapel.

In the recent visit to Santa Maria di Leuca and to Brindisi, the Pope has distributed Communion to the faithful in the mouth while kneeling. Is this a practice destined to become habitual in the papal celebrations?

I really think so. In this regard it must not be forgotten that the distribution of Communion in the hand still remains, from a juridical point of view, an indult [that is, an exception] to the universal law, granted by the Holy See to those bishops' conferences who have requested it. The manner adopted by Benedict XVI aims to underline the validity of the norm valid for the whole Church. In addition one could perhaps even see a preference for using this manner of distribution which, without taking away anything from the other [manner], better highlights the truth of the Real Presence in the Eucharist, helps the devotion of the faithful, and introduces [them] more easily to the sense of the mystery. These are aspects which, in our time, pastorally speaking, it is necessary to stress and recover.

How does the Master of Liturgical Celebrations respond to those who accuse Benedict XVI of thus wanting to impose preconciliar models?

First of all I like to stress the cordial and convinced adhesion which is also noticeable regarding the liturgical teaching of the Holy Father. As far, then, as terms like 'preconciliar' and 'postconciliar', used by some, are concerned, it seems to me that they belong to a language already overcome, and, when used with the intent to indicate a discontinuity in the path of the Church, I think they are wrong and typical of very reductive ideological visions. There are 'things old and things new' that belong to the treasure of the Church of always [sic] and should be considered as such. The wise man knows to find in his treasure the one and the other, without invoking other criteria than the evangelical and ecclesial ones. Not everything that is new is true, as on the other hand also not all that is ancient [is true]. The truth transcends the old and the new, and it is to it [truth] that we must strive without preconceptions. The Church lives according to that law of continuity by virtue of which she knows a development rooted in tradition. What is most important is that everything comes together so that the liturgical celebration is really the celebration of the sacred mystery, of the crucified and risen Lord who makes Himself present in his Church, re-actualizing the mystery of salvation and calling us, in the logic of an authentic and active participation, to share up to the extreme consequences of his own life, which is a life of the gift of love to the Father and to the brethren, a life of holiness.

Today the motu proprio Summorum Pontificum, on the use of the Roman liturgy prior to the reform carried out in 1970, still seems to give rise to contrasting interpretations. Are celebrations presided by the Pope according to the extraordinary form, which is this old one, presumable (ipotizzabili)?

That is a question to which I cannot give an answer [literally: do not know to give an answer; a very guarded response]. As for the motu proprio referred to, considering it with serene attention and without ideological notions, together with the letter addressed by the pope to the bishops of the entire world to present it, a twofold precise intention becomes apparent. First of all, the [intention] to facilitate the achievement of 'a reconciliation in the bosom of the Church', and in this sense, as has been said, the motu proprio is a very beautiful act of love for the unity of the Church. Secondly—and we should not forget this fact— its purpose is to encourage a mutual enrichment between the two forms of Roman Rite: in such a way, for example, that the celebration according to the missal of Pope Paul VI (which is the ordinary form of the Roman Rite) 'will be able to demonstrate, more powerfully than has been the case hitherto, the sacrality which attracts many people to the former usage.'

C) *Excerpts from an interview from Le Figaro prior to the papal visit in France in 2008*[4]

'Why the Pope Renews the Traditional Liturgy', by Jean-Marie Guénois, special envoy to Rome.

'Catholics will discover on Saturday at *Les Invalides* the Return of Forgotten Practices'

In the sacristy, it is he who watches over the vestments of Benedict XVI. The pope enters, they exchange a smile, already focused on the Mass which the successor of Peter is preparing to celebrate. Monsignor Guido Marini, a young Italian prelate of forty-three years, is the Master of Papal Liturgical Celebrations. His childlike face shows a very precise look. No detail seems to escape him. Thin, tall, he respectfully assists the pope in putting on his vestments. Then there comes a time of prayer. The Mass can begin.[...]

In his bright office at the Vatican, at the corner of St Peter's Square, Mgr Marini explains [the recent changes to papal liturgies]: 'Benedict XVI wants to emphasize that the norms for distributing Communion [on the tongue] in the Catholic Church are still in force. One has indeed forgotten that the distribution of Holy Communion in the hand is due to an indult, an exception, one might say, given by the Holy See to the episcopal conferences that request it.' He recognizes that Benedict XVI has a 'preference' for communion in the mouth but that 'the use of this modality does not detract from the other modality, to receive the host in hand.' However, he observes, 'to receive the host in the mouth highlights the truth of the Real Presence in the Eucharist, it helps the devotion of the faithful and introduces more easily into the sense of mystery. It is important today to stress so many aspects, and urgent to recover them.' Nothing, therefore, is a papal fantasy. These changes in liturgical forms are part of a clear vision of Benedict XVI, which is explicitly expressed in Rome by several

---

4. Translation available from http://www.newliturgicalmovement. org/2008/09/papal-mc-explains-changes-in-papal.html; accessed 9 December 2010.

interlocutors close to him: 'To achieve, ultimately, a liturgical synthesis between the Mass of Paul VI and that which tradition can contribute to it as enrichment.'

Monsignor Guido Marini is formal: 'It is not a battle between the old and the modern, much less between the preconciliar and the conciliar ones. This kind of problematical ideology is today outdated. The old and new belong to the same liturgical treasure of the Church. The liturgical celebration must be the celebration of the sacred mystery, of the crucified and risen Lord. It is our task to find, in the heritage of the liturgy, a continuity to serve this sense of the sacred.'

D) Office of the Liturgical Celebrations of the Supreme Pontiff: Interview of Mgr Guido Marini in the periodical Radici Cristiani no. 42, March 2009.

'Without words before the greatness and beauty of the mystery of God'
by Maddalena della Somaglia [excerpts][5]

The Holy Father seems to have the liturgy as one of the basic themes of his pontificate. As you accompany him closely, can you confirm this impression?

I would say yes. It is noteworthy that the first volume of the *opera omnia* of the Holy Father, soon to be published in Italian, is that devoted to those writings which have as their object the liturgy. In the preface to that volume, the same Joseph Ratzinger emphasizes this fact, noting that the precedence given to the liturgical writings is not accidental, but desired: in the same way as Vatican II, which first promulgated the constitution dedicated to the sacred liturgy, followed by the great Constitution on the Church [*Lumen*

---

5. Translation available from http://www.newliturgicalmovement. org/2009/02/msgr-guido-marini-speaks-again-on.html; accessed 9 December 2010.

Gentium]. It is in the liturgy, in fact, where the mystery of the Church is made manifest. One can then understand the reason why the liturgy should be one of the basic themes of the papacy of Benedict XVI: it is in the liturgy that the renewal and reform of the Church begins.

Is there a relationship between the sacred liturgy, art and architecture? Should the call of the pope to continuity in the liturgy be extended to art and sacred architecture?

There is certainly a vital relationship between the liturgy, sacred art and architecture. In part because sacred art and architecture, as such, must be suitable to the liturgy and its content, which finds expression in its celebration. Sacred art in its many manifestations, lives in connection with the infinite beauty of God and toward God, and should be oriented to his praise and his glory. Between liturgy, art and architecture there cannot be then, contradiction or dialectic. As a consequence, if it is necessary for a theological and historical continuity in the liturgy, this continuity should therefore also be a visible and coherent expression in sacred art and architecture.

Pope Benedict XVI recently said in an address that 'society speaks with the clothes that it wears.' Do you think this could apply to the liturgy?

In effect, we all speak by the clothes that we wear. Dress is a language, as is every form of external expression. The liturgy also speaks with the clothes it wears, and with all its expressive forms, which are many and rich, ever ancient and ever new. In this sense, 'liturgical dress', to stay with the terminology you have used, must always be true, that is, in full harmony with the truth of the mystery celebrated. The external signs have to be in harmonious relation with the mystery of salvation in place in the rite. And, it should never be forgotten that the actual clothing of the liturgy is a clothing of sanctity: it finds expression, in fact, in the holiness of God. We are called to face this holiness, we are called to put on that holiness, realizing the fullness of participation.

In an interview with L'Osservatore Romano,[6] you have highlighted the key changes since taking the post of Master of Papal Liturgical Celebrations. Could you recall and explain what these mean?

I was just saying that the changes to which you refer are to be understood as a sign of a development in continuity with the recent past, and I remember one in particular: the location of the cross at the centre of the altar. This positioning has the ability to express, also by external sign, proper orientation at the time of the celebration of the eucharistic liturgy; that the celebrant and the assembly do not look upon each other but together turn toward the Lord. Also, the unity of the altar and cross together can better show forth, together with the 'banquet' aspect, the sacrificial dimension of the Mass, whose significance is always essential. I would say that it springs from it, and therefore, always needs to find a visible expression in the rite.

We have noticed that the Holy Father, for some time now, always gives Holy Communion upon the tongue and kneeling. Does he want this to serve as an example for the whole Church, and an encouragement for the faithful to receive our Lord with greater devotion?

As we know the distribution of Holy Communion in the hand remains still, from a legal point of view, an exception [indult] to the universal law, granted by the Holy See to the bishops conferences who so request it. Every believer, even with an exception [indult], has the right to choose the way in which they will receive Communion. Benedict XVI began to distribute Communion on the tongue and kneeling on the occasion of the Solemnity of Corpus Christi last

---

6.   See text 'B', above.

year, in full consonance with the provisions of the current liturgical law, perhaps intending to emphasize a preference for this method. One can imagine the reason for this preference: it shines more light on the truth of the Real Presence in the Eucharist, it helps the devotion of the faithful, and it indicates more easily the sense of mystery.

The motu proprio Summorum Pontificum *is presented as the most important activity in the papacy of Benedict XVI. What is your opinion?*

I do not know whether it is the most important but it certainly is an important document. It is not only so because it is a very significant step towards a reconciliation within the Church, not only because it expresses the desire to arrive at a mutual enrichment between the two forms of the Roman Rite, the ordinary and extraordinary, but also because it is the precise indication, in law and liturgy, of that theological continuity which the Holy Father has presented as the only correct hermeneutic for reading and understanding the life of the Church and, especially, Vatican II. [...]

Addendum

The Instruction *Universae Ecclesiae* on the application of the Apostolic Letter *Summorum Pontificum* of Pope Benedict XVI

Just before the publication of this book, the long-awaited instruction concerning Pope Benedict XVI's motu proprio *Summorum Pontificum*, from the Pontifical Commission *Ecclesia Dei*, was released on 13 May 2011. The opening words of the instruction are *Universae Ecclesiae*.[1] It is dated 30 April, the feast of Pope St Pius V in the new liturgical calendar, and of Our Lady of Fatima, and has received papal confirmation (8 April).[2] *Universae Ecclesiae* contains a number of important, official clarifications concerning the correct interpretation and application of *Summorum Pontificum*. It is evident, from our discussion of the spirit and general principles of the motu proprio in chapter four, that these are underlined and strengthened by the instruction. *Summorum Pontificum* is for the whole Church, as the opening words of the instruction indicate. However I do not intend to repeat again these general principles, and

---

1.   The full official Latin text of *Universae Ecclesiae*, which will later appear in the *Acta Apostolicae Sedis*, and translations in several languages, including English, may be found on the website of the Holy See, currently at http://press.catholica.va/news_services/bulletin/news/27407.php?index=27407&lang=en; http://www.vatican.va/roman_curia/pontifical_commissions/ecclsdei/.

2.   *Summus Pontifex Benedictus PP. XVI, in Audientia die 8 aprilis a. d. MMXI subscripto Cardinali Praesidi Pontificiae Commissionis 'Ecclesia Dei' concessa, hanc Instructionem ratam habuit et publici iuris fieri iussit.* Apparently, this confirmation is *in forma commune*.

the 'spirit' of the motu proprio, here in detail, nor give a detailed commentary on the instruction. I simply wish to highlight some points of interest, especially in relation to the canonical commentary on the motu proprio in chapter four,[3] which compares very favourably with the instruction, and specific points which have been clarified or changed. The emphasis which *Universae Ecclesiae* places on the importance of *Summorum Pontificum* in the life of the Church, and in the celebration of the liturgy, could be summarized from no. 8 of the instruction:

> The motu proprio *Summorum Pontificum* constitutes an important expression of the Magisterium of the Roman pontiff and of his *munus* of regulating and ordering the Church's sacred liturgy. The motu proprio manifests his solicitude as Vicar of Christ and Supreme Pastor of the universal Church, and has the aim of:
>
> a. offering to all the faithful the Roman Liturgy in the *usus antiquior*, considered as a precious treasure to be preserved;
>
> b. effectively guaranteeing and ensuring the use of the *forma extraordinaria* for all who ask for it, given that the use of the 1962 Roman Liturgy is a faculty generously granted for the good of the faithful and therefore is to be interpreted in a sense favourable to the faithful who are its principal addressees;
>
> c. promoting reconciliation at the heart of the Church.

Numbers 9-11 of the instruction confirm the authority and power which Pope Benedict XVI has given to the Pontifical Commission Ecclesia Dei—including the means of legitimate recourse to the commission where there is conflict—as well as indicating that it has the task of supervising future editions of the liturgical books of the *usus antiquior*, with the approval of the Congregation for Divine Worship and the Discipline of the Sacraments. Reference to 'future editions' of liturgical books is another very positive

---

3.   See pp. 145-57.

sign, demonstrating that the *usus antiquior* is a 'living and breathing' liturgy of the Latin Church. The competence of diocesan bishops in the implementation of *Summorum Pontificum*, 'always in agreement with the *mens* of the Holy Father' — that is, concerning the mind/intention of the legislator regarding the motu proprio — is related in numbers 13-14. The minimum number of the *coetus fidelium* ('existing in a stable manner'), who wish the celebration of the *usus antiquior* in a church or chapel, is not specified in the instruction : canonical opinion indicates at least three persons. Instead it says, very favourably, nevertheless, that the *coetus fidelium* could be 'some people of an individual parish who, even after the publication of the motu proprio, come together by reason of their veneration for the liturgy in the *usus antiquior*, and who ask that it might be celebrated in the parish church or in an oratory or chapel'. It can also be composed of persons 'coming from different parishes or dioceses, who gather together in a specific parish church or in an oratory or chapel for this purpose' (no. 15 : cf. art. 5 §1 of the motu proprio).

Numbers 16-18 of *Universae Ecclesiae* indicate that groups or priests, wishing to celebrate the *usus antiquior* when visiting another church, are to be favourably welcomed and facilitated by the pastors concerned, and that 'in sanctuaries and places of pilgrimage the possibility to celebrate in the *forma extraordinaria* is to be offered to groups of pilgrims who request it (cf. motu proprio *Summorum Pontificum*, art. 5 § 3), if there is a qualified priest' (no. 18). Concerning the interpretation of a celebrant of the *usus antiquior* as *idoneus* (cf. motu proprio *Summorum Pontificum*, art. 5 § 4), this largely follows what we have already said in chapter four of our canonical commentary (no. 20, a-c). Significantly, the instruction says that, 'regarding knowledge of the execution of the rite, priests are presumed to be qualified who present themselves spontaneously to celebrate the *forma extraordinaria*, and have celebrated it previously' (no. 20, c). Ordinaries — for example, bishops — are 'encouraged' (actually *enixe rogantur* : 'strongly requested'), 'to offer their clergy the possibility of acquiring adequate preparation for celebrations in the *forma extraordinaria*. This applies also [*potissimum*] to seminaries, where future priests should be given proper formation, including [the] study of Latin and, where pastoral needs suggest it [*adiunctis id postulantibus*], the opportunity to learn the *forma extraordinaria* of the Roman Rite' (no. 21). The instruction emphasizes, and clarifies, the stipulations of *Summorum Pontificum* (art. 2), in that priests, secular or religious, are not required to ask permission to celebrate the *usus antiquior*—*sine populo* or only with the assistance of one minister - from their ordinaries or superiors (*ordinariorum vel superiorum* : no. 23).

Concerning liturgical and ecclesiastical discipline, provision will be made in the near future for new prefaces and the celebration of newer saints in the *usus antiquior*, as the Holy Father indicated in his letter to the bishops, which accompanied *Summorum Pontificum* (no. 25). This is undoubtedly a welcome enrichment of the *usus antiquior*, which is already a liturgical treasury for the Church. Clarification is also given concerning the readings used at the *usus antiquior*—that is, those in the *Missale Romanum* of 1962—and the (optional) use of the vernacular : 'As foreseen by article 6 of the motu proprio *Summorum Pontificum*, the readings of the Holy Mass of the Missal of 1962 can be proclaimed either solely in the Latin language, or in Latin followed by the vernacular or, in Low Masses, solely in the vernacular' (no. 26). Liturgical laws after 1962, which are incompatible with the rubrics of the *usus antiquior*—and which are currently permitted in celebrations of the *novum missale* (nos 4, 7)—do not apply to it : 'Furthermore, by virtue of its character of special law, within its own area, the motu proprio *Summorum Pontificum* derogates [that is, 'sets aside'] from those provisions of law, connected with the sacred rites, promulgated from 1962 onwards and incompatible with the rubrics of the liturgical books in effect in 1962' (no. 28). The *Codex Iuris Canonici* (1983) applies with regard to the disciplinary norms connected to celebration, for example, the Eucharistic fast of one hour (no. 27).

Concerning the liturgical books and rubrics of the *usus antiquior*, number 24 stipulates that 'the liturgical books of the *forma extraordinaria* are to be used as they are. All those who wish to celebrate according to the *forma extraordinaria* of the Roman Rite must know the pertinent rubrics and are obliged to follow them correctly.' The lawful use of the old formula and rite of Confirmation, discussed above (pp. 170-71), and which was already confirmed by *Summorum Pontificum*, is emphasized in the instruction (no. 29).[4]

Number 32 indicates that 'Art. 9 § 3 of the motu proprio *Summorum Pontificum* gives clerics the faculty to use the *Breviarium Romanum* in effect in 1962, which is to be prayed entirely and in the Latin language'. The Latin text reads, *Omnibus clericis conceditur facultas recitandi Breviarium Romanum anni 1962, de quo art. 9, § 3 Litterarum Apostolicarum Summorum Pontificum, et quidem integre et Latino sermone*. The words *et quidem integre et Latino sermone* can be literally translated 'and indeed [or 'even'] [this recitation] wholly and in Latin'. This appears to specify that clerics who freely choose to use this breviary, fulfil their obligation by reciting it in its entirety—that is, all the canonical hours—and in Latin. This would entail a modification in canonical opinion as regards the hours which are to be recited from this breviary, by those clerics who choose to use it and who are obliged to recite the divine office (see p. 151 above). The insistence on fulfilling the rubrics of the *usus antiquior* books in the instruction, and the derogation of contrary liturgical laws after 1962, in relation to the rubrics of the *usus antiquior* (1962), strengthens this interpretation (nos 24, 28 cited above). Other questions surrounding no. 32 require further clarification, and discussion among canonists.[5] The

---

4.   I omit here mention of the conferral of the tonsure, minor orders, the subdiaconate, major orders and the clerical state, indicated in nos 30-31 of the instruction, while not wishing to underestimate its importance.

5.   I am grateful to Dr. Gero P. Weishaupt for discussing this, and other priests and religious. One should also be aware that there are circumstances which can mitigate the office, in whole or in part,

instruction also indicates that the Easter triduum can be celebrated by a qualified priest 'for a *coetus fidelium...* which follows the older liturgical tradition', even in a church not specifically assigned for the *usus antiquior* : and even if this means that the triduum is to be repeated (no. 33). Finally, another significant point made by the instruction relates to those religious orders who had their own liturgical books in the Roman Rite, such as the Dominicans and Premonstratensians: 'The use of the liturgical books proper to the religious orders [actually *sodalibus ordinum religiosorum*] which were in effect in 1962 is permitted' (no. 34). Hopefully this will help religious orders—and individual members more specifically—who had, or still have their own liturgy, to rediscover any lost liturgical treasures from their patrimony. Clearly the instruction *Universae Ecclesiae* is a significant and much welcomed authoritative document concerning the interpretation of *Summorum Pontificum.*

---

or other situations—for example when one visits a monastery and uses that community's office—when there is clearly no obligation to repeat an office by reciting it from one's own breviary.

Bibliography

For the writings of Joseph, Cardinal Ratzinger (to 19 April 2005), see under 'Pope Benedict XVI.'

1. *Pope Benedict XVI/Joseph Ratzinger*

A. Books and articles

Benedict XVI, Pope/Ratzinger, J., *The Feast of Faith: Approaches to a Theology of the Liturgy*, translated by G. Harrison (San Francisco, Ignatius Press, 1986).

Benedict XVI, Pope/Ratzinger, J., *Principles of Catholic Theology*, translated by M. F. McCarthy (San Francisco, Ignatius Press, 1987).

Benedict XVI, Pope/Ratzinger, J., *Eschatology: Death and Eternal Life*, translated by M. Waldstein (Washington, The Catholic University of America Press, 1988).

Benedict XVI, Pope/Ratzinger, J., *The Theology of History in Saint Bonaventure* 2nd ed. (Chicago, Franciscan Herald Press, 1971, 1989).

Benedict XVI, Pope/Ratzinger, J., 'Preface', in Gamber, K., *The Reform of the Roman Liturgy* (California and New York, Una Voce Press and The Foundation for Catholic Reform, 1993).

Benedict XVI, Pope/Ratzinger, J., *Called to Communion: Understanding the Church Today*, translated by A. Walker (San Francisco, Ignatius Press, 1996).

Benedict XVI, Pope/Ratzinger, J., *A New Song for the Lord: Faith in Christ and Liturgy Today*, translation by M. M. Matesich (New York, The Crossroad Publishing Company, 1997).

Benedict XVI, Pope/Ratzinger, J., *Milestones: Memoirs 1927–1977*, translated by E. Leiva-Merikakis (San Francisco, Ignatius Press, 1998).

Benedict XVI, Pope/Ratzinger, J., 'Ten Years of the Motu Proprio *Ecclesia Dei*' (24 October 1998), translated by I. Harrison of the Oratory, available from http://www.sanctamissa.org/en/spirituality/ten-years-of-the-motu-proprio.pdf; accessed 8 December 2010.

Benedict XVI, Pope/Ratzinger, J., *Der Geist der Liturgie* (Freiburg, Basel and Wien, Herder, 2000): English translation *The Spirit of the Liturgy*, translated by J. Saward (San Francisco, Ignatius Press, 2000).

Benedict XVI, Pope/Ratzinger, J., 'Réponse du Cardinal Ratzinger au Père Gy', *La Maison-Dieu* 230 (2002), 113–20: English translation '*The Spirit of the Liturgy* or Fidelity to the Council: Response to Father Gy', translated by S. Maddux, *Antiphon* 11 (2007), 98–102.

Benedict XVI, Pope/Ratzinger, J., 'The Theology of the Liturgy', in Reid, A. (ed.), *Looking again at the Question of the Liturgy with Cardinal Ratzinger: Proceedings of the July 2001 Fontgombault Liturgical Conference* (Farnborough, St Michael's Abbey Press, 2003), 18–31.

Benedict XVI, Pope/Ratzinger, J., 'Assessment and Future Prospects', in Reid, A. (ed.), *Looking again at the Question of the Liturgy with Cardinal Ratzinger: Proceedings of the July 2001 Fontgombault Liturgical Conference* (Farnborough, St Michael's Abbey Press, 2003), 145–53.

Benedict XVI, Pope/Ratzinger, J., *God is Near Us: The Eucharist, the Heart of Life*, S. O. Horn and V. Pfnür (eds), translated by H. Taylor (San Francisco, Ignatius Press, 2003).

Benedict XVI, Pope/Ratzinger, J., '40 Jahre Konstitution über die heilige Liturgie. Rückblick und Vorblick', *Liturgisches Jahrbuch* 53 (2003), 209–21.

Benedict XVI, Pope/Ratzinger, J., 'Preface', in Reid, A., *The Organic Development of the Liturgy*, 2nd ed. (San Francisco, Ignatius Press, 2005).

Benedict XVI, Pope/Ratzinger, J., *Pilgrim Fellowship of Faith: The Church as Communion*, S. O. Horn and V. Pfnür (eds), translated by H. Taylor (San Francisco, Ignatius Press, 2005).

Benedict XVI, Pope/Ratzinger, J., *On the Way to Jesus Christ*, translated by M. J. Miller (San Francisco, Ignatius Press, 2005).

Benedict XVI, Pope/Ratzinger, J., *Waarden in tijden van ommekeer*, P. Mulder (ed.), translated by G. van der Weyde, G. Boer and S. van Wierst (Tielt, Lannoo, 2005).

Benedict XVI, Pope/Ratzinger, J., *Jesus of Nazareth*, translated by A. J. Walker (London, Bloomsbury, 2007).

Benedict XVI, Pope/Ratzinger, J., *Theologie der Liturgie, Gesammelte Schriften*, vol. 11. (Freiburg, Herder, 2008).

Benedict XVI, Pope, *Light of the World: The Pope, the Church, and the Signs of the Times: A Conversation with Peter Seewald*, translated by M. J. Miller and A. J. Walker (London and San Francisco, Catholic Truth Society and Ignatius Press, 2010).

B. Magisterium

Benedict XVI, Pope, 'First Message of His Holiness Benedict XVI at the End of the Eucharistic Concelebration with the Members of the College of Cardinals in the Sistine Chapel', 20 April 2005, in Benedict XVI, Pope, *Give Yourself to Christ: First Homilies of Benedict XVI* (London, Catholic Truth Society, 2005) 25–34.

Benedict XVI, Pope, 'Mass of the Possession of the Chair of the Bishop of Rome, Homily', 7 May 2005, available from http://www.vatican.va/holy_father/benedict_xvi/homilies/2005/documents/hf_ben-xvi_hom_20050507_san-giovanni-laterano_en.html; accessed 8 December 2010.

Benedict XVI, Pope, 'Address of His Holiness Benedict XVI to the Roman Curia Offering them His Christmas Greetings', 22 December 2005, available from http://www.vatican.va/holy_father/benedict_xvi/speeches/2005/december/documents/hf_ben_xvi_spe_20051222_roman-curia_en.html; accessed 8 December 2010.

Benedict XVI, Pope, *Encyclical Letter Deus Caritas Est*, 25 December 2005 (London, Catholic Truth Society, 2006).

Benedict XVI, Pope, *Post-synodal Exhortation Sacramentum Caritatis*, 22 February 2007 (London, Catholic Truth Society, 2007).

Benedict XVI, Pope, 'General Audience', 6 June 2007, in Benedict XVI, Pope, *The Fathers* (Huntington, Our Sunday Visitor, 2008), 51–56.

Benedict XVI, Pope, 'Homily on the Solemnity of Corpus Christi', 7 June 2007, in Benedict XVI, Pope, *Heart of the Christian Life: Thoughts on the Holy Mass* (San Francisco, Ignatius Press, 2010), 93–97.

Benedict XVI, Pope, 'General Audience', 28 November 2007, in Benedict XVI, Pope, *The Fathers*, (Huntington, Our Sunday Visitor, 2008), 157–62.

Benedict XVI, Pope, *Litterae Apostolicae Motu Proprio Datae 'De Usu Extraordinaria Antiquae Formae Ritus Romani' Benedictus XVI*, 7 July 2007, *AAS* 99 (2007), 777–81: English translation, *Summorum Pontificum* (London, Catholic Truth Society, 2007), 3–19.

Benedict XVI, Pope, *Letter to the Bishops on the Occasion of the Publication of the Apostolic Letter "Motu Proprio Data"* [*On the Extraordinary Use of the Ancient Form of the Roman Rite*] *Summorum Pontificum on the Use of the Roman Liturgy prior to the Reform of 1970*, 7 July 2007, in Benedict XVI, Pope, *Summorum Pontificum* (London, Catholic Truth Society, 2007), 20–27.

Benedict XVI, Pope, 'Homily for the Chrism Mass', 20 March 2008, in Benedict XVI, Pope, *Heart of the Christian Life: Thoughts on the Holy Mass* (San Francisco, Ignatius Press, 2010), 105–10.

Benedict XVI, Pope, 'General Audience', 14 May 2008, available from http://www.vatican.va/holy_father/benedict_xvi/audiences/2008/documents/ hf_benxvi_aud_20080514_en.html; accessed 8 December 2010.

Benedict XVI, Pope, 'Interview of the Holy Father Benedict XVI during the Flight to France', 12 September 2008, available from http://www.vatican.va/holy_father/benedict_xvi/speeches/2008/september/documents/hf_ben-xvi_spe_20080912_francia-interview_en.html; accessed 8 December 2010.

Benedict XVI, Pope, 'Meeting with French Episcopal Conference Address of His Holiness Benedict XVI, Hemicycle of Sainte-Bernadette's Church, Lourdes', 14 September 2008, available from http: // www.vatican. va/holy _father /benedict_xvi/ speeches/ 2008/september/ documents/hf_ben-xvi_spe_20080914_lourdes-vescovi_en.html; accessed 8 December 2010.

Benedict XVI, Pope, 'Homily at the Eucharistic Celebration and Dedication of the New Altar in the Cathedral of Albano', 21 September 2008, available from http://www.vatican.va/holy_father/benedict_xvi/homilies/2008/documents/hf_ben-xvi_hom_20080921_albano_en.html; accessed 8 December 2010.

Benedict XVI, Pope, 'General Audience', 7 January 2009, in Benedict XVI, Pope, *Paul of Tarsus* (London, Catholic Truth Society, 2009), 127–36.

Benedict XVI, Pope, *Apostolic Letter, Motu Proprio Ecclesiae Unitatem*, 2 July 2009, available from http://www.vatican.va/holy_father/benedict_xvi/apost_letters/documents/hf_ben-xvi_apl_20090702_ecclesiae-unitatem_en.html; accessed 8 December 2010.

Benedict XVI, Pope, *Apostolic Constitution Anglicanorum Coetibus*, 4 November 2009 (London, Catholic Truth Society, 2010).

Benedict XVI, Pope, 'General Audience', 29 September 2010, available from http://www.vatican.va/holy_father/benedict_xvi/audiences/2010/documents/hf_ben-xvi_aud_20100929_en.html; accessed 8 December 2010.

Benedict XVI, Pope, *Post-synodal Exhortation Verbum Domini*, 30 September 2010 (London: Catholic Truth Society, 2010).

Benedict XVI, Pope, 'General Audience', 6 October 2010, available at http://www.vatican.va/holy_father/benedict_xvi/audiences/2010/documents/hf_ben-xvi_aud_20101006_en.html; accessed 8 December 2010.

Benedict XVI, Pope, 'Message to the Italian Bishops' Plenary Session', 4 November 2010, available at http://www.zenit.org/article-30904?l=english; accessed 8 December 2010.

Benedict XVI, Pope, *Heart of the Christian Life: Thoughts on the Holy Mass* (San Francisco, Ignatius Press, 2010).

2. Magisterium

A. Ecumenical councils (in chronological order)

The Second Vatican Council, *The Constitution on the Sacred Liturgy Sacrosanctum Concilium*, 4 December 1963, in Flannery, A. (gen. ed.), *Vatican Council II: The Conciliar and Post Conciliar Documents*, rev. ed., vol. 1 (Dublin, Dominican Publications, 1988), 1–36.

The Second Vatican Council, *Dogmatic Constitution on the Church Lumen Gentium*, 21 November 1964, in Flannery, A. (gen. ed.), *Vatican Council II: The Conciliar and Post Conciliar Documents*, rev. ed., vol. 1 (Dublin, Dominican Publications, 1988), 350–426.

The Second Vatican Council, *Decree on the Catholic Eastern Church-es Orientalium Ecclesiarum*, 21 November 1964, in Flannery, A., (gen. ed.), *Vatican Council II: The Conciliar and Post Conciliar Documents*, rev. ed., vol. 1 (Dublin, Dominican Publications, 1988), 441–51.

B. Papal documents (in chronological order)

Pius XII, Pope, *Encyclical Letter Mediator Dei*, 20 November 1947, published as *Christian Worship* (London, Catholic Truth Society, 1947).

Paul VI, Pope, *Apostolic Constitution Missale Romanum*, 3 April 1969, available at http://www.vatican.va/holy_father/paul_vi/apost_constitutions/documents/hf_p-vi_apc_19690403_missale-romanum_en.html; accessed 8 December 2010.

John Paul II, Pope, *Apostolic Letter Ecclesia Dei of the Supreme Pontiff John Paul II given Motu Proprio*, 2 July 1988, available from http://www.vatican.va/ holy_father/john_paul_ii/motu-proprio/documents/hf_jp-ii_motuproprio_02071988_ecclesia-dei_en.html; accessed 8 December 2010.

John Paul II, Pope *Apostolic Letter Vicesimus quintus annus*, 4 December 1988: English translation, *Love Your Mass* (London, Catholic Truth Society, 1989).

John Paul II, Pope, *Encyclical Letter Ecclesia de Eucharistia*, 17 April 2003 (London, Catholic Truth Society, 2003).

John Paul II, Pope, *Apostolic Letter Spiritus et Sponsa of the Supreme Pontiff John Paul II on the 40th Anniversary of the Constitution of the Sacred Liturgy Sacrosanctum Concilium*, 4 December 2003, available from http://www.vatican.va/holy_father/john_paul_ii/ apost_letters/documents/hf_jp-ii_apl_20031204_spiritus-et-sponsa_en.html; accessed 8 December 2010.

C. Documents of the Roman Curia (in chronological order)

Sacred Congregation of Rites, *Instruction De Sacra Musica et Sacra Liturgica*, 3 September 1958, translated by J.B. O'Connell in *Sacred Music and Liturgy* (London, Burns and Oates, 1959).

Sacred Congregation of Rites, *Instructio ad Exsecutionem Constitutionis de Sacra Liturgia Recte Ordinandam (Inter Oecumenici)*, 26 September 1964, *AAS* 56 (1964), 877–900.

Sacred Congregation for Divine Worship, 'Unicuique suum ...' *Notitiae* 9 (1973), 48.

Congregation for Divine Worship, *Quattuor Abhinc Annos*, 3 October 1984: *AAS* 76 (1984), 1088–89: English translation, 'Use of the 1962 Missal', in *The Pope Teaches* (London, Catholic Truth Society, 1984/10), 303–304.

Congregation for the Doctrine of the Faith, *Instruction on the Ecclesial Vocation of the Theologian Donum veritatis*, 24 May 1990 (London, Catholic Truth Society, 1990).

Congregation for Divine Worship and the Discipline of the Sacraments, 'Editoriale: Pregare "ad orientem versus",' *Notitiae* 29 (1993), 245–49.

Congregation for the Clergy, *Directory on the Ministry and Life of Priests* (London, Catholic Truth Society, 1994).

Congregation for Divine Worship and the Discipline of the Sacraments, 'Responsa ad quaestiones de nova *Institutione Generalis Missalis Romani*', *Communicationes* [Pontifical Council for the Interpretation of Legal Texts], 32 (2000), 171–74.

Congregation for Divine Worship and the Discipline of the Sacraments, *Directory on Popular Piety and the Liturgy*, (London, Catholic Truth Society, 2002).

Congregation for Divine Worship and the Discipline of the Sacraments, *Instruction Redemptionis Sacramentum, On certain matters to be observed or to be avoided regarding the Most Holy Eucharist*, 25 March 2004 (London, Catholic Truth Society, 2004).

Congregation for Divine Worship and the Discipline of the Sacraments, *Compendium Eucharisticum* (Vatican City, Libreria Editrice Vaticana, 2009).

Congregation for the Doctrine of the Faith, 'Note of the Congregation for the Doctrine of the Faith On the Trivilization of Sexuality: Regarding certain interpretations of *Light of the World*', 21 December 2010, available from http://press.catholica.va/news_services/bulletin/news/26596.php?index=26596&lang=en#TESTO IN LINGUA INGLESE; accessed 21 December 2010.

D. Liturgical and rubrical books

Caeremoniale Episcoporum ex Decreto Sacrosancti Oecumenici Concilii Vaticani II Instauratum Auctoritate Ioannis Pauli PP. II Promulgatum, editio typica 1984, reimpressio emendata, (Vatican City, Libreria Editrice Vaticana, 2008).

Institutio Generalis Missalis Romani, in *Missale Romanum: ex Decreto Sacrosancti Oecumenici Concilii Vaticani II Instauratum Auctoritate Pauli PP. VI Promulgatum Ioannis Pauli PP. II Cura Recognitum*, editio typica tertia (2002), reimpressio emendata (Vatican City, Typis Vaticanis, 2008): English translation, *General Instruction of the Roman Missal* (London, Catholic Truth Society, 2005).

Ordinarius seu Liber Caeremoniarium ad usum Sacri et Canonici Ordinis Praemonstratensis (Tongerlo, Tongerlo Abbey Press, 1949).

E. Miscellaneous sources

Catechism of the Catholic Church, rev. ed. (London, Geoffrey Chapman, 1999).

Codex Iuris Canonici (Vatican City, Libreria Editrice Vaticana, 1983).

3. Books

Aillet, M., *The Old Mass and the New: Explaining the Motu Proprio Summorum Pontificum of Pope Benedict XVI*, translated by H. Taylor (San Francisco, Ignatius Press, 2010).

Aquinas, T., St, *Summa Theologica*, in three parts, ed. by the Dominican Order, Biblioteca de Autores Cristianos, 5 vols (Madrid, 1952).

Arinze, F., George, F., Medina Estévez, J., Pell, G., *Cardinal Reflections: Active Participation and the Liturgy*, (Chicago/Mundelein, Illinois, Hillenbrand Books, 2005).

Asci, D. P., *The Conjugal Act as Personal Act* (San Francisco, Ignatius Press, 2002).

Baldovin, J. F., *Reforming the Liturgy: A Response to the Critics* (Minnesota, The Liturgical Press, 2008).

Baumstark, A., *Comparative Liturgy*, rev. ed. by B. Botte, translated by F. L. Cross (London, Mowbray and Co., 1958).

Berger, D., *Thomas Aquinas and the Liturgy* (Ann Arbor, Sapientia Press, 2004).

Bouyer, L. C., *The Liturgy Revived: A Doctrinal Commentary of the Conciliar Constitution on the Liturgy* (London, Libra, 1965).

Bouyer, L. C., *The Decomposition of Catholicism* (London, Sands and Co., 1970).

Bugnini, A., *The Reform of the Liturgy (1948–1975)* (Collegeville, Liturgical Press, 1990).

Bux, N. and Vitiello, S., *The Motu Proprio of Benedict XVI Summorum Pontificum cura*, *Fides Service Dossier*, 1 August 2007 (Agenzia Fides: Agenzia della Congregazione per l'Evangelizzazione dei Popoli), available from http://www.fides.org/eng/documents/ dossier_motu_proprio_eng.doc; accessed 8 December 2010.

Cabié, R., *The Eucharist*, in Martimort, A. G. (ed.), *The Church at Prayer: An Introduction to the Liturgy*, vol. 2, translated by M. J. O'Connell (London, Geoffrey Chapman, 1986).

Cassingena-Trévedy, F., *Te Igitur* (Geneva, Ad Solem, 2007).

Crouan, D., *The History and the Future of the Roman Liturgy* (San Francisco, Ignatius Press, 2005).

Dobszay, L., *The Bugnini Liturgy and the Reform of the Reform*, *Musicae Sacrae Meletemata*, vol. 5 (Front Royal VA, Church Music Association of America, 2003).

Dobszay L. *The Restoration and Organic Development of the Roman Rite*, ed. and introduction by L. P. Hemming (London and New York, T. and T. Clark, 2010).

Edwards, R., *Catholic Traditionalism* (London, Catholic Truth Society, 2008).

Elliott, P. J., *Ceremonies of the Liturgical Year* (San Francisco, Ignatius Press, 2002).

Elliott, P. J., *Ceremonies of the Modern Roman Rite*, rev. ed. (San Francisco, Ignatius Press, 2005).

Evdokimov, P., *The Art of the Icon: A Theology of Beauty*, translated by S. Bigham (Redondo Beech, Calif., Oakwood Pub., 1990).

Flanagan, K., *Sociology and Liturgy: Re-presentations of the Holy* (London, Macmillan Press, 1991).

Gamber, K., *The Reform of the Roman Liturgy*, translated by K. D. Grimm (California and New York, Una Voce Press and The Foundation for Catholic Reform, 1993).

Gamber, K., *The Modern Rite: Collected Essays on the Reform of the Liturgy*, translated by H. Taylor (Farnborough, St Michael's Abbey Press, 2002).

Geffroy, C., *Benoît XVI et la Paix liturgique* (Paris, Les Éditions du CERF, 2008).

Gherardini, B., *The Ecumenical Vatican Council II: A Much Needed Discussion* (Frigento, Casa Mariana Editrice, 2009).

Giampietro, N., *The Development of the Liturgical Reform: As seen by Cardinal Ferdinando Antonelli from 1948 to 1970* (Fort Collins, Roman Catholic Books, 2009).

Guardini, R., *Vom Geist der Liturgie* (Freiburg, Herder-Bücherei, 1959).

Gy, P.-M., *The Reception of Vatican II [:] Liturgical Forms in the Life of the Church*, The Père Marquette Lecture in Theology 2003 (Milwaukee, Marquette University Press, 2003).

Hahn, S.W., *Covenant and Communion: The Biblical Theology of Pope Benedict XVI* (London and Rapid Springs, Darton, Longman and Todd, 2009).

Hemming, L. P., *Worship as a Revelation: The Past, Present and Future of Catholic Liturgy* (London and New York, Burns and Oates/Continuum, 2008).

Hermans, J, *Benedictus XIV en de Liturgie* (Brugge, Uitgeverij Emmaüs, 1979).

Hermans, J., *Het Getijdengebed: Liturgie en Spiritualiteit van het Getijdenboek* (Oegstgeest and Brugge, Columba and Tabor, 1995).

von Hildebrand, D., *Liturgy and Personality*, 4th ed., (Manchester, Sophia Institute Press, 1993).

Hitchcock, J., *The Recovery of the Sacred* (San Francisco, Ignatius Press, 1995).

Kocik, T. M., *The Reform of the Reform?* (San Francisco, Ignatius Press, 2003).

Lamb, M. L. and Levering, M. (eds), *Vatican II: Renewal within Tradition* (Oxford, Oxford University Press, 2008).

Lang, U.M., *Turn towards the Lord: Orientation in Liturgical Prayer* (San Francisco, Ignatius Press, 2004).

Marini, G., *Liturgical Reflections of a Papal Master of Ceremonies* (Pine Beach, Newman House Press, 2011).

Marini, P., *A Challenging Reform: Realizing the Vision of the Liturgical Renewal 1963–1975*, (eds) M. R. Francis C. S. V., J. R. Page, and K. F. Pecklers (Minnesota, Liturgical Press, 2007).

Marmion, C., Bl., *Christ in His Mysteries*, translated by A. Bancroft (Leominster, Gracewing Publications, 2008).

Mosebach, M., *The Heresy of Formlessness: The Roman Liturgy and its Enemy*, translated by G. Harrison (San Francisco, Ignatius Press, 2006).

Nichols, A., *Looking at the Liturgy: A Critical View of its Contemporary Form* (San Francisco, Ignatius Press, 1996).

Nichols, A., *Christendom Awake: On Re-energising the Church in Culture* (Edinburgh, T and T Clark, 1999).

Nichols, A., *The Thought of Pope Benedict XVI: An Introduction to the Theology of Joseph Ratzinger*, 2nd ed. (London and New York, Burns and Oates, 2007).

Nichols, A., *Redeeming Beauty: Soundings in Sacral Aesthetics* (Aldershot and Burlington, Ashgate, 2007).

Pickstock, C., *After Writing: On the Liturgical Consummation of Philosophy* (Oxford, Blackwell Publishers, 1998).

Reid, A. (ed.), *Looking again at the Question of the Liturgy with Cardinal Ratzinger: Proceedings of the July 2001 Fontgombault Liturgical Conference* (Farnborough, St Michael's Abbey Press, 2003).

Reid, A., *The Organic Development of the Liturgy* (Farnborough, St Michael's Abbey Press, 2004).

Robinson, J., *The Mass and Modernity: Walking to Heaven Backward* (San Francisco, Ignatius Press, 2005).

Rowland, T., *Ratzinger's Faith: The Theology of Pope Benedict XVI* (Oxford, Oxford University Press, 2008).

Roy, N. J., and Rutherford, J. E. (eds), *Benedict XVI and the Sacred Liturgy: Proceedings of the First Fota International Liturgy Conference 2008* (Dublin, Four Courts Press, 2010).

Rubin, M., *Corpus Christi: The Eucharist in Late Medieval Culture* (Cambridge, Cambridge University Press, 1991).

Schneider, A., *Dominus Est: It is the Lord!* (Pine Beach, Newman House Press, 2008).

Suarez, F., *The Sacrifice of the Altar* (London and New York, Scepter, 1990).

Van Dijk, S. J. P., *Sources of the Modern Roman Liturgy: The Ordinal by Haymo of Faversham and Related Documents (1243–1307)*, 2 vols (Leiden, Brill, 1963).

Weishaupt, G. P., *Päpstliche Weichenstellungen: Das Motu Proprio Summorum Pontificum Papst Benedikts XVI. und der Begleitbrief an die Bischöfe: Ein kirchenrechtlicher Kommentar und Überlegungen zu einer „Reform der Reform"* (Bonn, Verlag für Kultur und Wissenschaft, 2010).

4. Article and conference papers

Anon., 'More Decisions of the Ecclesia Dei Commission', available from http://saintbedestudio.blogspot.com/2007/04/more-decisions-of-ecclesia-dei.html; accessed 8 December 2010.

Baldovin, J. F., 'The Uses of Liturgical History', *Worship* 82 (2008), 2–18.

Bovens, P., 'Chronique inachevée des publications autour de la Lettre apostolique en forme de *Motu proprio* "Summorum Pontificum" de Benoît XVI"', *Ephemerides Theologicae Lovanienses* 84 (2008), 529–36.

Bretzke, J. T., ' In forma specifica', in *Consecrated Phrases: A Latin Theological Dictionary* [CD-ROM] (Collegeville, The Liturgical Press, 2000).

Brinkhoff, L. and Lescrauwert, J., 'Liturgische Beweging', in, Brinkhoff, L., et al., *Liturgisch Woordenboek*, vol. 2 (Roermond, J.J. Romen and Sons, 1965–68), 1598–1611.

Burke, R. L., 'Cardinal Burke's Homily at Solemn Mass of Thanksgiving on the Occasion of the Ordinary Public Consistory' (2010), available from http://stlouisreview.com/article/2010–11–24/cardinal-burkes; accessed 8 December 2010.

Capponi, N., 'Alcune considerazioni giuridiche in materia di riforma liturgica', *Archivio giuridico 'Filippo Serafini'* 190/2 (1976), 147–73: English translation, *Some Juridical Considerations on the Reform of the Liturgy* (Edinburgh, David MacDonald: n.d.).

Fink, P. E., 'Mystagogy', in *The New Dictionary of Sacramental Worship* [CD-ROM] (Collegeville, The Liturgical Press, 2000).

Folsom, C., 'The Hermeneutics of *Sacrosanctum Concilium*: Development of a Method and its Application', *Antiphon* 8/1 (2003), 2–9.

Folsom, C., 'Roman Rite or Roman Rites?', in Reid, A. (ed.), *Looking again at the Question of the Liturgy with Cardinal Ratzinger: Proceedings of the July 2001 Fontgombault Liturgical Conference* (Farnborough, St Michael's Abbey Press, 2003), 58–81.

George, F., '*Sacrosanctum Concilium* Anniversary Address: The Foundations of Liturgical Reform', in Arinze, F., George, F., Medina Estévez, J., Pell, G., *Cardinal Reflections: Active Participation and the Liturgy*, (Chicago/Mundelein, Illinois, Hillenbrand Books, 2005), 45–57.

Gribbin, J. A., 'Lay Participation in the Eucharistic Liturgy of the Later Middle Ages', *Ministerial and Common Priesthood in the Eucharistic Celebration: The Proceedings of the Fourth International Colloquium of Historical, Canonical and Theological Studies of the Roman Liturgy* (London, Centre International Etudes Liturgique, 1999), 51–69.

Gy, P.-M., 'L'Esprit de la Liturgie du Cardinal Ratzinger est-il Fidèle au Concile ou en Réaction Contre?', *La Maison-Dieu* 229 (2002), 171–78: English translation, 'Cardinal Ratzinger's *The Spirit of the Liturgy*: Is it Faithful to the Council or in Reaction to It?', translated by S. Maddux, *Antiphon* 11 (2007), 90–96.

Harrison, B. W., 'The Postconciliar Eucharistic Liturgy: Planning a "Reform of the Reform"', in Kocik, T. M., *The Reform of the Reform?* (San Francisco, Ignatius Press, 2003), 151–93.

Hauke, M., 'Klaus Gamber: Father of the "New Liturgical Movement"', in Roy, N. J., and Rutherford, J. E. (eds), *Benedict XVI and the Sacred Liturgy: Proceedings of the First Fota International Liturgy Conference, 2008* (Dublin, Four Courts Press, 2010), 24–69.

Haunerland, W., 'Ein Ritus in zwei Ausdrucksformen? Hintergründe und Perspektiven zur Liturgiefeier nach dem Motu proprio "Summorum Pontificum"', *Liturgisches Jahrbuch* 58 (2008), 179–203.

Heinz, A., 'Rencontre avec le cardinal Joseph Ratzinger', *La Maison-Dieu* 238 (2004), 45–49.

Huels, J.M., 'Interpreting an Instruction Approved *in forma specifica*', *Studia Canonica* 32 (1998) 5–46.

Hull Hitchcock, H., 'Pope Benedict XVI and the "reform of the reform"', in Roy, N. J. and Rutherford, J. E. (eds), *Benedict XVI and the Sacred Liturgy: Proceedings of the First Fota International Liturgy Conference, 2008* (Dublin, Four Courts Press, 2010), 70–87.

Jackson, P. E. J., 'Theology of the Liturgy', in Lamb, M. L. and Levering, M. (eds), *Vatican II: Renewal within Tradition* (Oxford, Oxford University Press, 2008), 101–28.

de Jong, E., 'Enkele overpeinzingen naar aanleiding van de buitengewone misorde', *Tijdschrift voor Liturgie* 92 (2008), 250–67.

Kollmorgen, G., 'Important Clarifications from Ecclesia Dei', available from http://www.newliturgicalmovement. org/2010/02/important-clarifications-from-ecclesia.html; accessed 8 December 2010.

Lang, U. M., 'The Crisis of Sacred Art and the Sources for its Renewal in the Thought of Pope Benedict XVI', in Roy, N. J. and Rutherford, J. E. (eds), *Benedict XVI and the Sacred Liturgy: Proceedings of the First Fota International Liturgy Conference, 2008* (Dublin, Four Courts Press, 2010), 98–115.

Lüdecke, N., 'Kanonistische Anmerkungen zum Motu Proprio *Summorum Pontificum*', *Liturgisches Jahrbuch* 58 (2008), 3–34.

Mayer, A., 'Concerning the Apostolic Letter Ecclesia Dei', available from http://www.ewtn.com/library/curia/CEDMeyer.htm; accessed 8 December 2010.

McNamara, E., 'Both Hands at Elevation of the Host', available from http://www.zenit.org/article-23760?1=english; accessed 8 December 2010.

Nichols, A., 'Salutary Dissatisfaction: An English View of "Reforming the Reform"', in Kocik, T. M., *The Reform of the Reform?* (San Francisco, Ignatius Press, 2003), 195–210.

Parsons, J. P., 'Reform of the Reform?', in Kocik, T. M., *The Reform of the Reform?* (San Francisco, Ignatius Press, 2003), 211–56.

Quoëx, F. M., 'Historical and Doctrinal Notes on the Offertory of the Roman Rite', in *Theological and Historical Aspects of the Roman Missal: The Proceedings of the Fifth International Colloquium of Historical, Canonical and Theological Studies on the Roman Catholic Liturgy* (London, Centre International Etudes Liturgique, 2000), 53–75.

Read, G., '*Motu Proprio Summorum Pontificum*', *Newsletter of the Canon Law Society of Great Britain and Ireland* 151 (September 2007), 9–22.

Read, G., '*Summorum Pontificum*: Questions, Answers, Issues', *Newsletter of the Canon Law Society of Great Britain and Ireland* 156 (December 2008), 32–36.

Read, G., 'SSPX Lifting of the Excommunications', in *Newsletter of the Canon Law Society of Great Britain and Ireland* 157 (March, 2009), 13–21.

Reid, A., 'Looking Again at the Liturgical Reform: Some General and Monastic Considerations' (2006), available from http://www.benedictines.org.uk/theology/2006/reid. pdf; accessed 8 December 2010.

Reid, A., 'Sacrosanctum Concilium and the Organic Development of the Liturgy', in Lang, U. M. (ed.), *The Genius of the Roman Rite: Historical, Theological, and Pastoral Perspectives on Catholic Liturgy: Proceedings of the Eleventh International CIEL (International Centre for Liturgical Studies) Colloquium held at Merton College, Oxford, September 2006* (Chicago/Mundelein, Illinois, Hillenbrand Books, 2010), 198–215.

Schumacher, J., 'The Liturgy as *Locus Theologicus*', in *Faith and Liturgy: The Proceedings of the Seventh International Colloquium of Historical, Canonical and Theological Studies on the Roman Catholic Liturgy* (London, Centre International Etudes Liturgique, 2002), 71–97.

Vijgen, J., 'Is de H. Mis in de Buitengewone Vorm een "Privé-Mis"?', *Vereniging voor Latijnse Liturgie Bulletin* 100 (2009), 208–19.

Index of Names